DESPITE THE
STATE

M. Rajshekhar started his career as a business reporter in 1997. He began reporting on environmental issues as a freelance journalist in 2005. After a brief stint with the World Bank, an MA at the University of Sussex, and two years of independent research—spent studying the village-level impact of an agribusiness model in central India and the drafting process which produced India's Forest Rights Act—he joined the *Economic Times* to report on rural India and environment in 2010. During this period, he won two Shriram Awards for Excellence in Financial Journalism (2013 and 2014).

He joined *Scroll.in* in 2015 to do a thirty-three-month-long reporting project, *Ear to the Ground*, which became the substrate for this book. This series won the Ramnath Goenka Excellence in Journalism Award (2015), the Bala Kailasam Memorial Award (2016), and two more Shriram Awards for Excellence in Financial Journalism (2015 and 2016).

He now writes on energy, environment, climate change, political corruption and oligarchy. His reportage can be found at www.mrajshekhar.in.

DESPITE THE STATE

WHY INDIA LETS ITS PEOPLE DOWN AND HOW THEY COPE

M. RAJSHEKHAR

AFTERWORD BY V. GEETHA

context

'With cases meticulously explored in six states spanning the length and breadth of the country, Rajshekhar conveys the resilience of people faced with the State's failure to deliver what it champions. Lacing its way throughout this book is evidence for political centralisation, domination, patronage and predation. This is the nearest to a holistic account of India's everyday economy and its development and democratic failings that we are likely to have for a long while.'

BARBARA HARRISS-WHITE, emeritus professor of Development Studies,
University of Oxford, UK

'When a sensitive journalist puts his ear to the ground, as Rajshekhar did for three years, travelling and living in six states, he can be expected to hear the heartbeat of the land. But *Despite the State* is far more than sensibility and reportage of development challenges. It is, to use the author's words, a hitchhiker's guide to democratic palsy, lucid and informed by a unique perspective shaped by inquiries into everything from the human brain to political philosophy.'

T.K. ARUN, consulting editor, *Economic Times*

'If the rich have ceased to belong to India, the Indian states have seceded from the poor; their object being to extract greater resources and accumulate power bereft of accountability. *Despite the State* is a frightening account of India's neglect of basic functions of governance and minimal democracy.'

TRIDIP SUHRUD, writer and translator, Ahmedabad

'This journey through six different states—not as a travelogue but as an effort to have a deep understanding on how peoples' lives have been changing, the emerging concerns and its connections with the State and its politics—makes for a fascinating reading. Each state is different, each page tells us a distinct story, each one of these is a Tolstoyesque story of unhappy family where the relationship between the citizens and the mai-baap sarkar, the government, is being redefined as a patron-client relationship, a customer-provider relationship, a dole seeker–provider relationship, or as an episodic relationship of gratification, and not necessarily the relationship between an empowered citizen and the sevaks, including the pradhan sevak.

It is a book full of stories: stories of real people making the best of their potential, uncomplaining and leading their lives towards contentment, and so self-contained—aatmanirbhar—that they do not even notice that the State is absent. There are no expectations, and thus there are no expectations to be met. It is a book that makes for an easy reading, just flows through, but at the same time makes you pause. Makes the reader introspect and wonder if the larger picture is indeed true. Or how much more worse it can get. This is deeply insightful, and therefore deeply disturbing.'

M.S. SRIRAM, IIM-Bangalore

'By turns provocative, serious and humorous, *Despite the State* unravels the facade that passes off as democracy in India. Written in a terse staccato, Rajshekhar's travelogue style is deceptively simple but backed by well-researched conclusions. Guided by the author through six states, the reader confronts the ways in which a democracy can be made dysfunctional, unnoticed by the people who believe in its existence. An important book for our times.'

MADHU RAMNATH, botanist and author of *Woodsmoke and Leafcups: Autobiographical Footnotes to the Anthropology of the Durwa People*

'*Despite the State* is a remarkable, involved, engaging narrative that captures the voices and lived experiences of people, their aspirations, their despair and the ways in which they find the next possibility when what they have begins to crumble. We see the State as the people encounter it, woefully, often, as the entity that dismantles what the people have crafted for themselves and for their survival. It parses political economy into more than just the formal and the informal, and introduces us to a precariat which is made by State action and inaction. It is not a pretty tale; but it does help us identify the fault lines in our politics, and in our economy, and urges us to do something about it, now.'

USHA RAMANATHAN, scholar on the jurisprudence of law and poverty

'This is a book that I saw develop ever since Rajshekhar began his project and asked me what to look for in the ability of state governments to deliver. In fact, I ended up learning much more from it than I could advise on. While state government priorities, their administrative capacity and centre-state fiscal dynamics were what I thought he should concentrate on, his findings on non-State actors were far more interesting. I suppose that is why the title: *Despite the State*. But can people cope with failures of the State? While not necessarily conclusive, what emerges is a fascinating and very well-written quilted story of hope, anxiety and guile. Do read on.'

ABHIJIT SEN, economist and former member of Planning Commission

cntxt

First published by Context, an imprint of Westland Publications Private Limited, in 2021

1st Floor, A Block, East Wing, Plot No. 40, SP Info City, Dr. MGR Salai, Perungudi, Kandanchavadi, Chennai 600096

Context, the Context logo, Westland and the Westland logo are the trademarks of Westland Publications Private Limited, or its affiliates.

Copyright © M. Rajshekhar, 2021

ISBN: 9788194879015

10 9 8 7 6 5 4 3 2

Typeset in Adobe Devanagari by Jojy Philip, New Delhi - 110015
Printed at Thomson Press (India) Ltd.

MIX
Paper
FSC FSC® C010615

For M. Lalitha and M. Madhu.
And in memory of M. Ramam, Shashi Rajagopalan and Samir Acharya:
How I wish they were around to see this book.

Contents

Introduction

The inner workings of Amul, India's much-loved milk cooperative, briefly became public in the winter of 2013. Directors representing fourteen of the seventeen district milk cooperatives in the state, which together made up the Gujarat Cooperative Milk Marketing Federation Limited (GCMMF) and owned the Amul brand, turned on chairperson Vipul Chaudhary. A member of the Bharatiya Janata Party (BJP), he had been part of a faction that broke away in 1996 to form a short-lived government with the Congress in Gujarat. He had returned to the BJP but was suspected of cosying up to the Congress-led United Progressive Alliance (UPA) government at the centre at the time.[1] Charges of financial impropriety were also levelled against him.[2]

It was, however, a time when public attention lay elsewhere. The 2014 elections were nearing. The UPA was on its last legs. Amul's boardroom tussle did not get the attention it deserved. In January 2014, Chaudhary's opponents won, and he was ousted.[3]

The curtain dropped back on Amul's functioning.

———

The story of Amul is the story of India.

The cooperative was created in 1949 when Tribhuvandas K. Patel, a freedom fighter who set up the Kaira District Cooperative Milk Producers' Union to secure better deals for dairy farmers in Gujarat's Anand district, persuaded Verghese Kurien, who had just returned after studying dairy engineering in Boston, to come aboard as its first general manager.[4]

Between them, they created an organisation that embodied the promise of newly independent India. In *Milkman From Anand*,

M.V. Kamath quotes Rudolf von Leyden, a senior executive roped in to distribute the cooperative's new product line in baby food: 'Here was the unique concept of taking the products of the land, processing them in modern industrial establishments owned by the producers, creating products for the consumer and bringing the profits back directly to the producers in the village in a continuous cooperative operation.'[5]

Between 1960 and 1973, writes Kamath, the Kaira cooperative infused as much as Rs 350 lakh to Rs 540 lakh into the district every year. Its growth inspired other districts to create their own milk unions. By 1973, Gujarat had six district milk unions, which came together to create the GCMMF at the state level. Leaders during this period, mostly freedom fighters and Gandhians, kept dairy farmers at the centre of management decisions. After 1975, the introduction of elections to choose the leaders of the cooperatives further strengthened the system of accountability—dairy farmers voted for village society heads, who voted for directors of the district milk unions, who chose the district chairperson, who in turn chose the GCMMF chairperson.

Like Amul, India too began in earnest. It sought to use the modern innovation of constitutional democracy to remake its millions— oppressed by gender and caste asymmetries, separated by religion and ethnicity, and drained dry of their blood by colonialism—into equal citizens. The country created a republic with universal suffrage, formalised separation of powers, instituted orderly transfer of power, and worked towards agricultural and industrial modernisation. It made mistakes too, like: the first amendment to the Constitution, which introduced curbs to fundamental freedoms; the retention and use of preventive detention; the incarceration of Sheikh Abdullah; and the dismissal of the E.M.S. Namboodiripad government in Kerala. But the country was very much a nascent, postcolonial democracy rising to its feet.

———

At Amul, the curtain lifted again after four years. In August 2017, Ramsinh Parmar, a Congress member of the legislative assembly (MLA) from Gujarat's Thasra constituency, moved to the BJP.[6] He was not just another politician quitting the Congress before state polls. He was also the chairperson of the Kaira milk cooperative and the last non-BJP chairperson in the federation. With his move, all district milk unions of Gujarat came under the BJP's control.[7]

It was the culmination of a takeover that had started in 1998 when BJP's Keshubhai Patel was Gujarat's chief minister, continued under his successors, and hit fever pitch once Narendra Modi took strike at the state in 2001. Under Modi, pressure on chairpersons of dairy and credit cooperatives to join the BJP went past blandishments into coercion.[8] At the same time, the party began putting up its own candidates for cooperative elections.[9] Control over cooperatives helps politicians dispense patronage while weakening local power structures and curbing the rise of local leaders.[10]

What facilitated this capture was the crumbling of Amul's fidelity to its founding principles. By the 1990s, as its Gandhian founders aged and district politics began to revolve around the dairies, regional bigwigs took over. Money spent on cooperative elections rose, and most farmers could no longer afford to contest. With winning candidates recouping their election expenditure through inflated labour contracts, purchase contracts and employment contracts, complaints of financial mismanagement began.

This decay set the ground for the entry of career politicians, and Amul's drift accelerated. Vipul Chaudhary's ouster was a sign that party politics was interfering in the dairies. Another sign surfaced in May 2018. Banas Dairy, helmed by the then state health minister Shankar Chaudhary, set up a 150-seat medical college. According to the *Indian Express*, he was accused of 'misusing his position' in the government to get permissions for the trust and the college.[11] What went unexamined was how the dairy, and the GCMMF, agreed to this diversion of funds.

———

The project of Indian democracy traced its own trajectory. Although it suffered elite capture, it curbed the worst asymmetries in the country. Democracy was still being deepened—with legislations like the

Right to Information Act, 2005—when India veered into right-wing majoritarianism in 2014. Countries like the United States lurched rightward because, losing their jobs to other nations, its people fell to the lure of nationalist demagogues. India, in contrast, was one of the fastest-growing economies in the world. Incomes were rising in real terms. And yet, it too voted against plural democracy.

To explain this swerve, some pointed at the rise of a new global playbook that sought to undermine the legitimacy of ruling establishments. Like the Philippines, India saw the rise of 'disinformation architectures'[12]—for instance, content farms projecting popular upsurges against the UPA government in the run up to the 2014 polls. Like Brazil, India too saw its ruling elite embroiled in corruption scandals, followed by similar rightward turns in the national elections.[13] People's impatience and disillusionment with democracy, however, was the substrate on which these processes capitalised. As the Hungarian thinker Tzvetan Todorov writes, 'Democracy secretes within itself the very forces that threaten it.'*

———

Early in 2015, I left the *Economic Times*—where I wrote on India's environment and its rural hinterland—to re-familiarise myself with the country by living in and reporting from six representative states.

The India of my imagination—from my work, spaces like Delhi's Nizammuddin dargah and books like Saeed Mirza's *Ammi*—was an imperfect country with much religious and caste violence but moving towards greater tolerance.† Even the Anthropological Survey of India's

---

* Deformities enter democracy, Todorov writes, when one of its three foundational promises—a government of the people, the freedom of individuals, and the promise of progress—becomes stronger than the others. The 'hypertrophy of one' threatens the rest. And democracy degenerates into populism, ultra-liberalism or messianism. See: Tzvetan Todorov, *The Inner Enemies of Democracy* (UK: Polity Books, 2014).

† That hopeful sense of the country had deepened in 2008, when I lived for eight months in two villages in central India, studying the ground-level impact of an

massive 'People Of India' project, which mapped the cultural, linguistic and biological profile of all communities in the country between 1984 and 1992, had reached similar conclusions. 'The survey's revelation [was] that instead of becoming Hindu, Islamic or Christian, the country was, in fact, evolving a spectacularly rich, syncretic culture and a liberal ethos vis-a-vis religion,' writes Dinesh Narayanan in his book *The RSS and the Making of the Deep Nation.*[14] And so, as the 2014 polls neared, many thought Modi was too polarising to be accepted as the prime minister. His landslide win, however, suggested that a decisive proportion of Indians found majoritarianism alluring or, at least, did not mind the heightened vulnerability of minority communities as long as economic growth was delivered.

Reporters need to belong to the times they live in. The cost of not doing so, as Steve Wick shows in *The Long Night*, can be dire.[15] The journalist William Shirer lived in Berlin for most of the Second World War but missed the Holocaust. He was not the only one. Even the *New York Times*, as Laurel Leff describes in *Buried by the Times,* woke up to the Holocaust only after allied forces discovered the concentration camps.[16] Instances like these illustrate the greatest professional risk journalism runs: of missing the largest changes of its time.

—

How does one update one's understanding of India?

Geographically, the country is the seventh largest in the world. Demographically, the second-most populous. Environmentally, with ten biogeographic zones, one of the most biodiverse places on earth.* Culturally, home to 780 spoken languages and myriad religious,

Indian agribusiness that bought wheat and soya from farmers. In both places, caste exploitation had shrunk as, leaving farm work for industrial clusters, dalits had freed themselves from the village economy. There was also little religious polarisation of the kind India sees now. See: M. Rajshekhar, 'A Development Chronology of Tihi', *Fractured Earth* (blog, 1 February 2008), mrajshekhar.wordpress.in/2008/02/01/a-development-chronology-of-tihi/.

* America, three times as large, has twelve biogeographic zones.

indigenous and ethnic communities—not to mention caste, class, gender and income-based stratifications. Administratively, 28 states, 8 union territories, 718 districts, 7,935 cities and towns, and anywhere between 6 lakh and 10 lakh villages.[17]

More than districts, towns or villages, a state is the unit where most of this complexity is visible. I moved to *Scroll.in*, a new online journalism start-up launched in 2014, and began a reporting project called *Ear to the Ground*. The idea was to study six states that, between them, capture a cross-section of India's diversity: one from India's hilly borderlands—Mizoram; one which is mineral-rich but poor—Odisha; one with irrigated agriculture—Punjab; another with rain-fed farming—Bihar; one relatively industrialised state from the north—Gujarat; and another from the south—Tamil Nadu. Large parts of India, however, are anything but peaceful. States like Manipur, Kashmir and Nagaland have long-running insurgencies and live under coercive military presence. So, after Mizoram, I went to Manipur to see if insurgency and army rule, and the interplay between these two and the state, had changed in recent years.* For better immersion, instead of travelling back and forth from Delhi, I lived in each state I was reporting from.

I focused on major processes shaping these six states, as opposed to covering events that occurred during my stay. This distinction between events and processes is essential. 'Like the tip of an iceberg rising above the water, events are the most visible aspect of a larger complex but not always the most important,' writes the systems theorist Donella Meadows in *Thinking in Systems*.[18] We are likely to learn more if we scan large changes for clues to the underlying structure. This, Meadows writes, is 'the key to understanding not just what is happening but why'.

To identify processes, I interviewed a representative slice of each state's political economy—businesspeople, politicians, activists, bureaucrats, religious leaders, reporters, academics, civilians and

---

* Given I chased only one question in Manipur, my stint there was shorter than those in other states. For this reason, I describe what I found in Manipur in an annexure.

others attuned to changes in a society, like authors or poets—about the biggest changes in their state over the last five to seven years. To avoid big-city bias, I conducted these conversations in various regions of the state. In Punjab, for instance, I did exploratory interviews not only in Amritsar, Jalandhar, Ludhiana, Chandigarh and Bhatinda but also in smaller towns like Nurmahal and Pathankot, and the countryside.

Whenever a significant change emerged, I drilled deeper to understand it better. Between 2005 and 2016, for instance, Tamil Nadu saw a huge spike in household borrowings. In parts of the state, debt had grown twenty-five fold even as annual incomes had climbed only five fold. In 2010, reporting on a similar explosion in household debt in the neighbouring state of Andhra Pradesh, I had zeroed in on predatory lending by microfinance companies, the end of a state lending programme and decreasing rural incomes as the reasons.[19]

However, living in Tamil Nadu for six months during the *Ear to the Ground* project helped me see a wider web of interconnections. Causal factors I discovered included changing rainfall patterns (partly due to warming seas) that had hurt traditional livelihoods; a rise in the number of migrant industrial workers from north India that pushed down wages; locals turning to debt to bridge a widening gap between earnings and expenses; and the consequent arrival of moneylending as one of the most profitable businesses in rural Tamil Nadu, so much so that even castes that previously looked down on moneylending entered informal lending markets.

For the most part, this methodology worked well. It faltered only on timelines. Initially pegged as a fifteen-month assignment, *Ear to the Ground* stretched to thirty-three months. By its end, I had filed a hundred and twenty reports, with seventy-seven of them focusing on major changes in these states. Along the way, I also found a bigger puzzle than the inchoate question I had set out with.

Democracy was malfunctioning in each state I reported from. Mizoram was financially unviable. Odisha was dominated by a handful of families. Punjab, while I was there, was entirely controlled by one family—the Parkash Singh Badal clan. Under J. Jayalalithaa, Tamil

Nadu had drifted from welfarism to messianic populism. In Bihar, the state was absent. And Gujarat? Majoritarianism was writ large.

Beneath these differences lurked similarities. All of them struggled to deliver health, education and justice, including Tamil Nadu, venerated for its social justice movements and policies. In all these states, there was concentration of political power, and a politically connected elite had gained much more than everyone else. There was a weakening of democratic practice and a loss of common purpose as old worldviews retreated without a new vision replacing them. People fell back on caste or religious identities as they tried to cope. The question wrote itself. How did six states—with different histories, natural resource allocations, economic and civil society structures, and political parties at the helm*—reach the same developmental cul de sac?

This is not a bloodless, abstract question. The structures and processes responsible for this convergence have left most Indians trapped in poorly realised lives—graduates driving cabs in Aizawl; students in a government school in Keonjhar having four teachers for eight classes; Harbans Singh Bhanwer wondering if he should relocate his machine tooling firm from Punjab to Himachal Pradesh; Alagiri Madhivanan struggling to find fish in Vedaranyam; Jilani Mobin spending sleepless nights trying to defuse communal tensions in Chhapra; and the leuva patel community in Rajkot no longer renting out houses to kadva patels.

---

* Three of these states—Odisha, Tamil Nadu and Bihar—were ruled by regional parties at the time. Gujarat and Punjab were under the BJP (in Punjab, it was the BJP's ally Shiromani Akali Dal). India's other national party, the Congress, was in power in two small states—Mizoram and Manipur. This typology was less than perfect. The states I covered did not include any Left-ruled states. It also did not include border states like Himachal Pradesh and Uttarakhand—which, unlike the Northeast, belong to India's ethnic majority. This imperfection left me on an emotional pendulum. On bad days, I wondered about the utility of the project. And then, the pendulum would swing again. Identifying even some processes, I would think, could be a useful addition to the understanding of emergent India.

I was quick to see the first cost of this decay: state after state had let its people down. Its other costs took longer to sink in. The resulting disillusionment with democracy pushed people towards a 'strong' leader who promised achche din, good days. The other was that, faced with a rampaging centre, state governments—poorly democratic themselves—failed as bulwarks.

———

Ear to the Ground was bracketed by two of the most consequential elections in India's recent history. The first, in 2014, installed Modi as the prime minister. The second, in 2019, at the end of a campaign that had less talk of development and more of minority-baiting and nationalism, gave him an even larger mandate.

The first five years of the BJP's rule were unnerving. The country saw ill-conceived demonetisation, which hurt lower-income groups, and the hasty rollout of the goods and services tax (GST), despite its fiscal costs for the states and small businesses. With the government favouring a few large business groups, the informal economy and small and medium enterprises suffered.[20] The economy slowed.

The party moved with greater purpose and clarity on social and political fronts. Approaching each state election as a battle, it outspent rivals and rapidly forged post-poll alliances when it did not emerge as the largest party or, as in Maharashtra, swore its state unit to power despite lacking numbers, trying to cobble up a majority by engineering defections of MLAs from other parties.[21] It also began a project of demonising and diminishing minorities.[22] In the first twelve months of Modi's prime ministership alone, India saw over 110 attacks on Christians and 95 on Muslims.[23] Lynchings of Muslims rose. Some attackers were felicitated by union ministers,[24] while others were let off after lax police enquiries.[25]

In its second term, the government doubled down. Article 370, which gave special status to Jammu and Kashmir, the only Muslim-majority state in the country, was hollowed out, and the state was bifurcated and reduced to two union territories. Fearing protests, the valley was put under a communication and military lockdown in August 2019,[26] which continues as this book goes to press in November 2020. After a rollout of the National Register of Citizens (NRC) in Assam, to identify so-called undocumented immigrants, yielded more Hindus than Muslims with inadequate documentation, the government passed a bill linking Indian citizenship to religion. The Citizenship Amendment Act (CAA), 2019, offers Indian citizenship to the Hindu, Sikh, Buddhist, Jain, Parsi and Christian minorities fleeing religious persecution in Pakistan, Bangladesh and Afghanistan but leaves out Muslim refugees. It was the Modi government's most direct attack yet on Indian democracy's secular character.

Most of these violations went unchallenged by watchdog institutions. Bodies like the Election Commission and the Supreme Court stayed mum. In a sting operation, some of India's biggest media houses, who believed they were speaking to a cog in India's right-wing ecosystem, were shown agreeing to stoke up communal tensions in return for cash.[27] At the same time, civil society organisations in India found themselves under deeper scrutiny of the government and faced mounting curbs on their access to funds.

Talk began about Indian democracy slipping into a crisis. This assertion is simplistic. As the kleptocratic capture of central and state governments by political parties deepened, India's democratic project was already in crisis. This left voters disenchanted with democracy and set the stage for Modi's rise. What we face now is a second, deeper crisis. This is not semantic quibbling. India's founders saw state governments as one check against an overweening centre. However, as this book shows, they are out of control themselves. Warding off the Hindutva brigade's project of recasting India into a Hindu Rashtra is necessary, but it is not sufficient to revive India's democratic project. We need a deeper reconstruction.

As you will see in this book, most Indians live despite the State, as opposed to flourishing under it. The structures and processes responsible for that outcome also threaten India's democracy—not just the greatest accomplishment in the subcontinent's history but also one of the most audacious experiments in the postcolonial world. Understanding them better is the first step towards securing a more just country.

1

The State That Could Not
Pay Salaries

Like most towns in Mizoram, Aizawl sits on a ridge. Its elevated perch
is a throwback to the state's tribal past when chiefs sited villages atop
steep ridges as a defensive strategy.[1] It is one reason why the state
capital's oldest parts, like the governor's colonial bungalow, occupy
its highest points. Only with growth did the city flow downhill,
unstoppably and transformationally, replacing old forests with a thick
warren of middle-income apartments, shops and churches. On yet
lower slopes and valley bottoms, as though to prove the accompanying
correlation between altitude and power, lie the slums.[2]

Somewhere in those middle reaches was the house of Malsawma Sailo.

When I reached Mizoram in March 2015, the state was in the throes
of a South Korean fever. Youngsters were mimicking characters from
Seoul's films and television soaps. Hairstylists and furniture sellers
were lifting styles from these. An eatery barely passable as Korean
had just opened. There was much excitement that a South Korean
boy band might perform in Aizawl. Much of this inordinate fondness
for South Korean culture was the handiwork of Mizoram's cable
television channels. Korean soaps and films dubbed into Mizo had
been their staple programming since 2010.[3] Sailo owned and ran one
of the first such channels—Nauban, named after a local orchid. So,
one afternoon, I journeyed down to meet him.

Sailo was a trim man in his mid-forties with short, black hair, clad in a grey polo and khaki cargos that ended halfway down his calves. Only the creases on his face showed he was older than his attire and frame suggested. We marched down the road for a bit from the local landmark—a large white church with a driveway wide enough for three cars to parallel park—and then up Aizawl's ubiquitous cement steps that wove between apartments and houses, connecting them to roads below and above, till Sailo ducked into an apartment block. Seconds later, we were at his door.

Dolls stood propped up in threes and fours against the fading blue walls of the living room. A Barbie-like one, with a wavy red line running from the corner of her right temple to the nose, stood next to a stuffed yellow doll in a pink jacket. Another, to the left of a white teddy bear, had black dots on her cheekbones, black painted lips and a thick, black 'V' running from the ends of her temple, down her forehead, to meet at the bridge of the nose. They looked quite striking, like superheroes from an edgy graphic novel.

Three computers shared the living room with the doll collection that belonged to his two daughters. In the adjacent room were more dolls and two more computers, one connected to a speaker, the other with earphones lying on top of it. Home was also where Sailo and his spouse, Pi Lalmuanpuii Sailo,* produced Nauban. While I inspected the dolls in the second room, Sailo settled into a brown plastic chair in front of the speaker.

'How did you get into Korean programming?'

'Because of *Kasautii Zindagii Kay*,' he said. And then, as though marvelling at how it had all started, he laughed.

The story dated back to 2004, when Zonet Cable TV, a local company, fixed the central contradiction in its business model. Mizos wanted programmes in their language but, numbering just 11 lakh, were too small a market for Zonet to recover the cost of original programming. As an experiment, it dubbed episodes from *Kasautii Zindagii Kay*, a

---

* In Mizo, Pu is the honorific for men, Pi for women.

(very) long-running Hindi television serial about two lovers destined to stay apart all their lives, into Mizo.

So eager were Mizos for programmes in their own language that the soap, written for India's Hindi heartland, became a runaway hit in the state. By 2008, both Zonet and LPS Vision, the other big cable company in the state, were airing dubbed episodes of the soap. Magazines, unwilling to sit out the mania, published transcripts of the episodes as they aired. Minor cable providers, working in smaller towns and hamlets below the radar of LPS and Zonet and far too puny to do their own dubbing, scouted for already dubbed films and serials.

At that time, Sailo was the principal of an English school set up by the Pentecostal Church in the district of Mamit, over to the west of Aizawl. It was his fourth job. Between 1991 and 1999, after completing his BA from Lunglei, the second largest town in Mizoram, he had run a grocery store, served as the principal of a church-backed school there and manned a cement store in Aizawl, before shifting to Mamit. In 2008, he left that school and returned to the capital.

A homespun attempt to rise in an economy that had only low-paying jobs followed. From local CD and DVD stores, he bought Hindi and English films, which he and his team of four—'two voice artistes, one editor and one translator'—dubbed into Mizo. When more voices were needed, Lalmuanpuii stepped in. By 2009, they were dubbing three movies a month and selling each for Rs 150 a DVD. 'We knew the sub-operator [local cable distributor] of Aizawl town. And then sub-operators from other districts also began asking me to send my DVDs to them.' By 2010, about a hundred cable operators across Mizoram were buying his DVDs, from which he and his team made Rs 45,000 a month.

And then, the business arched downwards. As word spread that money could be made dubbing movies into Mizo, competition grew. 'A lot of people got into dubbing, and they were quoting cheaper rates.'

Compounding matters, Mizos also turned to South Korean fare. Some people I met traced this switch to an evening in 2009, when, to fill time, a local cable company played the DVD of a Korean serial.

When it switched to news, its switchboard was said to have lit up with viewers calling to ask when the serial would resume. Others traced this craze back to a Korean romantic melodrama called *The Classic*. Built around the love stories of a mother and daughter, the film is said to have entered India through Manipur and then spread rapidly across the Northeast. Yet others said everything started in 2001, when South Korean channel Arirang—a part of what the journalist Euny Hong describes as the country's efforts to become a cultural soft power[4]— became freely available across Northeast India.

What is more incontrovertible is that, by 2010, South Korean serials with English subtitles had reached Aizawl's shops and street vendors, and cable operators were airing these. By 2012, dubbed DVDs were fetching Sailo just Rs 80. It was a familiar arc. In the hyper-competitive world of India's informal economy, businesses do not stay profitable for long. Because of the pervasive lack of opportunities, others rush in. Heightened competition results in price warfare. Booms end early. People hop from one unrelated business to another, hoping to land on their feet.

Sailo leapt too. In 2012, shuttering the old dubbing business, he signed up with Zonet to produce Nauban. The cable company charged Sailo a monthly fee to air the channel, while he had to produce the daily feed as well as generate advertising revenue from sponsors. Some parts of his dubbing business changed—he now downloaded Korean soaps from websites like HanCinema—while other aspects stayed the same. The dubbing team stayed small. Whenever needed, the Sailos continued to lend their voices.

'How do you know which soap will do well?'

'Romance and family drama work well. Like *Yellow Boots*. That did very well.'

'What's the story?'

'A woman is hit by a car and she dies. Our heroine is charged, so police take her into custody. While she's in jail, her fiancée leaves her and marries another woman. But our heroine is pregnant at the time, so she has a child in prison.'

That was Lalmuanpuii narrating the plot. Sailo had started on the answer but given up almost immediately. The script's evident enthusiasm for squeezing tear ducts had left him laughing again. 'The truth is, she has been falsely implicated in the accident,' she continued. 'It's the woman actually responsible for the accident who has married her fiancée. After she leaves jail, our heroine plots revenge.'

The script is ho-hum, as trite and manipulative as soaps elsewhere in the world. A deeper reason why Mizos watch Korean soaps lies in what Pu Vanneihtluanga, the programming head of Zonet, told me. Asked about their allure, he referred to 1966, when the Mizo National Front (MNF) rebelled against India and liberated Aizawl. 'I was nine years old. I remember standing in a forest watching Indian Air Force planes bomb Aizawl. We had been told by [MNF leader] Laldenga then—and we believed him—that a thlawhnavar [a white aeroplane] would come and drive these IAF planes away. None came.'

This, he said, was a turning point for the Mizos. 'Before that, we thought we were Westerners. We were born and raised in the lap of missionaries. In Zodin cinema hall, all the movies we saw were John Wayne, cowboys, Western films. We felt they were very near to us. But gradually, we came to learn that the West is far away. We were remote, very ignorant. The missionaries were gone. We had to depend on India.'

The society felt unmoored. 'This is because of where we are. On the western side of Mizoram, we see you. On the east, we see the Burmese Buddhists. Neither of you is us. We are an island in the Himalayan range.' When the Indian media came in, Mizos consumed what was available but could not identify with it.* 'We hate the Bollywood style of singing and dancing. Our face is different from that of most Indians. There are ethnic differences. We are Christians.' This, he said, explained the Korean wave. 'They look like us. Their facial structures are clean. The plots are conservative, ones that Protestants and Catholics can relate to. Even the way they talk, a slightly musical tone, is similar to ours.'

---

* Doordarshan, India's national broadcaster, began its Mizoram service in 1994.

It was a sharp insight into the state, touching on questions of ethnicity and identity, lingering alienation, the persistent fear of assimilation and the underlying yearning to identify with and belong to groups perceived as similar.*

Sailo revealed another perplexing thing about Mizoram's Korean programming boom. Its popularity notwithstanding, none of the channels were making money. He had started with modest ambitions, assuming that if Nauban got ten advertisers—government departments or local businesses—each willing to pay Rs 10,000 a month to sponsor either the channel or a serial, he would make Rs 1 lakh every month. Even these marginal numbers, however, proved elusive. After rising to Rs 50,000, monthly revenues began falling.

Over-competition was the culprit again. The number of channels climbed to ten. With all of them chasing the same sponsors, advertisement rates fell to Rs 5,000–Rs 6,000 per month. The number of sponsors fell too. It was inching towards five for Nauban, which meant a gross monthly income of Rs 25,000–Rs 30,000 for Sailo.

The strain showed. The house had not been painted for long. In less animated moments, Sailo looked anxious, wondering what to do next. 'If the number of sponsors comes down to five, it will be hard to survive. We might have to start some new business.'†

A few days later, I heard a similar tale from Pu Laldinmawia, the founder of another channel, Ainawn, named after a local flowering shrub. Disdainful of Korean programming, Laldinmawia dubbed documentaries from channels like National Geographic into Mizo. For him too, advertisement rates were not crossing Rs 6,000, and the number of sponsors was dropping.

---

* The academic Joy L.K. Pachuau alludes to this apprehension: 'The fear for many Mizos is in being *chim ral* (lit. "submerged to extinction") or overrun by *Vais* (outsiders).' See: Pachuau, *Being Mizo: Identity and Belonging in Northeast Asia* (New Delhi: Oxford University Press, 2014), 140–142.

† By 2019, the Korean boom had lost some of its vitality but was still around. One more new channel had come up. Profits from Nauban were down to Rs 20,000 a month. With expenses mounting, the Sailos started a taxi service.

It did not add up. Why could Nauban and Ainawn—aired on the biggest cable company in a state with an annual budget of Rs 5,500 crore—not find ten sponsors who would each pay Rs 10,000 a month? What did this say about economic activity in Mizoram?

———

At the time *Ear to the Ground* was conceptualised, what I knew about Mizoram would not have filled a paragraph. In the troubled periphery that is India's Northeast, mauled variably by insurgents, army rule, corrupt politicians and militant student unions, I knew that Mizoram was peaceful. The state was one of the most sparsely populated parts of India, being seven times the size of Goa but with just two-thirds its population. Talking to friends working in the Northeast, I learnt it was quite homogenous—most people were Mizos. Minorities were few and geographically concentrated. Tribespeople of the Lai, Mara and Chakma communities lived in Mizoram's southern reaches. Others, like the Brus, resided in the western part of the state.

Daman Singh's environmental history of Mizoram, *The Last Frontier*, narrates a tale of extraordinary change. Mizoram's people, writes Singh, 'entered the twentieth century as little known, but feared tribes; animists whose lives were ruled by sacrifice and superstition; wanderers through the hills with no permanent home, with neither plough, nor script, nor currency. Nearly a century later, 46 per cent of the population lives in urban areas, 83 per cent are Christians, and the state has an impressive literacy rate of 81 per cent, and even more strikingly, a female literacy rate of 78 per cent.'[5]

By 1854, as Singh writes, the British had most of the Brahmaputra plains under their control. The opposition they faced came from the hill tribes—the Nagas, Garos, and Lushais or Mizos. By 1880, only the Lushais continued to resist, descending on the plains to raid, plunder, kidnap and kill. In 1890, the British gave up on conciliatory measures and launched a fresh offensive. By 1900, they prevailed.

It was, however, a weak victory. Unlike neighbouring Assam, which had oil, timber and tea plantations, the Lushai Hills offered little economic prospects. The region lacked minerals, had few trees of commercial value, hardly any settled agriculture, and the locals, living off jhum, or slash-and-burn farming, were too poor to serve as a market for foreign goods.[6] All that the Mizos had was the capacity to disrupt trade in Assam and what was then eastern Bengal. These qualities set the contours of British rule in Mizoram. The new rulers focused on provoking as little resistance as possible and on investing as little as possible. They, however, allowed the Church and Christian missionaries to work in the region.

The years that followed reshaped Mizoram in lasting ways. The days of ranging widely to seek fresh lands for jhum ended for the clans. Instead, each was given territories. With the British taking over functions like defence, clan chiefs became subservient to the colonial power. At the same time, 'evangelism and education led to the propagation and spread of Christianity at a speed that had no parallel in the experience of Missions abroad'.[7]

After Independence, present-day Mizoram became part of Assam. In 1959, ties between Assam and the Mizo leadership frayed. That year, the state saw a famine and inadequate relief attempts by Assam. Discontent deepened after the state decided the very next year to make Assamese its official language, a move the hill people saw as an imposition on their cultural identities. In 1962, the Mizo National Famine Front, a communitarian outfit which took shape during the famine, dropped 'famine' from its name and became a political outfit. Its objective: an independent Mizo nation.[8] Training in East Pakistan, present-day Bangladesh, followed. In 1966, an armed secessionist movement—described in books like *Mizoram Marches towards Freedom* by Laldenga, Mizoram's first chief minister—began.[9]

The Indian government cracked down. Its excesses went beyond the much-discussed bombing of Aizawl in 1966 by the Indian Air Force. The next year, foreshadowing the Salwa Judum camps that Chhattisgarh would see in the 2000s, Mizo villages were forcibly relocated to sites controlled by security forces. Here too, the idea was to 'cut off food and shelter provided, willingly or otherwise, by the people to the insurgents,' writes Singh.[10] This affected as much as 87 per cent of the population. 'The villages were barricaded, and frequent checking of identity cards and searches of homes, patrols, restricted movements and alleged abuses by security forces caused immense resentment. Social relations were upset by the sudden heterogeneity of people from different villages. Relief measures were inadequate. Jhumming was totally dislocated.'[11] It was 1980 before compulsory residence in these camps was relaxed across the state. In 1986, the Mizo Peace Accord was signed. The next year, as part of the accord, Mizoram became a state, and Laldenga, its first chief minister.

Singh's book came out in 1996. Almost twenty years later, on my way from the airport to the government hotel at Chaltlang, a suburb on the same ridge as Aizawl, my first jumbled impressions were of vegetable sellers sitting under a concrete shed, the cab taking a detour because of a landslide, houses standing on stilts driven into steep mountain slopes, and Aizawl, high up on a ridge, visible in the distance.

In the days that followed, every morning, locals were out sweeping the streets. This was one way the ancient Mizo notion of 'tlawmngaihna'—putting everyone's welfare above one's self-interest—revealed itself in daily life. The state was intensely devout. Every evening, church bells called people to inkhawn zan or church night. On Sundays, life stood still. Opening for business was frowned upon. Public transport was minimal. Some general stores opened, but their shutters stayed down as observance. Only the door was left ajar for customers. Butchers opened early and closed by eight o'clock in the morning.

The workers at a butcher's shop I spoke to, all from Uttar Pradesh and Bihar, expressed apprehension towards the Young Mizo Association (YMA). A volunteer organisation most adult Mizo men belong to, the YMA sees itself as a custodian of the community. Its members, as the journalist Maitreyee Handique wrote for *Scroll.in*, make important local announcements such as 'the deaths of locals' and 'organise overnight wakes and make other funeral arrangements'.[12] There was also, Handique added, a darker side to this Mizo code of life.

'It is exceptionally severe on those who don't fall in line with rigidly structured social mores.'

Those initial days in Aizawl, smoke rose from the surrounding hills. The deadline set by the administration to stop the burning of forests was looming closer. Jhum cultivation was still the primary mode of farming in the state. I woke up every day to soot and burnt leaves twisting in the air and falling to the ground.

One evening, as Pu Vanlalruata, a veteran Press Trust of India reporter in the state, and I sat outside on a log in his farmstead, drinking rakzu, the local rice alcohol, a forest patch went up in smoke a couple of hundred metres to our right. It was dark. The ridge and the night sky blurred into each other. All we could see was a thin line of jhum fire, crackling as it moved uphill, eating the forest. Before us reared another ridge, its edges similarly indiscernible in the dark but silhouetted by a blanket of lights. Aizawl.

———

Rain was pelting down. Seven forest guards were sheltering in a wooden hut atop a gently sloping hill in the village of Damparengpui in the district of Mamit. Squatting before a fire, two of them were making lunch while the rest chatted as they sharpened their machetes.

We were near the core area of the Dampa Tiger Reserve. Sprawled over the hills to the east of the great Brahmaputra floodplains, Dampa is a remnant of a tropical forest that once connected forests in India and the Chittagong hill tracts of Bangladesh with those in Myanmar. The result is a unique assemblage of species—martens, clouded leopards, civets, golden cats, marbled cats, leopard cats, Malayan sun bears and binturongs.

It is also one of the more vulnerable forests in India. 'No less than twelve separatist groups are active here,' Priya Singh, a biologist camera-trapping small cats in the forest, told me. Among them are splinter groups of the Shanti Bahini fighting for the autonomy of the Chakma people in Bangladesh and the National Liberation Front of Tripura (NLTF) militating for Tripura to be an independent, Christian country. In February 2015, working with the Bru Democratic Front of Mizoram, the NLTF kidnapped twenty-two people. Two were held back as hostages and marched over into Bangladesh.[13] The troop had triggered one of Singh's camera traps.

Dampa is an insurgency corridor. Groups active in Bangladesh use it to access the relative safety of India. Those active in India use it to access the relative safety of Bangladesh. Forest guards, given their antiquated .303s, avoid parts of the park close to the border, making movement easier for these groups.

Travelling with Singh into Damparengpui, I saw a second reason this little forest was in trouble: human pressure. Villages here mainly comprised the minority Brus. After ethnic violence that saw Mizos attack Brus in 1997 and again in 2009, thousands fled Mizoram for Tripura. The ones who stayed back continued with the traditional livelihood of jhum. It, however, could not support households for an entire year. So, these families also lived off the forest, hunting and gathering minor forest produce. Since 2013, some families had been returning. Locals estimated Damparengpui's population to have swelled from 300 families in 2013 to about 500 in 2015. This increase was affecting the park. Most shifting cultivation used to take place in Dampa's buffer zone, but now, the newcomers were heading into the core area of 500 square kilometres.

The state's response to this second threat was unsatisfactory as well. The state Department of Environment, Forests and Climate Change (henceforth, Forest Department) had no more than seventeen permanent staff at the hilly 988-square-kilometre park.[14] Most patrolling was done by villagers drawn from Dampa's fringe. Guards, hired from the same villages and communities as the hunters, were unlikely to catch them. Compounding matters, at the time of my visit in March 2015, the little forest guards were paid—Rs 6,600 to Rs 6,700 a month—was running late by six months.

Something odd was afoot here. The state government allotted very little money to the Forest Department, an official of the department in Aizawl told me. So, the department used the funds from the central government's Project Tiger to pay forest guards. According to D.P. Bankwal, the Guwahati-based regional director of the National Tiger Conservation Authority (NTCA), which oversees Project Tiger, the institution had released money for salaries in June 2014. The allocation was sent to the state Finance Department, which had to release the money to the Forest Department. When I visited Dampa, it was yet to do so.* This delay came with large costs. With salaries coming late, I was told in Teirei village, some guards too had cleared plots in the forest for farming. When they could, they hunted as well.

It was not just the salaries of forest guards that were running late. Students in the state capital were on a strike protesting a delay in their scholarships. A Health Department staffer in the town of West Phaileng told me that salaries of Accredited Social Health Activists (ASHAs) were running late too. So were payments for those trying to slow the spread of the human immunodeficiency virus (HIV) in the state.

———

Given its proximity to Southeast Asia's golden triangle—where Thailand, Laos and Burma meet, a region infamous for opium and heroin production—the border district of Champhai is one of the primary routes through which drugs like heroin and methamphetamine enter India. Most of these drugs head to Aizawl, Silchar and beyond, but some circulate in Champhai as well. In 2015, with addicts sharing needles and turning to sex work to make money, the district was a hotspot for both drug use and HIV. The incidence of HIV in Mizoram was second only to Manipur in the Northeast. And within Mizoram, it was Champhai that stood out. Sixty per cent of all HIV-positive people in the district were drug addicts. The equivalent number for all of Mizoram was half that.[15]

———

* This problem of delayed payments extended beyond Mizoram. 'In Nameri National Park [in Assam's Sonitpur district], with great arm-twisting, we were able to get 2013–2014 salaries paid out a few months ago,' Rajesh Gopal, a former NTCA head, told me in 2015.

In the litany of India's medical crises, HIV is that rare public health emergency that saw a swift and proportionate response from the central and state governments. Targeted Intervention Centres (TICs), run by local NGOs, gave free needles and condoms to those at high risk of contracting HIV—like drug addicts and sex workers—and took them for regular HIV check-ups. A second node of response, Integrated Counselling and Testing Centres (ICTCs), tested the general population. In hilly Champhai, 230 kilometres long and 90 kilometres wide, the district AIDS Control Society also ran mobile ICTCs—white-coloured pickups, each with a driver, counsellor and lab technician—which roamed the district, screening remote communities.

This is where Pi Lalbiaki, a thirty-three-year-old postgraduate in social work from Mizoram University, worked. 'Because of my grandfather,' she said. 'It's good to work for the people, to help others, he told me.' In 2013, her pick-up had covered almost sixty villages. By 2015, things changed. Her team's travel budget was coming in fits and starts, and the testing schedule was in a shambles. 'Between January and March, we covered five villages.'

Or take Agape, a church-funded body running a TIC for female intravenous drug users in Aizawl. The centre received funds in September 2014, and then again only next February. In October 2014, said Pi Zothanpuii, its programme director, it borrowed from the parent NGO and carried on as usual. In November, fieldworkers, who met the centre's drug-user and sex-worker clients five days a week, began cutting back on trips. By February, they were heading out only once a week. A chart on a wall in its office showed that monthly expenditure, which stood at Rs 3.5 lakh in September, had fallen to Rs 1.3 lakh in October, Rs 25,837 in November, and then, an incredible Rs 1,569 in December. Phone and internet bills, said Zothanpuii. As field trips reduced, clients had to either visit Agape's office to get fresh needles or buy them in the market. Travelling cost money. So did the needles. While we spoke, a young sex worker, about thirty years of age but who looked much older, was listening to us. She had abscesses on both her feet, a result of shooting heroin into the veins there. Waiting for her feet to be cleaned and re-bandaged, she echoed Zothanpuii. 'When we don't get needles, we share with our friends.'

In Champhai too, another chart, on the wall of a TIC run by an NGO called Genesaret, showed similar decrease in activity. According to Pu Lalnunsanga, its accountant, no money came between April and September 2014. And then again, none till February 2015. 'We used to test clients' HIV status at least twice each year,' he said. As the centre began taking only acute cases for testing, the number of tests they did per month fell from forty-seven in April 2014 to four in March 2015.*

The fallout of these funding delays was nothing less than the haemorrhaging of hard-won gains.

Growth in new HIV cases in Mizoram had slowed to between 100 and 150 a month by 2010–2011, said an official in the AIDS Control Society at Aizawl. Until September 2014, there were some months when no client tested positive, added Pi Lalengmawii, a project manager at Agape. Since then, however, every month had yielded at least one positive case, even as the number of people getting tested fell.

Healthworkers were panicking. In 2014, Lalbiaki and her mobile ICTCs had identified eighty HIV-positive people in Champhai. With funds not coming but villagers calling her, she was taking personal loans. 'Depending on how much we raise, we do the outreach.' By April, her loans stood at Rs 13,600. Her monthly salary was Rs 13,000. 'We need to keep going to these villages. If there's one positive [person] in the village and if there's no test, then he or she can spread the disease easily to others.'

Yet, individual responses could not fill the gaps left by systemic failure. Sometimes, her team visited three to five villages in a month. 'These are mostly villages close to Champhai. At the most, we get into the middle of the district.' People living deeper yet in the district had

---

* Asked about the number of cases referred for testing by NGOs, Pi Zonunmawii, the programme manager at the district AIDS Prevention and Control Unit in Champhai, confirmed the number had fallen—from 2,507 in 2011–2012 to 987 in 2014–2015.

to travel to Champhai for testing. While pregnant women were willing, drug users were not.

––––

It was not just salaries that were late. Government schemes were beset by funding delays as well.

After coming to power in 2008, Chief Minister Pu Lalthanhawla's Congress government announced an ambitious plan to wean Mizoram off jhum farming. Under the New Land Use Policy (NLUP), his government promised Rs 1 lakh each to 1.35 lakh households, close to three-fifths of all households in the state, over five years to help them find other livelihoods. They were also promised technical help from state departments; families interested in setting up fish farms, for instance, would get not only cash but also technical advice about establishing hatcheries and building ponds, and would get stocks of fingerlings.[16]

It was an intriguing scheme. At the best of times, settling into a new occupation is hard. Opting out of jhum too engendered complex outcomes. While locals spoke of shrinking jhum cycles and falling yields, biologists were worried about the state pushing plantation crops, especially oil palm, on to the farmers. In clearings of one to three hectares, as ecologist T.R. Shankar Raman writes in *The Wild Heart of India*, 'each farmer [in Mizoram] plants and sequentially harvests between fifteen to twenty-five crops—indigenous rice varieties, maize, vegetables and herbs, chillies, bananas, tubers, and other species—besides obtaining edible mushrooms, fruits and bamboo shoots'. Switching to cash monocultures would undermine food security.

It would also threaten the local biodiversity. In 2014, surveying near Dampa, Raman recorded ten forest bird species in oil palm plantations, thirty-eight in teak plantations, fifty in jhum and seventy inside the rainforest.[17] 'The secondary forests that arise after jhum fields are rested are poorer than mature evergreens,' he said in an email to me. 'But the jhum landscape is still a mixed, dense forest of higher diversity than just about any of the other forms of agriculture or horticulture.*"

Six years after the NLUP was announced, according to the state finance minister Lalsawta's 2014–2015 budget speech, Mizoram had spent about Rs 3,000 crore and covered 1.2 lakh households. Results, however, seemed underwhelming. Not only did jhum continue, but also the scheme had been used to reward party supporters. A 2012 study by the Presbyterian church, covering ten villages in the districts of Aizawl, Mamit and Champhai, found that nine out of ten beneficiaries were connected to the Congress.

P.L. Thanga, a retired government official heading the NLUP's Implementing Board, in an interview to me, agreed that the first set of beneficiaries were predominantly from the Congress but said that the programme, as it scaled up, had spread beyond party supporters. A Forest Department official I spoke to aligned with Thanga but advanced a different reason: 'While only Congress supporters were given funds in the first round, Congress leaders used the opportunity to tell locals, "Loosen your stiffness [closeness] to the Mizo National Front."'

This created a fresh puzzle. According to the Forest Survey of India's 2013 report, between 2011 and 2013, Mizoram's moderately dense forests shrank by 263 square kilometres and 'open forests' grew by 103 square kilometres. The main reason was 'shifting cultivation, soil erosion and biotic pressure'.[18] If everyone was covered, why was jhum expanding?

In Vanhne, a village about twelve kilometres from Lunglei, only the first set of NLUP beneficiaries had got the entire amount when I visited. Payments to the rest were running late, said Pu Lallianbuanga, secretary of Vanhne village's south section. 'Those in the second or third group only got Rs 10,000–Rs 15,000. There's not too much that can be done

---

* There were other impacts. Jhum farming is done on community land. As individual farmers migrated to plantations, land commons shrank and fragmented. With individual land titles mostly going to men, gender equity took a beating. Crops like oil palm need a lot of water, and so, local hydrology got stressed as well.

with Rs 10,000. Sarusun Rai, who runs a small shop in Damparengpui, and his wife got one instalment of Rs 15,000 shortly after signing up in March 2013. A second instalment arrived that August but nothing more since. 'It's now March [2015], and there's no sign of the money,' he said.

What remained unanswered was the reason for these delays in government payments.

———

Finding it hard to sit at home, Pu Zalawma headed to work as usual.

But there was not much to do. When I saw him—a man in his mid-forties, clad in flip-flops, brown trousers and a red T-shirt with 'Coca-Cola' written across it—he was sitting on the stone steps of the district Health Department's office in the town of Champhai.

To provide health services to people living in the district's remote parts, the department ran a three-minibus cavalcade. The first carried doctors, while the other two hefted a laboratory and an X-ray machine. Zalawma, an army man for seventeen years before returning to Mizoram, drove the one with the X-ray. It made for a busy life. The cavalcade would tour at least twice every month, seeking to cover all eighty-three villages in the district as often as it could.

And then, in August 2014, Zalawma's salary stopped coming. By the time we met, the father of three—the youngest three years old, the eldest fourteen—had not been paid his salary of Rs 8,550 for eight months.[19] He was managing because of his pension of Rs 11,000 from the army. Those without such support, he said, were having a hard time. 'They are borrowing from everywhere.'

When asked why his salary was late, an administrative rabbit hole opened up. Money from the Mizoram Health Society, which decides how healthcare funds are used in the state, was coming in late. Champhai had not received funds for four months, Pi Lalnuntluangi, a medical superintendent in the district, told me, forcing officials like her to choose between supporting the district hospital, primary health centres (PHCs), programmes like immunisation or keeping mobile units on the road. They chose the hospitals, PHCs and health programmes, and the minibuses travelled only when funds were available. Even when they did, they could not venture beyond fifty to eighty kilometres from Champhai.

One evening in Aizawl, a senior official at the health society traced the problem back to an economic straitjacket the state should have been more mindful of. Like other states in the Northeast, Mizoram needs central government funds to support itself; its internal revenues are a fraction of central payouts. In 2014–2015, its total revenues stood at Rs 5,880 crore. Of this, state government revenues were Rs 549 crore and share of central taxes were Rs 1,031 crore, both of which the state could spend anyway it liked. The rest were grants from the central government, which came with preconfigured uses, for instance, wages for forest guards.

In 2010, the state government accepted the Sixth Pay Commission's recommendations and increased the salaries of government employees. By 2015, between staff salaries and subsidies on power, food and water alone, Mizoram was spending close to Rs 2,000 crore each year.

This created a cash-flow problem. The state had high monthly payments to make but unpredictable monthly receipts: it did not know when central allocations would come. Unable to balance both, it periodically ran out of money. In response, apart from borrowing more, the treasury held on to grants from the centre, putting them into civil deposits it could dip into whenever it fell short of cash.* When newer grants came, they were redirected as well, some to replace funds diverted earlier, the rest to fresher expediencies.

----

* By 2014, as Pu Lalsawta, the state finance minister, told the assembly, Mizoram's twenty-three government departments had stockpiled no less than Rs 535.23 crore in civil deposits. Apart from this, the state government was also taking more Ways and Means Advances—high-cost, short-term loans given by the Reserve Bank of India. See: PTI, 'Mizoram Government Depts Keeps Rs 535.23 Crore in Civil Deposit: Finance Minister', *Economic Times* (18 November 2014), economictimes. indiatimes.com/news/economy/finance/mizoram-government-depts-keeps-rs-535-23-crore-in-civil-deposit-finance-minister/articleshow/ 45189549.cms.

This dysfunction metastasised into a healthcare crisis when, during its dying months in 2013–2014, the Congress-headed UPA government changed how states got health funds from the centre. Under the old system, money directly moved from the central Ministry of Health and Family Welfare to state societies. But after the change, said the senior official at the health society in Aizawl, 'the ministry sends money to the state treasury, which releases it to the society'. These funds, he said, were getting stuck. A Rs 25 crore payment the society had to get in November, its third and final instalment for 2014, was yet to come in mid-April the next year.

Funds were needed for salaries, hospitals and clinics, fighting diseases like malaria and tuberculosis, immunisation, family planning, childbirth, care of new mothers and more. When funds came late, triage was the only option. 'My medical staff has not been paid since January. ASHAs have not been paid for six months. There's a shortage of medicines for drug-resistant tuberculosis. The only programme we are protecting till now is immunisation,' said the official.

In the state HIV programme too, the rot had set in once the UPA government decided to re-route AIDS funds from the state AIDS Control Society to the state Finance Department. Things worsened once the BJP-led National Democratic Alliance (NDA) came to power in the centre. It slashed the allocations for the National AIDS Control Organization (NACO) from Rs 1,785 crore to Rs 1,397 crore. J.P. Nadda, the union health minister, justified the move, saying, 'AIDS was a concern ten years back.'[20] Not only was the state's AIDS programme affected by this nationwide cut, but also the little funds that did reach Mizoram got stuck in the treasury.

The rest was predictable. Not just funding cuts, funding delays too imposed dire costs on people. In 2015, Mizoram had between 9,000 and 10,000 HIV-positive people. By November 2017, it climbed to 14,632.[21] The state, along with Meghalaya and Tripura, was one of three that posted an increase in HIV cases at a time India saw a national decline.[22] By 2019, it had a higher HIV prevalence, percentage of people living with the disease,* than all other states in India.[23]

Or take the NLUP. The Rs 1 lakh paid over five years was to cover villagers' expenses while the new livelihood took root. But, with cash coming at unpredictable intervals, villagers investing in new businesses found themselves stuck. People with existing businesses invested NLUP money in those. Others splurged. Several stopped jhum when the money came in but resumed once the cash ran out. With only the first set of beneficiaries getting the full payment, most of them Congress supporters, the NLUP came to be seen as a giveaway to party supporters.

All this could have been evaded if state revenues had been higher. Why were they not?

———

In Mizoram, agriculture is pre-modern and provides little more than subsistence. Manufacturing too, businessperson Michael Lalthanmawia told me at the local industry association's office in Aizawl, is small-scale.

A slender man in his late forties with large eyes and an earnest disposition, he had set up a steel rolling mill near Aizawl in 1995. Twenty years later, this unit was still struggling. Mizoram, with its population of 11 lakh, was not a large market. To grow, he needed to sell steel outside the state. However, given the distance between Mizoram and the rest of India, he could not truck the steel billets in, all the way from Assam—the raw material was also heavier than finished steel—process them, truck back the finished steel again and hope to be competitive. Instead, he found himself competing with rolling mills

---

* Between 2008–2009 and 2013–2014, the number of cases reported per day rose from 2.9 to 3.9. By 2018–2019, it stood at 9.2. See: Rahul Karmakar, 'With Nine Cases a Day, Mizoram Becomes State with Highest HIV Prevalence Rate', *Hindu* (13 October 2019), thehindu.com/sci-tech/health/with-nine-cases-a-day-mizoram-becomes-state-with-highest-hiv-prevalence-rate/article29674665.ece.

in Assam that were shipping finished steel to his state. This was the experience of most manufacturers in Mizoram.[24]

Logically, given its position right next to Myanmar, packed with products made in China, Mizoram should have a competitive advantage in trading. However, the pallets of Shock, an energy drink like Red Bull, that businessperson David Thangluaia tried importing from Myanmar, told a different story.

A stocky man in his late thirties with close-cropped hair, he lived in the town of Champhai. Twenty-two kilometres to its east was the sole trading outpost between Mizoram and Myanmar, the border village of Zokhawthar. By 2013, he had completed a postgraduate in science, gotten married and returned to Champhai, where his automobile repair workshop and the school set up by him and his wife—where they both taught—were running well.

Then, the young man's thoughts turned to trade. He saw an opportunity. Mizoram enjoyed advantages over neighbouring Manipur when it came to trade with Myanmar. Belonging to the ethnic group of Chins, Mizos could negotiate deals with their counterparts in Myanmar more easily than the traders from Silchar in Assam, who dominated trading in Manipur. And unlike insurgency-riddled Manipur, where extortion by underground groups was common, Mizoram was an oasis of calm. One of the products Thangluaia decided to import was Shock. Pallets could come from the Myanmar town of Tahan to the village of Tiao, cross over into Zokhawthar, and then skitter across to be sold in Mizoram and neighbouring states like Assam.

Two years later in 2015, when I met him, Thangluaia was in a reflective mood. He had just lost a chance to supply Shock to distributors in Assam; they had, after all, decided to buy via Manipur.

The roads in Mizoram were terrible and trucks could not move around the year. During the rainy season, which starts with intense pre-monsoon storms in March and continues till the end of October, traders could only use pickups. In contrast, roads in Manipur were better. 'Larger vehicles ply around the year there, moving at speeds up to 100 kmph, unlike the 15–25 kmph that vehicles in Mizoram manage,'

Thangluaia said. This asymmetry had ruined his plans. For distributors in Assam, sourcing Shock through Manipur helped save Rs 2–Rs 3 on every pallet of twenty-four cans, a considerable saving given the margin on each pallet was Rs 8–Rs 10. It was the same story with betel nut. Sent to Assam through Mizoram, it sold for Rs 238 a kilo. Trucked through Manipur, it sold for Rs 225–Rs 230. These economics skewed further in favour of Manipur during the rains as transporting through pickups cost more.

Low trade volumes were palpable in Zokhawthar as well. Most goods moved between Myanmar and India on pushcarts. The bridge over the river Tiau connecting the two countries was just wide enough for a pickup. The warehouse in the customs complex was the size of private grain warehouses in Madhya Pradesh. At the customs office in Champhai, A. Hangzo, superintendent of the Zokhawthar land customs station, confirmed that impression to me. 'The only legal trade we have here is betel nut. Everything else is illegal.'

Most of what traders in Champhai imported—a random grab bag of commodities like garments, sneakers, watermelons, cheroots and mobile phones—could be sold only in Mizoram. While bad roads stopped traders of Assam and Manipur from accessing the state's markets as well, given Mizoram's small population, importers found their growth capped. Hardly any trading house in the state, Lalthanmawia said, had a turnover above Rs 25 crore.*

And yet, these factors that dulled the business prospects of Thangluaia and Lalthanmawia were just a halfway reason for low economic activity in Mizoram. Across India's Northeast, with both manufacturing and trading being small in scale and agriculture at subsistence levels, the biggest economic engine is the state government. In Mizoram too, the task of driving economic activity fell upon the

---

* Trading margins in commodities were thin. Assuming a gross margin of even 5 per cent for these firms, we get an annual revenue of Rs 1.25 crore or Rs 1.25 lakh a month, out of which, these firms also had to meet other costs like staff salaries.

state. Its actions, however, managed the opposite, as road-building in the state, the government's biggest head of expenditure, showed.

———

The office of the Class One Contractors' Association in Aizawl was preternaturally quiet. Next to its unattended reception desk, two women were rolling vaihlos, the local cigarettes. Going by the small mountain between them, they had been at it for a while. Behind the desk was a plywood partition. On the other side, men were sitting around four tables, playing cards. In a tiny room next to the reception, Pu Zoliana, general secretary of the association, and Pu Ngurzamloa, its executive member, were talking to each other. Photos of the association's members hung on its fading pastel walls. In a grey pullover and a peach shirt, Ngurzamloa was frail with age. Zoliana looked younger and was more forceful. 'Ten years ago, I had two hundred plus employees. Now I have zero. We left the contract work. There isn't any,' said Ngurzamloa.[25]

Given Mizoram was seeing a road-building spree, this inactivity was surprising. In 2014–2015 alone, said its Economic Survey, Rs 2,000 crore had been spent on road-building and maintenance in the state. To put that number in perspective, the state government's total expenditure in 2014–2015 was Rs 6,951 crore.[26] The survey document was filled with details about old roads being improved and fresh ones being laid. And yet, big and small contractors alike complained about the lack of work.

Chalngura Jahau, a member of the BJP's fledgling unit in Mizoram, was one of the bigger road-building contractors in the state. He had a hot mixer for stirring stone, sand and bitumen into asphalt; a paver for spreading this hot mix along the road's surface; and a road roller for compacting. The only thing he lacked was a road-building contract.

Large tenders floated by multilateral bodies and the central government eluded him because his firm was not big enough. The estimated cost of the proposed road from Aizawl and Mamit in Mizoram to Tripura was Rs 500 crore. The winning contractor was to submit bank guarantees and security deposits adding up to a tenth of this project cost. Contractors like Jahau did not have that kind of cash. The state Public Works Department (PWD) officials had wanted the project to be broken into smaller stretches. But the centre awarded the tender to one company—Gayatri Projects of Andhra Pradesh.

Jahau was not getting state government road projects either. In the state too, eligibility norms for bigger projects were so high, local contractors could not qualify. Most of those contracts instead went to a small set of big firms run by non-Mizos—Silchar-based ABCI Infrastructures, Kolkata-based Tantia Constructions and Delhi-based Sunshine Overseas.* But these norms were new. 'Between 1998 and 2008, when the Mizo National Front was in power, contracts were broken into smaller pieces and given to 7–10 contractors,' said Zoliana. This changed after the Congress came to power. A senior PWD official concurred that it was better to break large contracts into smaller packages. 'If one contractor fails to deliver, another company can step in. The whole project doesn't suffer.'

In the past, links have been alleged between Chief Minister Lalthanhawla and ABCI Infrastructures.[27] During my reportage, a connection between Sunshine Overseas and the chief minister surfaced. In 2009, the company allotted a 21 per cent stake to Lalthanhawla's younger brother and minister in the government, Pu Lalthanzara. He held these shares for three years, before selling them back at

---

* Mizoram was far from unique. In Arunachal Pradesh too, trade and business in the state was mostly controlled by businesspeople outside the state. These arrangements were extractive. Most profits were invested outside the state—the local economy was too small to deliver good returns. A sleight of hand accompanied these arrangements. As the scholar Deepak K. Mishra describes in an essay, 'Since people other than those belonging to Arunachal Pradesh Scheduled Tribes are not issued with trading licenses, most of these businesspeople have to run their businesses through firms registered in—and in premises owned by—the local tribal people.' See: Deepak K. Mishra, 'Regions and Capitalist Transition in India: Arunachal Pradesh in a Comparative Perspective', in *Mapping India's Capitalism: Old and New Regions*, ed. Elisabetta Basile, Christine Lutringer, Barbara Harriss-White (Palgrave Macmillan, 2015).

an undisclosed price to the company's promoter. This transaction happened when Lalthanhawla was the chief minister.* The company grew after this transaction. In the financial year ending March 2009, Sunshine Overseas's income from operations was Rs 12.55 crore. Three years later, its revenues almost trebled and its profits were up eleven-fold.†

If bigger state contracts went to these companies, complained contractors, smaller ones were being pocketed by district- and block-level Congress leaders. According to state PWD norms, only firms with experience, equipment and manpower were eligible. How, then, were block- and district-level Congress leaders getting these? Were they all contractors?

No. Politicians were borrowing class one contractors' documentation to participate in tenders. 'Party workers come and ask for our documentation—the work we have done, our financial statement, our list of equipment,' a road contractor told me. In return, they offered

---

* Neither Lalthanhawla nor Lalthanzara responded to emailed questionnaires and text messages.

† This report had an instructive afterlife. First, another conflict of interest involving Lalthanzara emerged. Laltanpuia Pachuau, a Mizo activist living in Australia, found that another company owned by the minister, HP Food Products, had supplied high-protein biscuits to the state government between 2010 and 2014. This too violated India's Representation of People's Act, 1951, which forbids elected representatives from entering into trade or business contracts with the government while serving as MLAs or MPs. Institutions meant to ensure accountability—like the anti-corruption wing of the police and courts—turned a blind eye to both Pachuau's claim and the Scroll.in report, but local papers and Facebook groups picked them up. Next, a Youth Mizo National Front leader, K. Vanlalvena, called a press conference and demanded that Lalthanhawla step down.

As protests continued, Lalthanzara resigned in August 2015. It was a smart move. The resignation helped him evade an anti-corruption probe and escape a bar on contesting again by the Election Commission. In October, the Congress renominated him as its candidate for the by-poll. Later in the year, he won. The voters had chosen pragmatism over idealism—it was beneficial to have the chief minister's brother as their representative. Later, in December 2018, the party was voted out of power.

2 per cent to 5 per cent of the project's value as commission. Given their links to the state government, it was easy for them to win. After winning, added Jahau, they sold the project to other contractors, even those not empanelled with the state PWD, for as much as a fifth of the tender's value. A senior PWD official confirmed this. 'What you're talking about happens mostly in PMGSY [Pradhan Mantri Gram Sadak Yojana]. The party workers are taking these projects.'

Essentially, politicians had captured the road construction sector in the state. Even Gayatri Projects is owned, as Lalthanhawla told the state assembly, by a Congress leader, T. Subbarami Reddy.[28]

This is an old truth about Northeast India. As academics Deepak K. Mishra and P. Ghosh write about the politics of the region: 'Given the overwhelming significance of the government sector in the economy, the state itself becomes the primary site of rent extraction.'[29] The state's administrators spent so much on themselves through higher salaries, populist programmes and inflated road contracts that little was left for the people.

Contractors who refused to share documentation struggled to find work. When they did, said Jahau, it was in places 'where others do not dare to go—border areas—or where some contractor could not finish the work'. Others, more resigned, lent out their papers and, like Ngurzamloa, slowly saw their businesses reduce to paperwork.

With only a handful of companies bidding, the government paid more. The project to upgrade the road between Khadacherra and Tuilutkawn was sanctioned at an estimated cost of Rs 134.7 crore in January 2013. Only two companies bid. According to Mizoram's 2014–2015 Economic Policy, the lowest quoted rate was a third higher than the stipulated cost. The state, instead of re-tendering, prepared a revised detailed project report based on the bids. Its outlay, said Jahau, went up by as much as Rs 58 crore.[30] To put that number in perspective, the travel budget for Lalbiaki's HIV-testing pickup was Rs 11,000 a month.

As politicians retained a cut and subcontracted the projects out again, roads ended up being built for less than even the initial estimate. 'Work is given to an experienced company but is done by an inexperienced one,' the senior PWD official said. 'No one completes a project on time. In case they don't do these roads well, potholes develop within the first year itself.' With that, as Thangluaia found, it was hard to run a business.

That is not all. If these contracts had gone to local companies, the state's business sector would have been strengthened. A greater percentage of wages and profits would have circulated locally, boosting consumer demand and economic activity. This explained why jobs were hard to find in the state. I kept running into graduates driving cabs. And people like Sailo, who lived off economic niches so slim that others would not even try.*

---

* In 2015, for the first time in Mizoram, the BJP won seats in a local election. That was in the autonomous district council of the Chakmas. The two other autonomous councils, of the Lai and Mara communities, were also making overtures to the party. This development presented a chance to study relationships between the Mizos and the minorities, and I travelled over.

These autonomous councils were created when Mizoram was spun out of Assam, and for the same reason—to give ethnic minorities an administrative structure that gives them greater control over their region and protects their ways of life. A little over forty years later, the districts of Saiha (Maras), Lawngtlai (Lais) and Kamalanagar (Chakmas) rank amongst the most wretched in the country.

Take Saiha. Maras lived on both sides of the border this district shared with Burma in the southeastern end of Mizoram. After bustling Lunglei, it was the backwaters. Youngsters milled around. Buildings were small and rundown. This sense of neglect was reinforced by local health statistics. In 2014–2015, no less than 147 women died here for every 1 lakh live births; the equivalent maternal mortality ratio for all of Mizoram was 76. Dismal healthcare was something Saiha had in common with the Lai and Chakma councils. Council leaders blamed Aizawl. 'The three councils account for 10 per cent of the state's population,' said L.C. Chakhai, chairperson of the Mara council in Saiha. 'But between the Lais, Chakmas and Maras, we get just 4.5 per cent of the state budget.' The council leaders attributed this underfunding to ethnic discrimination.

This explained their overtures to the BJP. All three councils wanted the NDA to either make them union territories or fund them directly. In return, council leaders said they would join the BJP, giving it a foothold in Mizoram. Their claim of underfunding, however, did not survive scrutiny. Not only did Aizawl separately

Instead, in Mizoram, politicians got richer faster than others in the state. 'Our politicians' assets rose by 600 per cent between 2003 and 2008. And by 400 per cent between 2008 and 2013,' Zodin Sanga, an activist with a local accountability and transparency NGO called Prism, told me.[31] In the years since, this quicksilver rate of primitive accumulation continued. Between 2013 and 2018, the average value of assets declared by ministers in the state cabinet doubled from Rs 3.41 crore to Rs 6.93 crore.[32]

---

run development programmes in Saiha, Lawngtlai and Kamalanagar, but also the councils themselves were grossly mismanaged.

The Animal Husbandry and Veterinary Department of the Mara council, which was allotted Rs 41.62 lakh in 2014–2015, spent all of Rs 50,000 on medicines, after expenditure on salaries, wages and administrative heads. Or take the 2015–2016 budget of the Lai council. Of its Rs 808 lakh allocation for education, Rs 793 lakh went on salaries—not schools or libraries.

This pointed to a larger pattern. These were backward areas with little economic activity. For the local elite, the councils were the best way to access power and affluence. Once they came to power and were done rewarding the supporters and themselves—at the time of my visit, Mara council was building a sprawling residence for its chief executive member—little money was left for developmental work.

This failure was hidden by blaming the state government, which did exhibit majoritarian impulses. For instance, in Mizoram, 85 per cent of seats in technical courses like medicine and engineering were earmarked for local permanent residents, 10 per cent for settled-down migrants, and 5 per cent for those working in the central or state administration. In April 2015, the state government restricted the definition of local permanent residents to only 'Zo-ethnic people who are native inhabitants ... and have been residing permanently in the state', excluding Chakmas from the largest chunk of the seats.

The councils were perfect simulacrums for larger societies, showing clearly the forces that turned them towards elite capture, inequality and identity politics. See: M. Rajshekhar, 'Why the BJP Is Gaining Popularity in Some Parts of Minority-dominated Mizoram', *Scroll.in* (13 April 2015), scroll.in/article/719322/why-the-bjp-is-gaining-popularity-in-some-parts-of-minority-dominated-mizoram; M. Rajshekhar, 'Minority Councils in the North East Want Direct Funding But Will That Really Help Them Develop?', *Scroll.in* (21 April 2015), scroll.in/article/720942/minority-councils-in-the-north-east-want-direct-funding-but-will-that-really-help-them-develop.

Finally, with most gains flowing to a few, Mizoram's state revenues stayed low. As a result, state finances, the major pillar of such an economy, were at the mercy of the centre.

———

As my stint in Mizoram drew to a close, the state got another reminder of its vulnerability.

States in India run on a mix of their own revenues, their share of taxes collected by the centre, and on development programmes funded by the centre. States with high non-plan expenditure, like salaries, but low revenues—such as those in the Northeast—also get deficit grant funding.

Now, acting on the Fourteenth Finance Commission's recommendations, the NDA government tweaked this model.[33] Although the combined share of central tax collections of all the states went up from 32 per cent to 42 per cent, the centre reordered development programmes it would pay for. Some would be funded as before, states would have to pay more for a second set, and the centre would stop funding the rest. The resulting calculus varied from state to state. Some got more untied funds, others got less. States in the Northeast, like Mizoram, were amongst the losers. A state Finance Department letter listed twenty-two programmes where it had to shell out more and eight programmes the centre would no longer fund.

For the Rashtriya Krishi Vikas Yojana, one of the biggest agriculture programmes running in Mizoram, the centre-state ratio was 90:10. In 2014–2015, the state raised its share of Rs 14 crore, and the centre released Rs 128.9 crore. As I prepared to leave Mizoram, the central Ministry of Agriculture was yet to communicate the new ratio, but state Finance Department officials were apprehensive. To run the programme at the same size of Rs 140 crore, would they have to cough up Rs 35 crore, a 25 per cent contribution, or Rs 70 crore, at 50 per cent? At the same time, they also needed to find cash to maintain the eight schemes the centre would no longer fund. 'It will be hard for the Northeast states to manage more than 90:10,' a Finance Department official worried.

It was an insight into the unilateralism that characterises fiscal relations between India's centre and the Northeast states. The Finance Department official got teary-eyed. 'How do we do this? There are no state assets to sell. We will have to borrow against future remittances of the state.' Future payments like salaries, the official clarified.

In essence, borrow and repay from next year's central allocation. A debt trap if there ever was one. The state grubbed around for additional revenues. The Kaladan Highway, extending from Lawngtlai to the river port of Sittwe in Myanmar,[34] was meant to create a new road-and-sea link, which could boost trade between Mizoram and the rest of India. Work was underway in Mizoram, but the road was nowhere near completion in Myanmar. Meanwhile, the state's decision to grant exclusive rights to oil palm production in a district, apart from its implications for gender equity, village commons, food security, water scarcity and local biodiversity, also threatened to lock growers into local monopolies.[35] Instead of improving jhum by lengthening fallow periods, enhancing market access and instituting organic labelling, now, Mizoram would have to push cash crops harder.

Last gasp measures followed. Rates at ration shops were hiked. Hoping to make Rs 30–Rs 40 crore as excise, Mizoram repealed prohibition even at the cost of displeasing the church. People wondered which programmes would be retained and which would be shuttered. Others felt this cutback might be a blessing, that it might reduce the state government's profligacy. I felt less sure. Would the state cut back on schemes like NLUP, which it used to stay in power, or would funds keep flowing to leaders and populism, as in the autonomous councils, with little money for anything else?*

---

* In November 2015, after much protest by the Northeast states, the NDA relented and retained the 90:10 ratio for seventeen centrally sponsored schemes (CSS) and decided to follow an 80:20 ratio pattern for non-core CSS schemes. See: IANS, '90:10 Funding Pattern to Be Maintained for Northeast', *Business Standard*, (11 November 2015), business-standard.com/article/news-ians/90-10-funding-pattern-to-be-maintained-for-northeast-1151111003161.html.

2

The State That Wasted Its
Iron Ore Boom

It was the early 2000s. Truck owners and drivers across India were abuzz with chatter about a small village called Koira. It is in Odisha, they told each other. Located on a hill in the middle of forests, a hundred kilometres to the south of the steel town of Rourkela, a lot of iron ore was being dug out here, which China bought at high rates. Koira did not have enough trucks to move this ore, so miners were paying truckers rates they would not get elsewhere in India.

Uncoiling itself, first stretching across Odisha and then covering north and south India, one place this trucking grapevine reached was the holy town of Varanasi, 700 kilometres away on the banks of the Ganges. There, Sanjay Kumar Gupta, a truck owner in his thirties, told his family he had to go, and he rushed over for a look.

On reaching, he found a place almost primordial in its single-minded striving. Day and night, trucks crawled up and down the hills, some hefting ore to the railway yard below; others heading to the port of Paradip, where ore was loaded on to ships bound for China; and yet others rumbling towards steel plants in Odisha and beyond.[1] With as many as eighty to hundred trucks moving bumper to bumper, pile-ups were common. Traffic jams took days to clear. The road itself was an almighty mess. Heavy rains and overloaded trucks had left it a rutted dirt track. Yet, given the insatiable desire to ship more and more ore, trucks slithered in red mud, lurched in and out of potholes, kicked up large clouds of red dust that settled on trees and bushes, and kept moving.

Koira itself, coated with the same red dust, was taken over by truckers. Businesses geared to serve them lined its main street—rooms for rent, shops selling truck spares, roadside repair shops, a petrol pump, a new hotel with a liquor license. It was a frontier town in the throes of a gold rush.

Between 2000 and 2009, the price of a tonne of iron ore rocketed from Rs 100 to Rs 8,000. With such unequivocal signals from the market, the rate of ore extraction in Odisha went vertical—rising from 80 lakh tonnes in 1994–1995 to 700 lakh tonnes by 2008–2009. Exports, in this period, rose from just below 10 lakh tonnes to a little over 160 lakh tonnes.

Koira was one of the ground zeros of that boom. On especially busy days, it filled ten rakes or cargo trains, while on most other days, it filled five to six. This ore came from about twenty-five mines, almost all privately owned. To fill a rake, it took four hundred to four hundred and fifty tippers—trucks that tip the load into the rakes—each carrying nine tonnes. Vying to ship more and competing for trucks, mine owners paid truck owners as much as Rs 800 per tonne for the shorter railyard run and more for longer ones to Rourkela, Paradip and beyond. When owners were not looking, miners also paid truck drivers to take quicker routes along especially terrible roads and handed bonuses to drivers who did multiple trips in a day. A nine-tonne tipper doing two rounds a day, twenty-five days a month, made Rs 43 lakh a year, while a tipper cost just Rs 16 lakh.

Gupta settled in Koira. As business grew, he bought three new tippers. He was still paying his instalments when the boom, all of a sudden, petered out.

It was 2009. Home owners had defaulted on sub-prime loans in America. As house prices and stock markets fell, people saw their personal wealth erode. As they cut back on consumption, value chains feeding them got battered. In China, exports dropped by 18 per cent and—more consequentially for Odisha—imports by 40 per cent.[2]

Exploratory interviews in Odisha revealed an array of changes that had taken place since 2005. When I visited in 2015, Chief Minister Naveen Patnaik was in power for an incredible fourth consecutive term and would go on to win a fifth term. He had launched a subsidised meal programme called Aahaar, which gave rice and lentils at Rs 5 a plate to the urban poor. The number of gold and jewellery shops had risen steeply. Debt bondage continued. All the mining districts in the state had been declared Naxal-affected. In each, the number of paramilitary forces had risen sharply. The state's numbers on healthcare and education continued to be dismal. The iron ore boom was over.* Steel plants were shuttering. A number of other booms had ended as well. Engineering colleges were not finding students. Chit funds, which had mopped up deposits promising quick, high and safe returns, had defaulted.[3] The state's real estate had cooled as well. A mining contractor from Salem, Tamil Nadu, had emerged as the biggest miner in the state.†

A thread ran through most of these seemingly unconnected developments: the iron ore boom and bust. Everywhere in the state, its impress showed up. A handful of people had gained wildly, some were worse off than before, most were much the same. Peer into this Rorschach test of unequal outcomes and you will come close to understanding modern Odisha.

———

On reaching Koira, I found a scene unimaginable ten years ago, when I had first visited in 2005. At an ore-crushing unit just before the village, a crusher, rusted the same dark shade of red as the iron-rich soil here, stood abandoned. To the right stood a rusting truck and earthmover,

---

* In 2014, the industry received a second blow when, based on the findings of the Supreme Court–mandated Shah Commission, India's belated crackdown on illegal mining temporarily halted iron ore mining in the state.

† Odisha, like most of India, was also seeing a spike in the number of self-declared godpersons. 'In the last ten years, more than fifty maths have opened in Bhubaneswar alone,' Rama Ballabh Rath, a former Biju Janata Dal leader told me. 'They are all self-appointed babas.'

with three cows and a bull placidly grazing around them. The only person here was a teenaged adivasi boy. Clad in flip-flops, a light-blue shirt and a brightly patterned towel, he was the security guard.

Koira was a shrunken version of itself. Its mines now filled just one rake a day. With seven hundred tippers registered with their local association, truckers now chased miners for work. Gupta, his moustache turning white faster than his hair, had been pushed into a crisis. Rates had fallen. In 2015, a trip to the railway yard fetched Rs 415 a tonne. Longer hauls, which used to earn him as much as Rs 1,350 a tonne during the boom, now netted only Rs 700, too low to cover his equated monthly instalments (EMIs). 'The instalment for the big trucks is Rs 60,000 every month. At Rs 700, after accounting for diesel; repairs to the vehicle, given how bad roads are; and paying the driver, I'm left with Rs 25,000–Rs 30,000.'

Some owners had sold their trucks and left. He was staying on, hoping for a turnaround. In the meantime, aware of too many cases of finance companies impounding trucks for missed payments, he was dipping into his savings to avoid defaulting. To survive, he said, truck owners needed at least Rs 1,350 per tonne. 'That won't get us chicken, but we would be able to afford pulses.'

An educative contradiction lay ahead. In Rourkela, a similar story was playing out. Around 2002, the Kalunga industrial estate, a grid of plots with small steel plants outside the town, saw its version of Koira's trucking boom. Small and medium steel plants—sponge iron plants making raw iron, induction furnaces converting iron into steel, rolling mills converting steel into sheets and rods—mushroomed here. Thirteen years later, it was deserted. Most units I walked past were shut. Later that day, Subrata Patnaik, the secretary of the Rourkela Chamber of Commerce and Industry, confirmed that impression. 'Out of the fifty induction furnaces here, forty are closed.' It was the same story, he said, with sponge iron plants. Most of those had wound up as well.

This distress was not limited to Rourkela. P.L. Kandoi, the president of All Odisha Steel Federation, said that small and medium steel plants were shutting down across the state because the cost of iron ore at

Rs 2,500 a tonne was too high. Units could not buy ore at this rate, make steel, sell it and turn a profit. The cost of production of a tonne of ore, including royalty, stood at Rs 1,330. It should be sold close to this price, tacking on no more than a reasonable margin for the mine owner, a senior executive at Visa Steel in Kalunga added.

To survive, the steel industry needed ore at Rs 1,330 a tonne, while truckers could not do without a shipping rate of at least Rs 1,350 a tonne.

From his office, Uday Patel, the owner of Rourkela Fabrications, an engineering company that made machinery for steel plants, had observed this contradiction take shape. 'When the boom started, a bunch of people assumed that it would always continue.' Truckers had placed orders for tippers in the early 2000s thinking they would always get high rates per tonne. Steel makers had made the same assumption about steel prices. But India's steel industry is not a level playing field. Larger companies have captive iron ore blocks, while smaller ones have to buy costlier ore from merchant miners. During the boom, the demand from China had pushed steel prices so high that even small and medium companies were viable despite paying more for ore. The mistake they made, said Patel, was in assuming this was the new normal. When steel prices fell, their viability ended as well.[*]

But the roots of the crisis in Koira and Kalunga ran deeper than irrational exuberance. They lay in how Odisha, and India, frittered away the iron ore boom. We should have, said Patel, used the boom to beef up steel-manufacturing capacities. The country, and the state, should have helped mid-sized steel makers invest in R&D, or it should have created

---

* Several steel makers also turned to 'over-invoicing'. To qualify for a bank loan, they had to put in a small portion, around 25 per cent, of the project cost, with the bank paying the rest. This was subverted by those who either did not have enough money or did not want to risk their capital. They asked suppliers for inflated bills and pushed the whole cost on to the bank. The downside, as Patel explained, was that the size of the bank loan went up. Promoters' assumption, he said, was that 'the boom would last long enough for them to pay back the bank'. It did not always work out.

a competitive field by doing away with the extant arrangement where large business groups had captive mines, while small and medium ones did not. 'Instead of making Rs 4,000 per tonne exporting ore, we could have made Rs 45,000 per tonne exporting steel. That would have made domestic manufacturers more competitive and created a more robust industrial economy in the state,' Patel said.[4]

But that is not what happened. Like Goa and Karnataka, Odisha exported raw ore, a decision Patel described as 'a silent accommodation of mining interests'.

———

Sitting in the coffee shop of an opulent five-star hotel in Bhubaneswar, B. Prabhakaran, from Tamil Nadu, traced the story of his rise in Odisha's mining industry.

It was the mid-1980s, and a second wave of entrepreneurship was bearing down on the district of Salem in the south Indian state of Tamil Nadu. In the first wave, locals had bought borewell rigs and ranged across the country with them, renting them out to farmers and households seeking groundwater. By the 1980s, the long age of manual earthworks—digging pits, breaking stones and moving earth—was ending. Earthmovers came in. And the people of Salem, as they did with the borewell rigs, bought earthmovers and rented them out.[5]

Studying computer science in Coimbatore at the time, Prabhakaran was amongst those fascinated by this new opportunity. Just twenty-three years of age, he prepared meticulously for the life he planned to lead. Unlike his batchmates, who were preparing for campus interviews, he took a bank loan after graduation and bought a JCB excavator for Rs 19 lakh. To learn about these machines, he went to the engineering company L&T's campus in Powai, Mumbai, and enrolled in a six-month course for machine operators and mechanics. 'I wanted to be fully equipped to handle these machines. In this business, you should not be dependent on anyone else's knowhow,' he said.

His fellow students were engineers from firms like Coal India. He was the only one who owned a machine. When the machine came, he focused on hard-rock excavation, more remunerative than earthworks, even though it imposed greater wear and tear on the machine. His business grew rapidly. By 1994, he had ten tippers and four excavators. Then came a call from L&T, which was looking for contractors, and he expanded beyond south India. Between 1994 and 2000, he worked with the engineering firm on fifteen or so projects. He bought more machines. Cannily, he bought used ones and maintained them well.* By 1999, his turnover was close to Rs 100 crore.[6]

Then, the L&T project came to an end. Another project he was hoping to bag, the government-owned National Hydel Power Corporation's Upper Subansiri Dam in Arunachal Pradesh, went to a Hyderabad-based contractor. Prabhakaran was in a bind. Much of his equipment, given his work for L&T, were machines used for mining, so he could not pivot to other infrastructure projects like roads. 'More than 100—all mining—equipment. About 500 people. Where to go? What to do?' he said, his tone dropping as he recalled that time.

The Odisha Mining Corporation was floating tenders. He tried there, won a contract to mine iron ore in Keonjhar's Gandhamardan Hills, moved to the state feeling relieved, and then found that the state-run company had not obtained a forest clearance. Work could not begin. 'They kept saying, "It will come, it will come," but I had already moved my machines, and family, to Keonjhar. We didn't have surplus to sit on. How to survive?' The district had many private contractors and miners. 'We knocked on every door saying we have equipment, we can deploy. And they all said, "No, we have largely small-scale mining. We cannot accommodate."'

That was 2000. By 2015, Prabhakaran, taller and more muscular than the photographs on his company website suggest, was the biggest contract miner for iron ore in Odisha. The turnover of his firm, Thriveni Earthmovers, stood at Rs 1,300 crore in 2015. The company controlled a coal mine in Indonesia.[7] Along with Kolkata-based EMTA and the

---

* This gave Prabhakaran's firm a better asset to turnover ratio than its rivals—it could generate equivalent revenues with lower investment.

Adani group's coal-mining arm, it was one of the three biggest contract miners in India. As an iron ore transporter in the town of Barbil, one of the mining hotspots in Keonjhar, told me, 'He had nothing ten years ago. Now, forget Rs 2,000 crore. He has Rs 10,000 crore.'

Prabhakaran's remarkable rise was the talk of Odisha's mining sector. Around 2000, when the iron ore boom was just starting, Keonjhar had a well-developed local political economy of mining. Apart from large companies like Tata and Rungta, who ran tightly integrated mining operations, the district had a local, politically connected elite that owned iron ore mines, alongside raising contractors who mined for them, transporters who trucked the mineral and four regional musclemen. Kusha Apat, who started out as a truck driver, controlled the villages near Guali panchayat, close to the border between Jharkhand and Odisha. Jitu Patnaik, a miner who became the chairperson of the Joda municipality, dominated areas around the nearby town of Joda, twenty-five kilometres from Guali. Barbil, fifteen kilometres from Joda, was with Murli Sharma, a local BJP leader. And the area around Unchabali, twenty-two kilometres from Joda, was with Sanatan Mahakud, a one-time union leader.[8]

Within a few years of Prabhakaran's arrival, this arrangement broke down. He became the biggest mining contractor in the district. In the same period, Mahakud became the local hegemon. Elected as an independent MLA in 2014 from the Champua constituency in the district, Mahakud was giving anywhere between Rs 1,000 and Rs 2,000 a month to over half the families in his constituency. He was also funding independent MLAs contesting elsewhere in Keonjhar. These candidates presented themselves as Sanatan Mahakudna Samarthita Prarthi or Sanatan Mahakud–backed candidates.[9] He could evidently afford the largesse. According to Mahakud's election affidavits, his assets grew from Rs 3 crore in 2009 to Rs 51 crore in 2014, a seventeen-fold growth in five years.[10]

This reconfiguration was poorly understood. When I spoke to rival mining contractors, mine owners—those working with Prabhakaran as well as those avoiding him—state politicians and an investigator in the Shah Commission, which was set up to inquire into charges of illegal mining during the boom across India, one narrative emerged. As I reported then: 'According to a veteran employee of a mining company in Barbil, the town where Prabhakaran has his base in Keonjhar, he obtained a list of people with mining leases but without the permissions and environmental clearances required to mine. "He told them he would get them the clearances and do the mining," said the employee. "Most of these people had obtained their leases a long time ago and did not have the connections required to get these clearances."'[11]

A former minister in Naveen Patnaik's cabinet told me, 'You need a lot of clearances, from the Indian Bureau of Mines, Environment Ministry, [state] Mining Department … In this [Odisha] government, there's no one else who can get a mining lease done.'

Prabhakaran was linked to none other than Naveen Patnaik. In an explosive interview in 2014, a former finance minister of Odisha, Prafulla Ghadei, alleged that Prabhakaran was one of four people who controlled the state government.[12] The other three he named were Biju Janata Dal (BJD) leader and former Panchayati Raj minister Kalpataru Das, IAS officer and Patnaik's private secretary V. Karthikeyan Pandian, and Supreme Court lawyer and BJD leader Pinaki Mishra. After the interview, Ghadei was expelled from the ruling BJD.[13]

Mine owners, transporters and contract miners in Keonjhar pointed at another link as well, between Prabhakaran and Mahakud. According to a mine owner in Bhubaneswar, Prabhakaran initially worked with Jitu Patnaik, but after relations soured between the two, he began supporting others like Apat and Mahakud. Since then, his proximity to Mahakud had been remarked upon a lot.

One afternoon in Bhubaneswar, a transport contractor from Keonjhar, a middle-aged man with a fleet of trucks used for ferrying ore, willing to talk about Mahakud but unwilling to meet in a public place, spoke to me inside his SUV, with the windows rolled up. 'Prabhakaran made him what he is today. He was nothing before all this.' He claimed that the money Mahakud paid out every month came from the mining baron. 'Prabhakaran gives that money, but through Sanatan.' People in that area were poor. When they got Rs 2,000 a month, they started considering Mahakud their god, he said. 'They do what Sanatan tells them to do. If he says go sit at a mine, don't let them work, they'll go sit at a mine.'*

These allegations had been made before. In 2013, Nihar Ranjan Mahananda and Jogesh Kumar Singh wrote a letter to Naveen Patnaik alleging a 'mining mafia led by Sanatana Mahakud … has taken control of more than 10 mines in Joda mining circle in collusion with raising contractor Triveni Earth Movers,' as *Business Standard* reported.[14] The two Congress MLAs claimed that the mafia had disrupted the public hearings of more than ten mining projects over the previous two years in a bid to take over their mines.

That noon at the coffee shop, Prabhakaran denied each of these accusations, saying that he neither procured clearances for miners nor worked with Mahakud. Instead, he traced Thriveni's rise to its proficiency in mining and its ability to get what he called a 'social licence' from the local community, essentially winning them over through jobs and contracts.

This response, however, sat weakly with the company's economics. It charged rates the Shah Commission described as 'much above the industry bench mark or normal ore raising charges'.[15] In 2009–2010, for instance, the combined cost of mining, transport, salaries and depreciation accounted for 16 per cent of the turnover of the government-owned miner National Mineral Development Corporation. The rest was profit. In contrast, mine owners were paying Prabhakaran 35 per cent to 42 per cent of the ore's eventual price for just mining.[16] That was because, unlike other mining contractors in Odisha, Thriveni did not charge a flat fee for mining but took a percentage of the prevailing ore price. As the commission reported, the company charged Indrani

---

* I tried contacting Mahakud in several ways. I left visiting cards with employees at his homes in Unchabali and Bhubaneswar, asking them to pass these on to the MLA. I called several times on the phone and sent emails to the address provided in his election affidavit. Finally, I left a questionnaire at his house in Bhubaneswar. There was no response.

Patnaik, one of the bigger mine owners in Keonjhar, sums ranging from Rs 568–Rs 781 for every tonne of ore it mined in 2008.[17] That year, rival mining contractors, said a senior official at another large contract mining company in Barbil, were charging a flat rate of Rs 350 per tonne. 'This is a different way of making payments,' Prabhakaran countered. 'It is not on fixed terms. It is on revenue-sharing terms.'

It does not quite add up. Think of the mine owners, the investigator with the Shah Commission told me. 'They have to pay a royalty of 10 per cent, an income tax of 30 per cent, a VAT [value added tax] of 5 per cent. If they have to also pay 37 per cent to Prabhakaran, what is left for them?' Or see this another way. In this business of commodities, Thriveni, despite larger economies of scale* and better mining knowhow, was not undercutting rivals to get contracts. Instead, it got clients despite charging more.

One answer for the overcharging lay in the financials of Serajuddin and Co., one of the biggest mine owners in the state. In 2009–2010, the firm dispatched 6.67 lakh tonnes of iron ore lumps and 5 lakh tonnes of iron fines, and closed the year with a declared total revenue of Rs 98.56 crore. The commission found this number odd. Considering even a 'modest average of Rs 2,000 per MT for lumps and Rs 1,000 per MT for fines', the company's sales turnover should have been at least Rs 180 crore. That is not all. After pegging revenues at Rs 98.56 crore, Serajuddin reported operating expenses of almost Rs 70 crore. After accounting for other expenses, it declared a profit before tax of Rs 3.75 crore. The tax it eventually paid was Rs 1.5 crore.[18]

The commission challenged these numbers: 'Mining activity normally has very high profitability because of the low cost/expense involved in mechanised ore-raising. The PBT [profit before tax], as a

---

* 'We use twenty-five- to thirty-tonners of Indian make,' a mining contractor in Keonjhar told me. '[Thriveni uses] forty-tonners made by companies like Caterpillar and Komatsu.' This made a difference. While his company's cost of mining was Rs 60–Rs 70 per tonne, that of Thriveni was around Rs 47 a tonne.

percentage of turnover, reaches as high as 75% for even Government Company like NMDC.'[19]

At this time, its report showed that Thriveni, after charging an inflated cost to Serajuddin—for which it was the mining contractor— was also making payments to the latter's subsidiary companies.[20] So, Thriveni helped Serajuddin evade taxes by inflating expenses, while it too enjoyed a large margin. I emailed a questionnaire to Prabhakaran, following up on the interview, but he did not respond.

An intricate picture emerged. Mine owners needed the support of those who could get them nods from the state and central governments. Subsequently, contract miners and mine owners colluded to deny funds to the State. Monopolies formed in both the mining and transport of ore. As one contractor told me, 'Everyone's sitting unemployed. We aren't earning enough to eat. They are running a monopoly. Our business is now close to zero.'

Things got odder yet. In a country where political parties would do anything to control cash-spewing constituencies like Champua, the BJD let Mahakud come to power. In 2014, when he stood as an independent candidate, the party got a local comedian called Papu Pom Pom aka Tattwa Prakash Satapathy to stand as its representative against him.[21] Mahakud won handily, defeating Satapathy by about 55,000 votes.

———

The iron ore boom itself generated little gains for Odisha. Not only did the state lose revenues to illegal mining but also did not earn much from legal mining.

First, the state lost revenue by exporting ore instead of finished steel. This was all the more surprising because, till 2009, royalty on iron ore—which would accrue to the state government and was determined by the central government—stayed low, ranging between Rs 8 to Rs 27 a tonne, even as the price of ore climbed to Rs 7,000 a tonne. Back-of-the-envelope calculations yielded astounding numbers. Between 2004 and 2012 alone, over 5,240 lakh tonnes of ore were mined in Odisha. The Shah Commission pegged the value of that ore at Rs 199,847.5 crore.[22] Even at Rs 27 per tonne, Odisha would have earned all of Rs 1,415 crore. After 2009, as the boom ended, royalty rates were raised to 10 per cent of the sale price, but even that was low. Ore is a non-renewable commons held in common trust by the State. There is no reason why miners should be allowed to retain nine-tenths of its value.

Compounding matters, as the Serajuddin instance showed, Odisha did not clamp down on tax evasion either. These went unspotted till the Shah Commission discovered them. Since then, as the environmental activist Biswajit Mohanty writes in *Chasing His Father's Dreams*, the state government 'failed to collect a single rupee of the Rs 68,700 crore fine imposed on [iron ore] miners.'[23]

In all, gains from the mining boom congealed with a few. According to the Shah Commission, a total of seventy-nine mining leases were given out in Keonjhar and Sundargarh alone by successive state governments.[24] Apart from the leaseholders, the boom benefited their employees, vendors and business partners, along with the government officials and politicians who supplied clearances and permissions.

A glimmer of hope still remained. The state could have yet gained from the boom if even this Rs 200,000 crore had been invested locally, in productive activities like manufacturing. But that is not what Odisha did.

Its elite, in a move out of Thomas Piketty's *Capital*, instead put their money into financial speculation, creating a series of short-lived booms. Between 2000 and 2009, the number of gold and jewellery shops spiked. Land rates jumped. Real estate prices soared. There was a period when, former BJD leader Rama Ballabh Rath told me, they doubled each year. As real estate rates spiked, chit fund operators mushroomed across Odisha, figuring they could raise funds from investors, keep some for themselves, put the rest into real estate and deliver high returns.

The engineering college boom in Odisha illustrates this trend of speculative investments.

—–

In 2010, Bijay Mohanty* quit his low-paying job of Rs 20,000 a month with an IT company and hopped over to the Kruttika Institute of Technical Education (KITE), a new engineering college coming up in the outskirts of Bhubaneswar, the capital of Odisha. The twenty-seven-year-old was moving from a field with low gains to a sector seeing exponential growth. Indeed, till 2000, Odisha had just five private engineering colleges. Over the next ten years, as though a genie with a fondness for engineering colleges had been uncorked, ninety more sprung up. As many as sixty of these came up in Bhubaneswar alone.[25]

Even today, when I look at the transcript of my conversation with Mohanty, I find the numbers scarcely believable. 'In 2008, twenty-five new engineering colleges opened. The next year, another twenty-five or thirty colleges followed,' he had said. One reason lay in the students. Attracted by the growth in Odisha's mining sector and seeing in it the prospect of steady employment and an escape into affluence, demand for engineering education soared in the state through the 2000s. A second reason lay elsewhere: in the circulation of profits from the iron ore boom.

Once those benefiting from the mining boom decided to invest in land, Soumya Ranjan Patnaik, a former MLA and editor of Odiya newspaper *Sambad*, told me, they gravitated towards education. It was smart thinking. Land buys could convert black money into white— the initial payment could be made using unaccounted funds, but its subsequent value could be shown as legal. Colleges, apart from conferring respectability, also generated revenues, which opened up bank funding. Additionally, revenues from the college could be used to repay bank loans.

Within education, funding flowed where investments were low and returns high. Which is why Odisha saw a boom in engineering but not medical colleges. The latter would need parallel investment in hospitals as well. In contrast, the economics of engineering colleges seemed more compelling. One evening, another faculty member at KITE

---

* Name changed.

walked me through the thinking at work. 'In Odisha, an engineering
college with an annual intake of 300 students can sell 30 of those seats
as management quota every year,' he said. 'If a college charges Rs 8 lakh,
it will make Rs 2.4 crore each year. In addition, all 300 students pay
Rs 50,000 as annual fees. Which is another Rs 1.5 crore.' That is a total
of Rs 3.9 crore from the first-year students alone. Add fees from the
students of the second, third and fourth years, and the college would
make another Rs 4.5 crore. 'A college investing Rs 10 crore in a campus
will recover that money in a little over a year.'

This created a frenzy. The first set of private engineering colleges
in the state had the support of politicians, said Ashok Satpathy,* who
worked as the principal at two such colleges. From 2000 onwards,
mining and real estate people entered the sector. Institutions with
strange names, like Koustav Institute of Self Domain, came up. This
was also when the state saw colleges being run out of homes. 'When
that became too obvious a fraud, the government came out with norms
pegging minimum landholding for a campus,' said Satpathy.

Things went well for these colleges till 2009. Land banks in the guise
of education, they invested little in teaching. In 2003–2004, Satpathy
conducted interviews through which lecturers were hired on salaries
for Rs 2,000–Rs 4,000 a month. As per the norms of the All India
Council for Technical Education, 'engineering colleges are supposed
to have a ratio of one teacher for every ten students,' he said. 'Better
colleges have one for every eight. But here, the norm was one teacher
for every thirty to thirty-five students.'

And then, as the iron ore boom ended, the flow of funds into the
sector as well as the number of students fell. In 2009–2010, about 22,000
students had enrolled for engineering courses. That year, however, just
5,000 of the graduating students got jobs. As word spread, enrolments
dropped. Some colleges started paying HR departments at companies
to hire their students for six months; they could be fired later.[26] By the
middle of 2015, things were dire. Of the state's 46,000 engineering seats,

---

* Name changed.

as many as 30,000 were vacant. Twenty colleges had failed to reach even 'double digits' in student enrolment.[27]

The educationists responded by slashing costs. Some stopped paying teachers. Employees of the Bhadrak Institute of Engineering and Technology, without pay for four months, went on strike in the town of Baripada in early 2015. Crude bombs were thrown at them, allegedly at the behest of college authorities, during the fifth month of their strike.[28]

Marvelling at this chaos, I contacted Bijay Mohanty. He had joined an engineering colleges' employees association set up to fight for the rights of teachers and students. On the drive to the KITE campus on the outskirts of Bhubaneswar in August 2015, he painted a bleak picture of these colleges after the bust. College managements were grubbing around for students, many having appointed brokers for this. Others had told teachers not to show up for the next semester if they were unable to find students. 'The auto-flow is zero,' Mohanty said, referring to the number of students who approached colleges on their own. 'Enrolments happen only with marketing.' To keep costs low, only junior faculty were hired.

Even with that prelude, KITE was a shock. It had garnered 30 students in 2015 instead of the targeted 300. Its promoter, a builder, had stopped investing. It showed. The college functioned out of a half-built red-and-cream building with iron rebar bristling from its top. The lobby stood unfinished, open to the elements, its girders exposed, with dark stains of mildew. Just as unfinished was the water fountain in the front—a square pit filled with rainwater, with the local white-topped kasatandi, a wild grass, growing around it. The library was housed in a large hall that was almost entirely empty. Bookshelves stood at the far end, forming a small rectangle that had six bookshelves running its length and four running its width. Peering into one classroom, I saw thin, nervous-looking students occupying the first four or so rows of a large lecture hall. Two new professors had joined work that day. Newly minted graduates themselves, both were twenty-two years old, and their starting salary was Rs 8,000 a month. Mohanty was desperate to get out. 'I'm thinking of working on SAP [a software]. I think I'll go to Delhi and look for work.'

Amidst this meltdown, the state government sided with college promoters, not the students. As enrolment fell, private colleges successfully lobbied for measures that broadened the pool of eligible students. The eligibility percentage for engineering entrance exams was lowered.[29] Promoters also got the state to resume its own Joint Entrance Exam, which was less rigorous than the All India Joint Entrance Exam for engineering colleges.[30] These measures, said Satpathy, weakened the quality of education further. 'This is not quality. It is kwality. Give money, take ice cream.'

One reason for this cavalier attitude of the state lay in the ownership of these institutions. The college at Baripada, whose employees had gone on strike, was linked to MLA Prafulla Samal.[31] His son was its chairperson. Or take Soumya Ranjan Patnaik. He was the chairperson of the KMBB College of Engineering and Technology.[32]

This construct engendered clear winners and losers. The miners, businesspeople and politicians who set up colleges had their bottom lines protected. Even if the institution collapsed, the real estate it squatted on would accrete value. The building itself could be repurposed.* As Satpathy said, 'KITE? It will be a hotel someday. Or a godown.' Students fared less well. Engineering graduates were sitting for bank entrance exams. Some had given up on education itself. One refrain came up often in Bhubaneswar. 'What is the use of spending Rs 4 lakh and four years to get a job which earns you Rs 8,000 a month? I'm better off buying a tempo.'

———

* The story of chit funds was similar. At its peak, Odisha, with 55,000 villages, had no less than 2 lakh chit fund agents. Lakhs of investors, who, like the truckers and engineering students, saw a few in the state making a lot of money and wanted to participate as well, rushed in. What they missed was the precarious edifice on which these booms stood.

In one of its more impassioned parts, the Shah Commission divided the value of the mineral produced in one year in Keonjhar and Sundargarh with the number of adivasi families living in the two districts. If the value of the mineral had been evenly distributed, it said, each family would have been richer by Rs 9.42 lakh.* Seen another way, even a 10 per cent slice of the mining companies' annual earnings from these two districts between 2004–2005 and 2011–2012 worked out to Rs 2,498 crore. If this amount had been used for these districts, said the commission, they would have been at the same level as any well-developed district in any developed state.[33]

What the state got was something very different. By 2015, the union Ministry of Environment had granted enough environmental clearances for Odisha to mine 1,542.63 lakh tonnes of iron ore a year. Odisha's iron ore reserves, as the commission said, were estimated at 47,040 lakh tonnes.[34] At that rate of annual production, the state would exhaust its mines in just thirty years with little improvement in how its people lived.

Yet, the nonchalance I encountered was extraordinary. A police officer I met in the city of Bhawanipatna claimed that there was progress. 'Twenty years ago, no one here used to wear chappals. Now, they all do.' Improvement, he said, was always slow.

Two lakh crore rupees in exports. Such marginal uptick in people's lives.

———

Pradip Kumar Behera was worried about his students. Twelve years had passed since the thirty-five-year-old joined the government school in Unchabali, a village in the iron-ore rich district of Keonjhar.[35] When he first came here, only motorcycles could tackle the road leading down

---

* Odisha is far from unique in showcasing such inequality. 'In Goa, the declared profits of mining—amounting to around Rs 12,000 crore—was shared by a handful of people. ... If you take the fact that there are 2 lakh families in Goa, this could have meant a 6 lakh-rupee windfall for each family.' See: Hartman de Souza, *Eat Dust: Mining and Greed in Goa* (India: Harper Litmus, 2015), 75.

the local hill to the village. There was a tar road now. On the hilltop, the MLA Sanatan Mahakud was building a house that ran its width. The village had changed as well. The lane leading to the school was a showcase of inequality. Interspersed among old, collapsing houses of bricks and tiles were two- and three-storeyed mansions, some almost fluorescent shades of pink and yellow. Most had trucks parked outside. One had a six-tonner standing in its porch. This signalled a shift in economic activity. While Unchabali, with its lush green fields and hills, in these rain-soaked monsoon months of 2015, continued to look pastoral, it was mining that now drove its economy and society, not farming.

The school, which taught kids from the first to the eighth standard, had changed as well. Its 144 students, mostly from poorer families in the village, got free afternoon meals, notebooks, underwear and uniforms. Whenever Principal Behera—bespectacled, wearing black sandals, baggy black trousers and an untucked white shirt that day—needed help, local mining companies emerged as an alternative to slower-moving government machinery. It is they who redid the school's wiring and built its latrines and boundary wall. 'I told a company there's no facility [of water] for the midday meal programme, and they sent a plumber and a mechanic,' he said. 'They were measuring for a Sintex [tank] when I told them I want a boring so we can water our trees too. So, they provided that facility too.'

What had not changed was staff levels. In 2003, when Behera got here, the school had three teachers. Between 2005 and 2014, it scraped along with two. In 2015, it had four teachers. Two of these, however, were shiksha sahayaks, matriculates hired as teaching assistants but now conscripted into teaching. 'We need at least six to seven teachers,' said Behera.

To manage, he made two classes share a room, each sitting on either side of the aisle. Teachers tutored one class for an hour, gave them an assignment, crossed the aisle and taught that batch for another hour before hopping back. The arrangement haunted Behera. 'The children are getting an education for less than three hours a day. How can they compete with students from bigger cities? The education we got was better.' He kept asking his superiors in the state Education Department for more teachers but to little effect.

It was the same story elsewhere in Keonjhar. On the road between Unchabali and the mining towns of Joda and Barbil was the tiny settlement of Jaribahal. It was strikingly located. All around it were man-made tabletop mountains of overburden—soil and rocks dug out from mines and deposited on rising mounds. Its primary school had five classes but just two teachers, one of whom was not coming to work. She had a young child, the residual teacher helpfully explained. There were two other teachers, their salaries paid by mining companies in this age of corporate social responsibility. But they were underpaid at Rs 2,000 a month, so one had not shown up for a year. The other came once a week.

Keonjhar, with its iron mines, red ferric soil and green hills, was an interior district, and, therefore, underdeveloped. Coastal parts of Odisha were said to be more developed. But similar understaffing showed up there too. In Kendrapara, closer to the coast, a government-run primary school had sixty-nine students across five classes but just three teachers. It had no desks or benches. The children sat on the floor. A 2014 report in the *Times of India* pegged vacancies in the state's primary schools at 36,137 teachers.[36] In 2020, even after the state shut down hundreds of schools[37] and redistributed their students and teachers, the shortage of primary school teachers stood at 21,000.*

---

* In 2017, Odisha closed 735 primary schools. In 2020, it was planning to close another 11,500 schools. 'The integration of primary, upper primary and high schools with the nearby bigger schools … would lead to fully functional schools with increase in number of teachers per class and concentrated investment of resources.' See: 'Odisha to Close Down 11500-odd Schools for Better Learning Outcome', *Hindustan Times* (14 March 2020), hindustantimes.com/education/odisha-to-close-down-11500-odd-schools-for-better-learning-outcome/story-zCaQifPc9IBfLcbQN5DWUL.html.

This is warped bureaucratic logic: to improve schools, shutter them. What gets missed in such transitions is the longer distances students have to travel to school. Some cannot—and so, drop out.

Lack of state government support showed in other ways. 'In all schools here, buildings are not in good condition. There are no boundary walls or they are broken. Some schools have latrines, tables and chairs. Others don't. Teaching equipment is not there. There is usually a very small library but that is kept locked in the principal's office,' a Sarva Shiksha Abhiyan official in Kendrapara told me when I visited her school.

State hospitals were no different. Kandhamal, one of the poorest districts in India, made headlines in 2008 after attacks on adivasi Christians.[38] While I was in Odisha, it made headlines again. In a ninety-day period between April and July 2015, 154 infants died in its hospitals. One factoid surfaced: government hospitals in the district, home to 731,951 people per the 2011 census, did not have even one paediatrician at the time.[39]

This was a state-wide phenomenon. A senior doctor in the state's anti-malaria project told me, 'We need 11,000–12,000 doctors, but the sanctioned posts are just 4,000. Of that, we have just 2,500–3,000 doctors.' As for other positions, like lab technicians, 'half the sanctioned posts have been filled. And that is [just the] sanctioned strength. The real shortage is probably four times as much.'

———

Like Mizoram, Odisha was failing to deliver healthcare and education. The reasons, however, were different. Mizoram had cash-flow problems because government spending had outpaced revenues, making it divert funds from programmes in health and education for more expedient needs like repaying loans and staff salaries. Odisha was different. In 2014–2015, state government revenues were a shade over Rs 30,000 crore. With funds coming in from the centre too, total revenues swelled to Rs 83,181 crore. In fact, the state was aiming to close 2015–2016 with a Rs 5,100 crore revenue surplus.[40]

Yet, there was such understaffing and neglect. The reason, said bureaucrats at the state and the centre, was Odisha's fixation on fiscal conservatism. Afraid of going broke, it hesitated to spend. The state settled on this tack in the late 1990s, Abhijit Sen, a former member of the erstwhile Planning Commission, told me. Back then, the state's finances were a mess. Revenues were low, expenditures were high, and borrowings were out of control. It took Odisha five years to effect a turnaround. At that time, to cut costs, it stopped appointing staff. Since then, the state government had frozen most recruitments. At the most, it hired contract employees.

'The government is telling us to outsource [government functions],' said a senior IAS official in Odisha. 'But that has quality issues. The people we can outsource to do not exist. Instead, they have sprung up as a business in response to the decision to outsource. We have a lot of people coming into the government who would not get in otherwise.'

This accelerated the decay of administrative capacities.

———

During the iron ore boom, the state had supported capital at the cost of its own people. While the boom had ended, this trait persisted.

In the districts of Kalahandi and Rayagada—home to dense forests, vulnerable adivasi communities and some of India's biggest bauxite reserves—paramilitary camps were rising. At Niyamgiri, sacred to the Dongria Kondhs, the number of central reserve police force (CRPF) camps had climbed from one in 2010 to three by 2015. More were expected. While government officials attributed the security build-up to rising Naxal activity, the Kondhs said that the state was trying to force them off the land.[41]

In an interview to KBK Samachar, a small independent collective of video journalists, Lado Sikoka, a young and articulate Dongria Kondh leader, had said, 'When they [government forces] meet us, they beat us. They take away our local weapons. They say things like "Go to Vedanta, you will get money for free". But we don't want free money. Our god is here.' The nature of police complaints was changing too. 'At one time, FIRs used to be lodged by the company against protesters,' Mahammad

Ashlam, a respected local journalist, told me. 'Now, these are being lodged by the state, listing leaders as Naxals.'

One such FIR, filed on 28 July 2011 at the police station in the town of Muniguda after the murder of a man called Dadhi Sikoka, accused six people and alleged they were accompanied by another forty to forty-five Naxals. Only two of those six, Ashlam told me, were Naxals. 'The others were Dongria Kondh leaders. One of them was Lado Sikoka.' Whenever the police wanted to clamp down on protests against mining, said Ashlam, it used these FIRs to put leaders behind bars. 'People like Lado did not even know their names are in the FIRs. They are branding everyone as Naxals.'

It was the same story in Rayagada. At a village called Kupakal, near Utkal Aluminia's bauxite mine, villagers described the oppression they faced from both the CRPF and the state police. 'We want a school, a hospital, drinking water, a road and daily wage work. But anyone who asks for anything is put in jail,' said the villagers. Earlier that year, they said, Section 144 of the Criminal Procedure Code, banning gatherings of more than five people, had been imposed for three months. Officials at the local police station claimed this was untrue; it was imposed only for a month, they said.

A rise in Naxal activity was not an exaggeration. As the number of companies wanting to mine rose, people's movements came up. Naxals entered the fray as well, hoping to win cadre and expand their geography. The CRPF followed. And, as in Chhattisgarh and elsewhere, the adivasis got stuck between Naxals and State forces. The superintendent of police in Kalahandi, expressing the more widespread State sentiment that is pro-industry and anti-adivasi, said, 'How is it fair for 10,000 people to deny the country bauxite?'

———

Bewilderment was the major leitmotif of my months in Odisha. Despite the persistence of debt-induced migration, the state did not implement the central government's Mahatma Gandhi National Rural Employment

Guarantee Act (MGNREGA).* It gave students cycles but not teachers. It gave people doles when someone passed away but no paediatricians.

---

* Every year, after the kharif harvest, the town of Kantabanji in the district of Balangir becomes the largest migrant labour market in western Odisha. Its guesthouses and hotels fill up as brick-kiln owners called 'seths' come to recruit workers with the help of local labour contractors called 'sardars'. A little later, in November, anywhere between 1 to 2 lakh villagers catch trains to Andhra Pradesh and Tamil Nadu, where they spend the next five or six months working in brick kilns. Workers suffer abuse, long working hours, severe beatings and even rape. Yet, they continue to go.

Three reasons, two old and one new, are at play. Between falling forest produce and weakening farm soils, the district struggles to support its people through the year. Lack of cheap credit is the other perennial reason. People like Thiru Gour Rana, a farmer from Haldipatrapalli village, borrow—in his case, to get his daughter married—and are saddled with high-cost debt. Rana borrowed Rs 20,000 at 10 per cent monthly interest from local lenders. To repay, he signed up with a sardar.

From 2006, MGNREGA, which provides employment during the post-kharif months when people travel out, could have been an alternative. A household working all 150 days would make about Rs 20,000. But when I visited, it was not being implemented. One reason, as I found in Kuibahal village in Balangir's Turekela block, were village sarpanches. Kuibahal's sarpanch was also the local sardar. He earned more if people migrated.

The state government was complicit. Statistics for Balangir suggested spotless MGNREGA implementation. According to state government data uploaded to the centre's MGNREGA portal, 57,916 people demanded work under the programme in 2015–2016 and 57,154 got work. In Kuibahal, it showed that all 42 asking for work got it. These numbers, strikingly immaculate given the state's dismal show on all other welfare fronts, did not match what the villagers said. 'We don't get MGNREGA work,' said a young man in Kuibahal. 'Not this year. Not the previous year.' An IAS officer in the union Ministry of Rural Development explained later, 'Odisha is passing off works approved as total demand for work.' A better way to assess implementation, he said, was to compare the number of work days provided against the demand for MGNREGA as estimated by the state government and the central ministry.

This revealed that against a probable district-wide demand of 90,508 days of work by August 2015, the state government provided 15,495 days. Or take Kuibahal. Its latent demand for work was pegged at 5,953 days. What it got was 90 days. See: M. Rajshekhar, 'Why Lakhs of People Leave Odisha to Work in Distant, Unsafe Brick-Kilns', *Scroll.in* (8 September 2015), scroll.in/article/747416/why-lakhs-of-people-leave-odisha-to-work-in-distant-unsafe-brick-kilns.

It fretted about fiscal conservatism but did not maximise gains from the iron ore boom. Despite this litany of failures, outcry from its people seemed to be surprisingly muted. This was a running theme through *Ear to the Ground*—people opposed expropriation far more than the under delivery of services by states.

Over the years, Odisha has seen several people's movements but most of them were localised, coalescing around specific projects in Niyamgiri, Hirakud or Kalinganagar. A majority of these, added Sudhir Pattnaik, an activist who also brings out a magazine on social issues called *Samadrusti*, were started by adivasis. 'They are more assertive than the rest of the population.' Apart from these, Odisha has not seen many political movements that straddle the state.[42]

Every evening, at a tea stall in Bhubaneswar's abandoned old bus stand, which had been taken over by garment stalls, Kedar Mishra, poet and editor of Odiya monthly *Sachitra Vijaya*, and a clutch of veteran reporters got together for an adda. As my stint in Odisha came to an end, one evening, Mishra and his friends traced one reason for this passivity to the state's history. An agglomeration of small princely states, Odisha was always feudal. This mode of thinking persisted, said Mishra. 'You get a mindset which says, "I don't want to understand politics, rights, political rights, democracy, etc. I operate on the belief that the people I am choosing understand them." It's a very lethargic society.'

In recent years, he added, Odiya society had seen further depoliticisation. This was partly the failure of institutions that should have created a political consciousness—political parties, civil society and the media.

Apart from the ruling BJD, Odisha had the Congress, the BJP and the Left parties. All of them were so weak—Chief Minister Patnaik periodically poached their leaders, and being out of power for long, they were bankrupt—that, by 2020, the BJD had been in power for twenty straight years.

Although, the rot ran deeper than the lack of a functional opposition. 'In Odisha, senior leadership of all parties is drawn from the same group. Even communist and socialist leaders are from

the same high-caste groups and feudal families,' said Mishra. Take
Balangir's member of parliament (MP), Kalikesh Singh Deo. Hailing
from the royal family of Balangir, he worked as an investment banker
and then at the disgraced energy firm Enron before entering politics—
an elected representative with little in common with the people who
voted for him. Newer entrants into politics were no different. Most
of them were businesspeople entering politics to grow their firms. A
veteran politician who left the BJD after a disagreement with Naveen
Patnaik told me, 'Being an MP or an MLA gives you access inside the
government.' It was a phenomenon in which candidates were not in
a party for ideology but to be elected as MLA or MP, Mishra told me.

Another stimulant to political discussion, Mishra continued,
could have been the media. But in Odisha, as in other parts of India,
a sizeable portion of the press was owned by political families. Indeed,
one curious aspect of Odisha was the almost hegemonic presence of
a few families. According to an IAS official in the state, these families
straddled 'the media, business and politics'. The politician Baijyant
Panda owned the mining and steel company IMFA as well as the news
channel OTV. *Samvad*, an Odiya newspaper, was owned by Soumya
Ranjan Patnaik, not only a former MLA and chairperson of the KMBB
college but also the brother of Niranjan Patnaik, a former head of the
Congress in Odisha. He was also related to Indrani Patnaik, who owned
mining leases in the state.

In this situation, said Mishra, where businesspeople or politicians
are owner-publishers, 'publications function as mouthpieces. They
provide MPs and MLAs with a chance to promote themselves', or to
protect themselves. At the time I was there, Serajuddin and Co. was
planning to start a newspaper. One reason, said a journalist who had
now joined the mining group, was the need for security. The business
family 'wanted a paper as they were being targeted by others'. The idea
was to have a medium they could use to defend themselves, he said.

The lack of political opposition hamstrung the media further. 'All
papers are overtly or covertly pro-BJD,' said Mishra. 'The journalism
this creates is subdued and subservient. Small questions become very

large. Even when there's a large issue, the debate will be on something else.' The Shah Commission report, for instance, did not get coverage, he added. 'What gets discussed are religious babas. Should the new IIT come up in Cuttack or Bhubaneswar? The run-up to Jagannath Rath Yatra itself went on for four months.'

The state government's crackdown on people's movements— slapping cases on activists and branding them as Naxals—also chilled dissent. Protest movements, said the activist Pattnaik, were being linked to Naxals to make it easier for the government to deal with them. 'So far, tribals have been very firm but peaceful in their protests. In order to crush them, you [the State] have to call them militant.'[43]

3

The State Controlled by One Family

Punjab was simmering when I reached in October 2015.

Farmers were out protesting.[1] In the northern Majha region, a slash in minimum support price (MSP) for basmati had brought them to the streets. In the central region of Doaba, they were protesting the closure of sugar mills and non-payment of dues. In the southern Malwa region, where a whitefly attack had decimated the cotton crop, there was near unanimity amongst farmers that the pesticides sold to them were fake. Compounding matters, in multiple villages since June, locals had found torn pages from the Sikh holy book, the Guru Granth Sahib.[2] Angry at this desecration, protesters had blocked roads and railway tracks. At a village called Behbal Kalan, near the town of Faridkot, the state police had opened fire, killing two.[3]

Elsewhere in the country too, these were dark times. A fortnight had passed since fifty-two-year-old Mohammad Akhlaq was lynched by a Hindu mob in his village near Dadri, Uttar Pradesh.[4] A week later, hearing of another mob attack in the state in the town of Karhal, again on the charge of 'gau hatya', killing of a cow, I had travelled over. Little about this attack, I found on reaching, had been spontaneous. The mastermind was a local Samajwadi Party leader who, hoping to become an MLA, had tried to polarise the Hindu vote in his favour. Quick diffusion of tensions by elders, local leaders and police officials had saved the victims and prevented a riot.[5] Now, a day after reaching

Amritsar, I learnt about another attack in Karhal, on a Muslim leader who had demanded police action against the instigators.[6]

———

It is from Punjab that the Green Revolution, which used irrigation, high-yielding varieties of crops and chemical inputs to make India self-reliant in foodgrains, began in the 1960s. The state also had a thriving manufacturing sector at the time. Supported by policies like freight rationalisation—which, seeking equal growth of industry across India, kept prices of inputs like coal and steel the same across the country—towns like Mandi Gobindgarh became centres of iron and steel production. Thousands of units in Ludhiana and Jalandhar made farm implements from this steel. Others processed local cotton into yarn and clothes. Yet others built the machines these factories ran on. Punjab was quite an exemplary mixed economy.

In its heyday, per capita incomes were rising in the state, so were life expectancy and government expenditure on public services like health.[7] There was, as Sumail Singh Sidhu, a former professor at Delhi University and former state convenor for the Aam Aadmi Party, told me when we met at his house in Bhatinda, a certain Nehruvian idealism in the state. 'To make Punjab something.'

What happened next is well-known. Agricultural growth peaked in the early 1980s and then dipped.[8] Removal of freight rationalisation in 1993, on complaints from mineral-rich states that it hurt their prospects for industrialisation, left towns like Mandi Gobindgarh struggling to compete. Insurgency and counter-insurgency between the late 1970s and early 1990s, as a section of the state demanded an independent Khalistan, hammered government and economic functioning, and left the people scarred.

In the years that followed, as in every state I reported from, the gulf had widened between Punjab's post-insurgency realities and how the rest of India saw it. In *Panjab*, author Amandeep Sandhu describes this well.

'A few weeks back an institute in Bangalore called me to talk about Panjab. I asked the participants to give me the first word

that came to their mind when they heard the term "Panjab". I
wrote them on the board.'

'And?'

'A strange word-picture emerged. Its edges rough, at war
with itself ...'

'What did they say?'

'The participants gave words like: Sikh, bhangra, Sufi,
terrorist, gurdwara, *langar*, Khalistan, Green Revolution,
soldiers, Dalit, tandoori chicken, Gurus, Partition, dhol, salwar
kameez, mehndi, Bhindranwale, five rivers, deras, butter chicken
... and so on.'[9]

In conversation with Satnam, the pseudonymous Punjabi writer and
activist, Sandhu calls this word salad problematic.

'None of these words give a central idea about Panjab. Placed
next to each other, they confuse. How does *"langar"* sit with
terrorist? How does "Sufi" sit with "Bhindranwale"? If the Sikh
religion is supposed to be equal and just, why do we have the
highest percentage of Dalits in Punjab? What are deras? Why
female foeticide? Why does the breadbasket of the nation have
the highest number of per capita farmer and labour suicides?
Why do only half the children in government schools pass
matric? Is Panjab on drugs? What is this new and renewed talk
of Khalistan? I feel lost in these micro-worlds.'

In May 2015, Hazara Ram rolled the dice again. Like his fellow farmers
in Baluana, a village of about 5,000 people near the town of Bhatinda,
the sixty-year-old planted cotton on his two-killa, or two-acre, plot in
the kharif season.* Wheat would follow as the rabi crop in winter.[10]

---

* Location determined the choice of cash crop. During the kharif season, up
north in the districts around Amritsar in the Majha region, farmers usually
planted paddy. In the state's eastern areas, running along Jalandhar, Ludhiana and

As the cost of farm inputs rose faster than crop yields or prices, this was how small and medium farmers, comprising 60 per cent to 70 per cent of all farmers in the state, lived. Wheat was the safety net. It would feed Hazara Ram and, if sold, fetch a moderate but stable price. As for cotton, it injected cash into farming households like his. It made for a meagre life. A killa yielded 20 quintals, or 2,000 kilos, of wheat. Hazara Ram would make Rs 10,000 if he chose to sell it. From cotton, he would earn 4 to 4.5 times as much. In a good year, he made just enough to survive another year. If either crop failed, he ran short of food or cash, opening the doors to hunger and indebtedness. Every summer, as he tilled his field in this state that had once made farmers rich, life hung in the balance.

Kharif planting had been delayed in 2015. After unexpected rainfall in the normally dry months of March and April, the previous crop of wheat had taken longer to ripen, pushing its harvest to the end of April. This left Hazara Ram with less than six months to prepare his fields, plant and reap the cotton crop, which would take five months to mature, before planting wheat again in November. In a rush, he harvested the wheat, tilled the fields, sowed cotton and begun watching it grow.

And then, the weather turned truant again. In June, when the mercury would normally touch 47°C and the hot summer wind, loo, would blow, it rained. Most days that month, temperatures stayed below 40°C. In July and August, when the monsoons would normally arrive, the skies stayed overcast but let out little rain. The first three weeks of September stayed dry as well, followed by heavy rains in the fourth.

The stage was set for the great whitefly crisis of 2015. Most years, these tiny insects that suck the sap from plants during the nymphal stage of their life are a minor pest. Both the loo and monsoon rains keep a lid on their numbers. In 2015, however, as skies stayed overcast with little rainfall, humidity remained high and temperatures relatively

---

Doaba, farmers planted potatoes and cane. Over in the south, where Hazara Ram lived, soil was sandier and the water brackish. Mostly cotton, which needs less water than paddy, was grown here.

low, their numbers built up from June itself. Delayed harvest of the rabi crop compounded the problem. The cotton plants were only about a month old when the whiteflies started to multiply. At this age, cotton plants have no more than twenty leaves, an entomologist at the Punjab Agricultural University, who wanted to remain anonymous, told me. 'A forty-five-day-old plant has about fifty. Even twenty whiteflies can overwhelm the smaller plant.'

That was just the start. Whiteflies do not live more than a month. They grow inside eggs, hatch into larvae, grow into adults, mate and die in that tiny stretch of time. So, in the absence of controlling factors, not one but three generations of whiteflies attacked Hazara Ram's cotton plants.

That summer, variants of this story played out across the cotton-growing belt. By October, three-fourths of the crop was ruined. Production dropped from 13.42 lakh bales in the previous year to 3.93 lakh bales.[11] By mid-October, fifteen farmers killed themselves. A farmers' agitation demanding compensation from the state began. Pesticides failed to control the outbreak, giving rise to speculation that they were fake. The director of the state Department of Agriculture and Farmer Welfare and several pesticide dealers were arrested.[12]

Along the way, both the state and society blew a chance to identify the real reasons for the whitefly infestation—changing rainfall patterns in Punjab. Which was what Surendra Paul, director of the Indian Meteorological Department's office in Chandigarh, was seeing from his large room in the weather-tracking agency's red-brick office. 'In the last fifteen years, we have seen a fall in the volume of rain. Between 2005 and 2015, rainfall has been 25 per cent below normal for six years. Monsoon, which used to reach Punjab around 30 June, now comes five days sooner. It also stays longer, leaving seven to eight days after the earlier departure date of 30 September. Rain is also getting more concentrated across time and space. In 2015, most of the rain fell in just ten days. Only six of the twenty-two districts in the state got the normal volume of rainfall,' he told me.

These changes, he said, were the result of a new interaction between the southwest monsoon and mid-latitude westerlies. The former starts from the Arabian Sea, covers south India and then heads north, curving up along the eastern coast, moving towards the low-pressure area that develops over central India due to the summer heat. As for the mid-latitude westerlies, these blow at a greater distance from the equator, starting from about latitude 32°North—the northern tip of Punjab and above. From 2005 onwards, mostly in the monsoon and winter months, Paul and his fellow meteorologists saw something new. Mid-latitude westerlies were swinging farther and farther south. Since 2010, they had reached as far south as latitude 25°North—the northern reaches of Madhya Pradesh. As a result, India was seeing greater interaction between them and the monsoon. 'We have seen as many as forty instances of western disturbances affecting the monsoons this year,' he said.

It was unclear yet why westerlies were swinging south. What was clearer was the effect of these swings on the monsoons. 'The monsoonal trough—the low pressure area which attracts monsoon clouds—is coming to depend on the interplay between the westerlies and the monsoon winds. Their collision now results in the formation of a large cloud mass and abrupt, short-lived but intense cloudbursts like the ones India saw in 2015 in Jammu and Kashmir, Himachal Pradesh, Uttarakhand and Gujarat. Elsewhere, rainfall tends to be low.'

This was just half the story. Like every year, in 2015 too, Paul's department had prepared pre-monsoon and weekly bulletins for local authorities like agricultural colleges, district collectorates and the Agriculture Department officials. But these alerts and updates had not reached the farmers.

During the Green Revolution, Punjab had created a large agricultural extension bureaucracy to inform farmers—through camps, lectures and visits—about new crops, seeds, fertilisers, implements and pesticides. In each district, gram sevaks, responsible for a few villages, reported to chief agricultural officers. This system was not working any more. The state had seen a 50 per cent to 60 per cent reduction in the number of extension workers, the entomologist at the Punjab Agricultural University said. As for the remaining staff, it was often deputed for other work, like conducting local elections.

Baluana, Hazara Ram's village, illustrated the costs. In the absence of visits by extension workers to check on the crop, the infestation was spotted only when the first generation of whiteflies began flying around. At this stage, with skies overcast and rain seemingly imminent, farmers did not spray pesticides. Companies making these cautioned farmers that the fields needed to stay dry for four to six hours after spraying, said Jagdish Kumar, who ran a fertiliser shop near the village gurudwara. The cost of the spray, Rs 1,800 a litre, made the farmers even more cautious. They waited for clear skies. Undisturbed, the whitefly eggs grew into nymphs, with concentrations per leaf much higher than previous infestations. It was only when the plants had visibly weakened and their leaves turned black that desperate farmers began looking for medicines.

At which stage, a fresh suboptimality arose. In the absence of advice from extension workers, farmers turned to adatiyas, or agricultural traders. In Punjab, as in the rest of India, adatiyas not only buy the harvest from farmers but also lend money and sell farm inputs. In a 2015 paper published in the *Economic and Political Weekly*, Sukhpal Singh of Punjab Agricultural University had estimated that as many as 89 per cent of all farming households in the state were in debt, and adatiyas were a primary source of credit. [13] He also estimated that 15.01 per cent of pesticides in Punjab were supplied by them. Another 80 per cent were sold by shops owned by people connected to these traders.

This introduced fresh risks. Lacking knowhow—were the whiteflies in egg, nymph or adult stage?—some traders pushed the wrong pesticides. Others sold those with fatter margins. At the same time, seeking to keep debt low, farmers bought cheaper ones. In Baluana, Sukhdev Singh showed me a can of the fungicide he had sprayed—it was for parasitic fungi and of no use on whiteflies. Hazara Ram too, watching his cotton crop plateau out at two feet instead of growing to the usual metre, tried everything. 'There are four medicines for whiteflies. I sprayed them all,' he told me. With each dose costing Rs 600 to Rs 800 per acre, he spent Rs 5,000 in all.

Nothing worked. The plants yielded only 80 kilos per acre—Hazara Ram had been hoping for 500 kilos per acre—which sold for Rs 4,000. He had hoped to make Rs 80,000 to Rs 90,000.

The whitefly infestation was not about fake pesticides or erratic rains one year. It was about missing adaptation and mitigation in the face of climate change. Recalling the chatter about fake pesticides, a passage from the anthropologist Akhil Gupta's *Postcolonial Developments* came to mind. Asked why manure was better for soil than fertilisers, farmers in his study site told him that fertilisers released their 'heat' suddenly, while manure released it slowly, strengthening the soil.[14]

In Punjab too, in the absence of updated farming information, farmers had fallen back on old patterns of thinking to make sense of the new.

———

A thread, invisible to the eye, linked businessperson Harbans Singh Bhanwer and Ludhiana. They came together in 1965, when the now ageing patriarch of a family today mostly settled in Canada, set up Craft Tools, a small company making machine parts, in the city. That was a time of great promise. Ludhiana provided a large part of the engineering underpinning for the Green Revolution—from making farm implements to processing cotton into yarn and fabrics—and units like Craft Tools built the bearings, hydraulic systems and motors these factories ran on.[15]

Over the next fifty years, Bhanwer and the city moved in tandem. Both grew fast through most of the 1960s. And both saw their growth ebb due to bank nationalisation in the late 1960s, the Emergency years of the mid-1970s and then again during the years of separatist terrorism. Each time, both dusted themselves off and got back to the serious business of growing. By 1991, products from Ludhiana were being exported to countries in Europe and the Middle East. Craft Tools followed suit. 'By 2002–2003, we had customers not just in India but also in the United Arab Emirates and Italy,' said Bhanwer.

When I met Bhanwer in November 2015, he and Ludhiana were back in another slump. Craft Tools had lost its global clients. Its revenues were dropping, from Rs 85 lakh in 2012–2013 to Rs 37 lakh by 2014–2015. As for Ludhiana, its biggest manufacturers were moving beyond Punjab. The local textile giant Nahar Industrial Enterprises, which made cotton yarn, garments and woollens, was now producing 40 per cent of its yarn and denim in Madhya Pradesh. The city was also home to some of India's largest bicycle makers—firms like Hero, Atlas and Avon—and accounted for about 90 per cent of cycle production in the country.[16] These companies too, were now spreading their manufacturing capacities beyond Punjab. Expansion, a Nahar official told me, could easily become the prelude to an exit. 'As our machines in Ludhiana get older, we will have to decide whether to replace them or not.'

Most of the manufacturing cluster, however, comprised small and medium firms supplying components to bigger ones. Not deep-pocketed enough to relocate and start anew, they were slashing costs to survive, and several had shut down. Rajinder Singh used to run a business making pedals for bicycles. When I met him, he was pushing a cycle laden with two-litre soft drink bottles and less recognisable smaller ones, all filled with phenyl, through Ludhiana's industrial area. It was a tough life for someone in his mid-fifties. The combined weight of the bottles was about 100 litres. Selling them netted him about Rs 300–Rs 400 a day. 'I work from half past seven in the morning to two in the afternoon,' he said. 'I cannot work longer than that.'

This contagion of businesses shuttering was not unique to Ludhiana. Jalandhar's sports goods industry had become a shadow of its earlier self. In Amritsar, the textile industry was closing down. In Mandi Gobindgarh, the number of furnaces in its steel industry had halved between 2012 and 2015.

Jalandhar, with its export-focused sporting goods industry, is a good starting point to understand this decline. As recently as the 1990 FIFA World Cup, its inflatable goods, like volleyballs, basketballs, footballs and beachballs, sold around the world. It was a head start India failed to capitalise on. Cheaper inflatables from China took over by 2010. 'We produce at $2 and they at $1.50. How do we compete? Today, 90 per cent of the market is theirs,' said Vipan Mahajan, secretary general of the city's Sports Goods Manufacturers and Exporters Association.

Companies selling in the domestic market, like cycle makers, had a similar refrain. Into the mid-2000s, Hero, Atlas and Avon made some parts—like frames, handlebars and forks—in-house and outsourced the rest to suppliers. This was how cities like Ludhiana came to have thousands of companies making pedals, spokes, ball bearings and more. This complex produced about 90 per cent of all cycles sold in India. Since 2008, however, cheaper Chinese imports have replaced indigenous manufacturers of cycle parts, most of which have shut down too.

These are familiar tales. India failed to prepare small and medium enterprises for import liberalisation, leave alone exports.[17] Take what happened when the industrial cluster at Mohali, making engineering components and bathroom fittings just outside Chandigarh, sought government funding to set up an R&D centre. It was to have a design centre, a tool room and a lab, said Kanwaljit Singh Mahan, a former president of the Mohali Industries Association. The proposal faced disinterest from both the centre and state. The union government eventually sanctioned the budget but, for years, the state government did not finish the paperwork. Getting money out of Punjab, said Mahan, was like 'getting milk out of a bull. By the time the lab comes up, China will have moved farther ahead.'

Complicating matters, the cost of doing business in Punjab was also higher than in other states. LED manufacturers in Punjab paid 13.5 per cent as VAT, while their peers in neighbouring states paid 5.5 per cent. Power cost more too. A unit cost Rs 8 in Punjab, while other states charged Rs 5, said Bhanwer. Since 2005, industrial units in the state had been paying octroi—levied elsewhere in the world only on physical goods entering a city—on electricity. That is just the start. Bhanwer slammed a file with power bills on his table and jabbed a finger at the column next to octroi. 'What is this?' It read cow cess. Levied on power consumption.

There was also electricity duty and infrastructure cess. In the days that followed, speaking to power corporation officials, I learnt that from March 2016, water and sewerage charges would also find their way into the state's power bills. Octroi, electricity duty and infrastructure cess alone added about Rs 1.27 per unit to power bills in the state, an official in the Punjab State Power Corporation Ltd (PSPCL) told me.[18] Cow cess swelled it up further. Water charges would push it up even more.

This was administrative jugaad. During the insurgency years, tax collection, like agricultural extension and other government functions, had crumbled in the state. When peace returned, successive governments did not revive these systems. The only state bill the people of Punjab paid was for power. So, whenever strapped for funds, the state government turned to PSPCL, with its 99.9 per cent collection rate, and got it to add cesses, duties and surcharges.

Electricity duty was introduced because the state needed more revenues. Cow cess came in because cities like Ludhiana faced a problem of abandoned cows. As 'gau rakshaks', or cow protectors, moved around, farmers struggled to sell ageing cattle and abandoned them in the cities. Ludhiana's municipal corporation, consequently, had to set up more cow shelters, but it was cash-strapped. People might not voluntarily give money for the shelters but, as a municipality official said, 'Electricity is a compulsion.'

This two-step logic, reminiscent of the politicians' syllogism outlined in the TV show *Yes, Prime Minister*—'We must do something. This is something. Therefore we must do this'—also drove the decision to port water and sewerage charges, which municipalities were unable to collect. People would not default on power bills. Therefore, the two should be clubbed.

It was a mind-numbing solution. PSPCL could not charge per actual water consumption. Linking its systems to water meters, where they existed, would have been almost impossible. Instead, water charges were to be levied as a percentage of the power bill—Rs 20 for 500 units of power consumption, Rs 50 for 1,000 units and so on. Punjab has entered, like the rest of India, a future of water shortage. Yet, in this new system, there was no link between water use and what users paid. It also dumped additional costs on industrial units already struggling to stay competitive.

High tax and power rates were still not the complete reason why Punjab was shedding its competitiveness. Two more factors, both linked to politics in the state, were also at work. The first was predatory extraction. As I reported: 'Punjab-based companies talk about the political pressure to share profits with the ruling Akali Dal. One businessperson, who wanted to set up an atta factory, said the party asked him for a 3–4% chunk of his turnover. "My margins are 10–15%. 3–4% was too high," he said.'[19]

The second was foregone revenue. States in India have three major sources of revenue, as K.R. Lakhanpal, a former chief secretary of Punjab, explained when I met him in Chandigarh. 'There is excise [like on alcohol], transport [like motor vehicle tax] and real estate [like levies on construction materials such as sand and stone]. Some states also levy professional tax and payroll tax.' After coming to power in 2007, the Badal family, of the then ruling Akali Dal's Parkash Singh Badal, and those close to it took over these three sectors.

With that, tax collections dropped. 'Each of these [sectors], controlled by people close to the ruling dispensation, either evades taxes or gets tax benefits,' said Lakhanpal, who had worked as principal secretary, finance, before becoming the chief secretary. This was another reason the state was cash-strapped. Trying to meet its costs, Punjab levied taxes and power bills so high that firms like Craft Tools struggled to survive.

Although he had waited out the bad times in the past, this time around, Bhanwer was wondering if he should relocate. 'Himachal, Jharkhand and Uttarakhand are offering ten-year tax holidays, power at Rs 5 per unit and no infrastructure tax. Between all these, our margins will rise by 10 per cent to 15 per cent,' he said. It was not an option he contemplated lightly. Getting old, he knew the efforts and risks involved in starting up again elsewhere. Some companies shifted, he said, but had to come back. Politicians there too had asked for a share in the business. 'They were bled dry.'

———

Late one evening, as dusk melted into night over Amritsar, I met a former liquor wholesaler in a storeroom above a fast food joint. There was a reason for meeting furtively amidst cartons of napkins, ketchup sachets and other future debris of the trade: the wholesaler wanted to talk about the Akali Dal's takeover of liquor distribution in the state. I had waited in a contact's office, talking to him and another businessperson who ran liquor vends, till the wholesaler called with directions. On reaching the eatery, I was directed to the storeroom.

Over the next two hours, the businessperson and his friend, also in the liquor wholesale trade, reconstructed the capture by the Akali Dal. Till 2002, the liquor distribution trade in Punjab had resembled a squat, broad triangle. Distilleries at the top, wholesalers in the middle and small businesspeople running thekas, or liquor vends, at the base. Wholesalers were chosen through the state Revenue Department's district-level auctions. As for the thekas, bids were invited per circle, an administrative subset of the Revenue Department. Entry barriers were low, and bids were keenly contested. Districts wound up with anywhere between four to twenty wholesalers. Circles had as many as twelve thekas each. Between multiple distilleries and over a thousand firms with wholesale and theka licenses, it was a competitive market.[20]

This structure first weakened under the Congress. In 2002, shortly after becoming the chief minister, Amarinder Singh gave a state-wide wholesale licence to liquor baron Ponty Chadha. Over the next four years, said Sarabjit Singh Verka, an investigator with the Punjab Human Rights Organisation, Chadha's private army waged war on liquor, desi or foreign, that did not flow from his organisation. His storm troopers would 'raid marriage halls and parties to check the booze being served,' he said. In 2006, with elections approaching, Amarinder Singh ended Chadha's contract. The liquor business reverted to its earlier model with multiple wholesalers in every district.

And then, the Akali Dal came back to power in 2007. The business changed once more. First, said the wholesaler, the number of wholesale licenses for a district was slashed to two. As I reported:

> The ability of the remaining wholesalers to put pressure on distilleries and retailers increased. 'Distilleries were told to offer higher trade discounts and longer payment periods,' [the wholesaler] said. 'Stores were put under pressure by slashing trade discounts and insisting on immediate payments.' Of the two wholesalers, one was usually an old player, the other one was a new entrant allegedly known to the Akalis. This split averted complaints of monopolisation. But, according to the former wholesaler, the new entrant called the shots: he would sell most of the stipulated quota and the holder of the renewed licence could sell the rest.[21]

Five people, the wholesaler said, controlled over 80 per cent of the liquor trade in the state. Of these, at least three had direct links to the ruling Akali Dal government. As I reported:

> Bikram Majithia's family owns Saraya Industries, which has operations in liquor and energy. He is the brother of Union Minister Harsimrat Kaur and brother-in-law of Sukhbir Badal, the Deputy Chief Minister, and the son of Chief Minister Parkash Badal. … Deep Malhotra heads the liquor-manufacturing Oasis Group and is the Akali Dal MLA from Faridkot. Shiv Lal Doda set up Gagan Wines and was the halka in-charge (local leader) of the Akali Dal in Abohar.[22]

If the liquor industry saw smaller companies elbowed out by a few large ones close to the ruling party, stone quarrying saw something different. Here, while the industry structure was not meddled with, an outsider took most of the profits.

Stone quarrying was concentrated in a few districts. In Pathankot and Gurdaspur, rivers like the Ravi were a major source of stone. 'When it rains,' said the owner of a crushing plant near Pathankot, 'the Ravi swells as wide as three kilometres. When it recedes, it leaves behind boulders on the fields of farmers.' Crushers also operated in districts with rocky outcrops and hills, such as Ropar. This too was a fragmented industry, partly because crushing units did not cost much to set up, no more than Rs 1.5 crore, according to a Congress councillor in Pathankot who also ran one.

Till 2007, plots were awarded through auctions. Contractors collected and crushed stones deposited by the river. The construction industry from Amritsar and elsewhere bought its requirements from them. The market price of a tractor-load of crushed stone was Rs 700 to Rs 800.

Around 2010, once the union government mandated environmental clearances for stone crushing, things began to change. According to a 2012 petition filed by the lawyer Gurbir Singh Pannu in the High Court of Punjab and Haryana, Punjab held very few auctions thereafter. On paper, the business almost stopped. In the real world, however, crushing continued. Travelling through this area in January 2016, I saw stone-laden trucks and crushers at work. At one crushing unit at Kathlour, a village near Pathankot, workers were matter of fact about the source of their stones. 'From the river,' one said. I reported on the mechanics at work:

> 'Mining continues,' said a quarry owner. 'It is just that now the stones are shown as coming from Jammu and Kashmir.' He claimed that crushers can now mine and transport their stones only on the payment of Rs 500 per tonne to a local called Kuldip Singh Makkar. 'On paying this money,' said the owner, 'we are given J&K ki *parchi*'—a document which attests that the stones being transported are from Kashmir and, therefore, legitimate.
>
> Kuldeep Singh Makkar, the local who is allegedly collecting levies from quarry owners, is the brother of Akali Dal MLA Sarabjit Singh Makkar. When contacted, [Kuldeep] Makkar

denied any wrongdoing. '*Sab ke paas permit hain*,' everyone has a permit, he said. 'There is so much police. How can anyone do illegal mining?'[23]

I saw a copy of that parchi. Makkar's claims about the absence of illegal mining were challenged by both local media reports and businesspeople in the crushing industry.[24] 'For every Rs 200 the crusher makes, the goonda tax is Rs 500,' said the councillor.

In an award-winning series, the *Tribune* mapped similar processes through which a handful of people close to the ruling Badal family came to control bus transport and cable distribution. The first used to be a fragmented industry too, with several companies plying buses. Not any more. '[Sukhbir] Badal-associated transport companies not only hold a virtual monopoly in the luxury bus segment, but are clearly the dominant player in the private sector,' the paper reported. 'Out of the 84 luxury bus permits operating in Punjab, at least 52 are with transport companies patronised by the Badals.'[25] This happened in two ways. People close to the Badals acquired stakes in private transport companies such as Indo-Canadian Transport Company, which ran Mercedes Benz intra-city buses. At other times, as the *Tribune* reported, companies associated with the Badals bought out permits from other private transporters.

As for cable, like in the rest of India, the business started in Punjab around the first Gulf War in 1990–1991, with a bunch of entrepreneurs rigging up dish antennae in streets and neighbourhoods. These were small businesses, feeding as few as 500 to 600 households, and subsisting on monthly subscription fees and local advertising. The business slowly began formalising as national cable networks like Hathway, owned by Mumbai's Rahejas, Zee's Wires & Wireless India, and Digicable entered the state. The market was still being split between them and local cable operators when Fastway Transmissions, headed by Gurdeep Singh, entered in 2008–2009.

What happened next is educative. Big and small cable operators were forced to join Fastway. A 2015 report by Sukhdeep Kaur in the

Hindustan Times, showed how cable operators were forced to fall in line, "'Fastway created a monopoly not only through its control over signals and big investment in digitisation, but also political and police patronage. They cut wires, beat up people and destroyed equipment of local operators who refused to fall in line. The police used to threaten us with false cases under the anti-piracy law or possessing CDs of X-rated films. They used to switch off set-top boxes (STBs) any time without giving notice to harass us. It was an option between becoming a part of the cartel [or] perishing," said a cable operator of Ludhiana requesting anonymity, who later switched to Fastway.'[26]

These processes also pushed larger rivals, like Hathway and Wires & Wireless India, into losses. Hathway sold out to Fastway. The latter granted rights over 'collection, distribution and dealing with broadcasters to Creative Cable, a sister company of Gurdeep Singh'. [27]

By 2012, as a judgement by the Competition Commission of India said, Fastway had captured 85 per cent of the cable TV market in the state. Since then, echoing the stone crushing industry where a newcomer captured most of the profit, cable operators in the state had been complaining that Fastway was squeezing them out. As it happens, Fastway too had a Badal connection. Two of its directors, Jagjit Singh Kohli and Yogesh Shah, also showed up in the statutory filings of two media companies owned by Sukhbir Singh Badal—G-Next Media and Gur-Baz Media. Sukhbir Badal owned 67.32 per cent of a company called Orbit Resorts. Orbit Resorts owned 99.98 per cent of Gur-Baz Media. Gur-Baz owned 99.98 per cent of G-Next. And G-Next owned the PTC Network of television channels,[28] more on which later.

———

Most cases of corruption in India are about politicians misusing power to enrich themselves. In Mizoram, politicians made money from road building. In Odisha, they grabbed the gains from the iron ore mining boom. Punjab was different. What one saw here was not just political rent extraction but an ambition to take over the state itself. What also deserves comment were the legal and extralegal mechanics at work. As academic Nicolas Martin writes in an essay in *The Wild East*:

> Many informants alleged that in the past corruption in the state happened only at the highest levels. Congress leaders in the state, they claimed, only took money from big business, whereas the Akali government—then in its second term—took money from everyone. The party leadership allegedly had shares in every business in the state, from media outlets to *dhabas* (roadside restaurants) and bus services to commercial property and industry. Businessmen who refused to pay tribute to the party leadership faced bureaucratic hurdles that caused their businesses to shut down.[29]

If a lucrative dhaba did not pay tribute, Martin adds, its license might be withdrawn, or police might discourage customers by not allowing them to park near it. The editors of this book, scholars Barbara Harriss-White and Lucia Michelutti, describe such a phenomenon as '*intreccio*'. 'Italian scholars of organised crime use the term *intreccio* (intertwinement) to signify that the world of crime does not exist in an alternative domain to that of the state but is deeply entangled with the actually existing state.'[30] These are not failed states, they write, but criminalised states.

In Punjab, intreccio created a business model almost impossible to compete against. It was, as Harriss-White and Michelutti write, a form of capital that could 'ignore state regulative law or selectively manipulate it to [its] advantage. These formations control party politics, simultaneously depriving the state of resources while plundering it of the resources it receives from others; they control the sectors they invest in, using violence whenever necessary.'[31]

This was new. Even during the previous reigns of the Akali Dal, the lines between business and politics were never so blurred. The people I spoke to placed the onus for this shift on Sukhbir Badal, who was made the deputy chief minister in 2009, under his father's chief ministership. A cabinet minister in the state government told me, 'Sukhbir is mainly a businessman. He is running the state like a private limited company.'

The growth in his declared net worth was astronomical. As I reported: 'In 2004, when he stood for Lok Sabha elections, he and his wife—current Union Minister for Food Processing Harsimrat Kaur Badal—pegged the value of their assets at Rs 13 crore. In 2007, when he contested state elections, the couple's assets stood at Rs 67 crore. Seven years later, in the run-up to the 2014 Lok Sabha polls, Harsimrat Kaur Badal declared joint assets of Rs 108 crore. That's an eight-fold increase in 10 years. In contrast, a person who invested, say, Rs 1 lakh in fixed deposits in 2004, would have seen a 2.3-fold increase—not factoring in taxes.'[32]

If only Indians could invest in politicians as an asset class, poverty might end in no time at all.

––––

The costs of this economic capture ran deep.

First, the government went easy on tax collection from companies and industries dominated by the Badals. For instance, it charged a higher tax on ordinary buses than on luxury buses—like the one run by Indo-Canadian—even though luxury buses charge passengers more. As the *Tribune* reported, 'The MVT [Motor Vehicle Tax] per km per vehicle in a day is Rs 3 for ordinary buses and on luxury buses … it is as little as Rs 1.75.' The state government also favoured luxury bus operators while allotting time slots at its bus stands.[33] In tandem, state revenues fell. As their profitability eroded, the dividends paid by state-owned bus transport companies to the government went down. As for the liquor industry, Lakhanpal estimated that half the alcohol in Punjab was sold illegally. By 2015, the state earned about Rs 5,000 crore from excise, which meant it was losing an equivalent amount. Pannu's petition to the high court estimated annual profits from stone crushing at Rs 10,000 crore. However, as stones crushed in Punjab were passed off as stones from Jammu and Kashmir, the state lost revenues. If proper auctions had been held, a part of that Rs 10,000 crore would have accrued to the state.[34]

Apart from the loss of revenue to the state, there was also a wider weakening of businesses. Firms like Craft Tools were saddled with high tax and power rates. Others, like liquor wholesalers and bus operators, were squeezed out. Yet others, like stone crushers and local cable operators, ceded profits to political actors. The price of both sand and stone went up, people in the construction industry complained. In 2005, sand cost Rs 400 a trolley, Master Mohan Lal, a former transport minister in the Akali Dal government, confirmed to me. By 2016, it cost Rs 4,500.

At the same time, government money flowed into the Badal business complex. Take the PTC Network owned by Sukhbir Badal's company G-Next. As *Firstpost* reported, the network got government ads worth Rs 78.32 lakh between 2007 and 2008. This was the time 'when it had just been launched, and needed financial support'.[35]

Shockwaves from the Akali Dal's inroads into Punjab's business sector extended far beyond the state economy. One morning in January, shortly after returning from Pathankot, I read this news report: 'Finance Minister Parminder Singh Dhindsa told *The Tribune* that the state had paid over Rs 1,500 crore to the Centre against the special term loan given to it during the militancy period. "We have asked the Centre to refund this amount so that the state's fiscal health can improve and more money can be used for development works," the minister said.'[36] No less than 65 per cent of Punjab's budget, the report added, goes into salaries, pensions, retirement benefits and other establishment costs. With another 22 per cent going as interest payments for loans, very little was left for the state's larger developmental functions.

———

The biggest healthcare crisis facing Punjab was not cancer, as is generally believed. As the medical journal *Lancet* reported, cancer mortality per 1 lakh people in Punjab was 80.6 in 2010, below the national average of 97.6 and far below the Northeast with 237.4.[37] Punjab's actual albatross was understaffing in the health sector. As per the 2011 census, the state had 2.77 crore people. For this population, the state's Health Department had 3,121 doctors, 1 for every 8,875 persons.[38] These numbers compared unfavourably with neighbouring states like Himachal Pradesh with 1 for every 1,419 persons and Jammu and Kashmir with 1 for every 3,386 persons. The World Health Organization (WHO) norm is 1 for every 1,000 persons.[39]

Worse, critical specialisations were entirely missing in the public health machinery. The state did not have even one neurosurgeon, said an overworked doctor at the subdivisional hospital at Jagraon, a town near Ludhiana. 'There is only one cardiologist in Faridkot. There is no angioplasty anywhere in Punjab. There is only one endocrinologist in the state.' In the civil hospital at Bhatinda, a single nurse oversaw seventy-nine beds. 'We manage,' said the nurse on duty at the time of my visit in 2015, 'because of students getting practical training from the local nursing college. The third-year students can give injections. The first- and second-year students change bedsheets. But it gets very hard at times, like when there is a dengue outbreak.' The hospital's intensive care unit was renovated two years ago, but at the time of my visit, it was not in use as there were not enough doctors and nurses.[*]

The proximate explanation for understaffing was low salaries. The entry level salary for a doctor in the public system was Rs 18,000 a month. A surgeon, who was drawing Rs 48,000 a month at the trauma centre in Ludhiana, had just moved to a private hospital for three times what he was making, another doctor at the hospital told me. The state's health budget, about Rs 3,400 crore in 2013–2014, did not permit it to pay higher salaries. The state had no money because of foregone revenues.[†]

---

[*] Given this shortage of funds, the state Health Department turned to increasingly desperate innovations. In 2006, mirroring Odisha's Education Department, Punjab closed as many as 70 of its 173 subdivisional hospitals and redeployed staff across the rest in a bid to boost staffing levels. The ailing, however, had to travel greater distances.

[†] Illegal sand and stone mining continued in Punjab even in 2019, well after the Akali Dal government had been replaced by the Congress. See: Prabhjit Singh, 'Head in the Sand', *Caravan* (31 October 2019), caravanmagazine.in/reportage/punjab-government-looks-away-illegal-mining-unabated.

Education was the same story. As Sandhu writes: 'A bird's eye view of the education system reveals that in the last decade and a half, there has been nearly a 70 percent shortfall of teaching staff in government colleges. As of 2018, per the education minister's statement in the Panjab assembly, in the forty-eight government colleges in the state, where 73,241 students study, 1,873 lecturer posts are sanctioned, but 1,292 are lying vacant and are being managed by 251 part-time lecturers and 882 guest faculty lecturers. This, despite the fact that per UGC guidelines, 90 per cent of the teaching staff should be regular across all streams.'[40]

Government schools were even worse off. In 2016, the shortfall stood at 32,000 teachers. Things had reached a pass where panchayats and parent-teacher associations were hiring locals to work as volunteer teachers.[41]

This zero-sum outcome posed a fresh question.

———

That the Badals owned businesses was not a surprise. Overtly or covertly, many Indian politicians do. What was intriguing was that most of this business complex, spanning not firms but entire sectors, came up in just nine years. Despite operating in a democratic set-up, how did the Badals manage this economic capture without facing a backlash? Through tight control over the state, from the cabinet down to the villages.[42]

Of the eighteen ministers in the state cabinet, five belonged to the Badal clan: Chief Minister Parkash Singh Badal, Deputy Chief Minister Sukhbir Singh Badal, Parkash Badal's son-in-law Adesh Partap Singh Kairon, Sukhbir Badal's brother-in-law Bikram Singh Majithia, and another Badal relative Janmeja Singh Sekhon.[43] Between them, they controlled twenty-one government departments. Parkash Badal held seven portfolios, including Power, Personnel and General Administration. Sukhbir Badal held another seven, including Home, Housing, Taxation and Investment Promotions. Kairon handled IT as well as Food and Civil Supplies. Majithia handled four, including Non-conventional Energy, and Information and Public Relations. Sekhon had Irrigation.[44] The remaining thirteen ministers looked after a total of thirty-two departments—some of them embarrassingly minor, like Printing and Stationery.*

What enabled this control was their grip over the Akali Dal. Anyone in the party who opposed the Badals was expelled or poorly supported by the party during the elections and made to lose, said Sucha Singh Gill, director general of Chandigarh's Centre for Research into Rural and Industrial Development.

Through the Akali Dal, the Badals also controlled the apex religious bodies of the state—like the Akal Takht and the Shiromani Gurudwara Prabandhak Committee (SGPC). The Akal Takht is the highest seat of the Khalsa, the collective body of the Sikhs, and the seat of the jathedar, the highest spokesperson of the community. The SGPC, which oversees all gurudwaras, is the apex religious body in the state.

The autonomy of the Akal Takht started eroding when 'Jathedar Bhai Ranjit Singh was replaced by eight members of SGPC executive loyal to Parkash Singh Badal in their meeting in Amritsar Circuit House in December 1998', noted I.P Singh in the *Times of India*.[45] As for the SGPC, Sandhu wrote in the *Caravan*, the capture began in 1999. 'Just before the tercentenary celebrations of the Sikh religion, Prakash Singh Badal, then and current chief minister of Punjab, removed the

---

* For my first report, I emailed questions to Parkash Badal, Sukhbir Badal and Kairon. I texted the questions to Majithia. Five days later, when there was no response, I sent consolidated emails (with questions for all four leaders) and faxes to Jangveer Singh and Harcharan Bains, media advisors to Sukhbir Badal and Parkash Badal. Both Singh and Bains were alerted about these questionnaires— the former by phone and the latter by text when he did not answer his phone. Subsequently, I faxed these questions to the offices of Parkash Badal, Sukhbir Badal, Majithia and Kairon. There was no response. For my report on the Badals' control over Punjab, I emailed my questions to Parkash Badal and Sukhbir Badal. When there was no response, I sent consolidated emails to Singh and Bains. Both were alerted—the former by phone, and the latter by text when he did not answer his phone. Subsequently, I also faxed these questions to the office of Majithia, who was in charge of the Department for Information and Public Relations. There was no response.

SGPC's longest tenured chief Gurcharan Singh Tohra from his post.' In the years that followed, Sandhu wrote, the Badals continued to control the body. 'It is an open secret that the SGPC's leaders are chosen by infamous "parchis" (chits) that arrive, sealed in envelopes, from Badal's desk.'[46]

Exploiting its control over the SGPC, the Akali Dal pushed its political requirements. When the religious leader Gurmeet Ram Rahim angered the Sikh community by dressing up as Guru Gobind Singh, the tenth Guru of Sikhism,[47] the party—which was wooing him, a senior member of the SGPC told me—got the Akal Takht to take back the fatwa it had announced against him, and the SGPC asked the Sikh community to support the decision.[48]

There was also its control over the news media. As *Firstpost* reported, the biggest cable distributor in Punjab, Fastway Transmissions, 'arbitrarily stopped beaming some channels which telecast stories against the Akali Dal, including channels like Punjab Today [and] Day and Night.'[49] What it did air, however, was PTC, owned by Sukhbir Badal's G-Net.

The Badals' control over the state extended even beyond the cabinet, the Akali Dal, the state's apex religious bodies and airwaves. They also marginalised political rivals on the ground. The party crowned its candidates who had lost in assembly polls as halka in-charges of their constituency, and its state government directed police and local bureaucracy to obey them. 'If the (Congress) MLA does good work, why would the people vote for us?' an Akali Dal cabinet minister asked me. 'That is why we have the halka in-charge—to make sure the Congress doesn't grow, and to protect our base in the state.'

Wherever the Congress won, the former transport minister Master Mohan Lal told me, 'not one paisa worth of work gets done as per the instructions of the local MLA.' Even in police matters, nothing got done without a nod from the halka in-charge, who, however, sanctioned action only if politically favourable. With this, the Akali Dal ruled every constituency, whether it had won or not.

Topping it all off was intimidation. As Nicolas Martin wrote in the *Economic and Political Weekly*, 'Ruling SAD politicians use harassment and intimidation when they seek to secure their party's stranglehold over particular panchayats, or when they are determined to give power to a particular village leader.'[50]

Violence need not always be physical. The government deployed the Unlawful Activities (Prevention) Act (UAPA) against all opposition, whether it was those demanding an independent Khalistan or fighting for farmers, said Ludhiana-based lawyer Jaspal Singh Manjhpur.[51] The lawyer too had been charged under UAPA, and it took five years for him to get acquitted. 'There is an unwritten instruction from the state that bail will not be given,' he said. 'One result is the number of agitations has come down. This is a process of suppressing people. The atmosphere is one of dread.'

This fear extended all the way to the ministers. According to the Akali Dal cabinet minister, 'Phones of all MLAs are tapped. There is surveillance.' The bureaucracy was equally stricken. 'At one time, the cost of not cooperating with politicians was inconvenient postings,' said the former secretary Lakhanpal. 'But now, people fear bodily harm, or, at the least, a vigilance case. The threat is enough. Hang one, and the message to the rest is very clear.'

————

A wider precarity accompanied this political capture. Most households lived close to the margins. One afternoon, after visiting the Nurmahal dera*, I met Gandharva Sen, a veteran communist leader in the town,

---

* In 2014, the religious leader of Nurmahal's Divya Jyoti Sansthan, Baba Ashutosh, passed away. Within hours of him being declared clinically dead, the dera backtracked and claimed instead that he was in samadhi, or deep meditation, and would be 'normal' very soon. Refusing to cremate him, the dera placed his body in a freezer at -22°C. Every six months, as the *Hindustan Times* reported in 2019, 'a panel of three doctors, formed on the orders of the Punjab and Haryana high court, inspects the body to check for decomposition'. See: Ravinder Vasudeva and Parampreet Singh Narula, '5 Years On, "Clinically Dead":

and his daughter Surinder, who was in her sixties. Kuchapakka Colony, where they lived, used to be an artisanal colony that had fallen on bad times. In the 1970s and 1980s, people from here went to Iraq and elsewhere seeking work in civil construction.[52] When they came back, said Surinder, they looked gaunt and were incapable of working more.

By 2015, most families here were either in trades like driving horse carts for weddings, or worked as labour in Ludhiana. Four out of five families were poor. Six years ago, when Surinder got haemoglobin levels of the people here tested, she found that 75 per cent of the women were anaemic. Earlier, Gill had explained the larger phenomenon: 'In Punjab, people who earn Rs 10,000 but have their own home live at subsistence levels. Those making Rs 10,000 but living in a rented house live at semi-starvation levels.' State failure pushed people deeper into poverty. Given the under-delivery of health services, households in Punjab had the highest out-of-pocket expenditure on healthcare in the country of Rs 28,539, against the national average of Rs 18,628, according to the National Sample Survey Office (NSSO)'s 2015 numbers.[53]

Political capture added its own costs. 'We cannot go to the police,' said Kishan Chand, a horse cart driver. 'I can complain, but the police might get tapped by the other side, and they might register a case against me instead.' People were discouraged, agreed the human rights lawyer R.S. Bains. 'If you get into trouble with a powerful person, your life is destroyed.'

Unlike Odisha, I saw more anger among the people in Punjab. This anger, however, lacked direction. Professor Sidhu said that before militancy, Punjab had not only the old Nehruvian idealism but also an ethos from progressive Left movements. Much of this was crushed in the years of militancy, leaving a void.

Nurmahal Dera Head Ashutosh Maharaj's Body "Lives" in Freezer', *Hindustan Times* (28 January 2019), hindustantimes.com/india-news/5-years-on-clinically-dead-nurmahal-dera-head-ashutosh-maharaj-s-body-lives-in-freezer/story-kDLBrRNyYNnUAm5HhGVIVI.html.

With that, the state's capacity to understand change had eroded. A gap that the poet Paash used to fill so well, Sidhu said. 'He could impregnate the vernacular with these ideas and broaden the horizons of society's imagination.' Such voices were missing now. 'You have the rabid sectarian Sikh identity. NRIs are the driving force here. There are also those who talk about the [Arcadian] past. The Left in the state is very predictable. And then, there is the youth. For a short while, they coalesced behind the Aam Aadmi Party. For a while, they got this courage, that they could resist, that the Badals could be broken. But this was mismanaged too.'

In all, he said, the state and its people were still seeking a fresh political reimagination, one that would address the precarity that surrounded them. 'They are taking to the streets, clear about some of the immediate targets but unable to weave a full tapestry.'

How do societies make sense of where they are, course-correct and coalesce around a new common purpose?

Most responses I saw were individual answers to systemic crises. Young cab drivers spoke of their plans to illegally enter other countries. IELTS (International English Language Testing System) centres were everywhere. The state, judging by its pop culture, was awash in nostalgia about a more masculine past. Punjabi pop videos told tales of imperilled romance, in which the hero brandished a gun, launched into fights and set things right. 'The songs have guns, big houses, open jeeps, Royal Enfields,' said the novelist Desraj Kali. 'Even as people struggle, they draw arrogance from their caste.'

There was also rage. Fuelled by the party's excesses over the last nine years and snowballing faster and faster after the desecration of the Guru Granth Sahib, people were out in the streets.*

But the most striking of these responses was religious.

---

* In the next assembly elections, the Akali Dal was voted out.

A middle-aged Sikh man in jeans, mustard-yellow turban and a beige sweater; a woman in a red jacket that extended till her knees, worn over a purple salwar. Both paused at the entrance, bowed their heads and prayed. To their right, another Sikh man, clad in brown trousers, black turban and a brightly striped sweater, sank to his knees and prayed. As they finished and stepped on to the courtyard, three more women halted at the entrance. They too bowed their heads to pray.

I followed the devotees into the white-tiled, trapezium-shaped courtyard that led into the gurudwara of Baba Deep Singh near Amritsar's Chatiwind Gate. After washing my feet and covering my head, I stepped through the double-storeyed, white-coloured deori that led to the shrine.

According to legend, Baba Deep Singh was decapitated while battling the forces of Ahmad Shah Abdali, who had ordered the holiest of Sikh shrines, Harmandir Sahib, also known as the Golden Temple, to be blown up and the sacred tank desecrated. A painting in the Golden Temple depicts the fabled aftermath: Deep Singh, holding his severed head with his left hand and swinging a massive sword with his right, continued to fight, dying only after reaching Harmandir Sahib.

The gurudwara was small and intricate. Pristine white, single-storeyed, rectangular in shape, its roof studded with six cupolas. In their middle stood a small double-storeyed tower topped with a dome. Being one of the more important gurudwaras in the pantheon, the dome was golden. A newly constructed six-storeyed guesthouse loomed nearby.

Since 2000, this shrine, also known as Gurudwara Shaheed Ganj, had seen a spike in the number of visiting devotees. This surge was part of a larger religious change that the novelist Kali saw in the state. A growing number of people in this predominantly Sikh state, he said, were now visiting Hindu temples. Not those of principal deities like Vishnu, Shiv and Ram, but of Shani, the elder brother of the god of death Yama, notorious for his malefic influence. More people than before were placing chadars, made of cotton or fine cloth, at the mazaars of pirs, the graves of Sufi saints. There was a 'thousand-fold' increase, said Kali, in the number of tantrik ads in the local media. Punjab was seeing a mushrooming of self-declared godmen. Even orthodox Sikhs like the Amritdhaaris were visiting non-traditional deras, religious centres with living gurus, although Sikhism expressly forbids worship of individuals.[54]

To understand why something as fundamental to a society as religious practice was seeing such large shifts in a short period of time, I took a closer look at the deras. Oppressed classes, as Mark Juergensmeyer shows using the instance of Punjab's Ad Dharm movement, in *Religious Rebels in the Punjab*, leave existing religions to create new faiths that would put them on a more equitable footing with the larger society.[55] What was happening now was different. It was more tactical.

Village life in Punjab had become faction-ridden and hard, said Jagrup Singh Sekhon, a professor of political science at Amritsar's Guru Nanak Dev University. At the same time, formal institutions for welfare, like administration and healthcare, and grievance redressal, like the police and judiciary, had weakened. 'In such a construct, who can save people from the police and patwari? That is what takes people to the sants.' They form a protective buffer between the powerful and the individual, since local leaders listened to the sants. Laxmi Kanta Chawla, a former health minister and BJP member, said that the nature of political leaders in the state was changing as well. 'These [leaders] are people who haven't done anything to build a following of their own.' Consequently, they cultivated dera leaders in the hope that a leader's followers would be told to vote for them.

Take Dera Sacha Sauda's Gurmeet Ram Rahim. By 2014, as Mulinja Narayanan, a Central Bureau of Investigation (CBI) sleuth who investigated the self-proclaimed godman told reporter Anurag Tripathi, the Baba of Bling 'was in a position to swing the fate of political parties with his influence on twenty-eight seats ... in Punjab, Haryana and Rajasthan.'[56] Once locals saw leaders visiting the dera, they recognised it as a power centre and began going there as well.

This influence of spiritual leaders over politicians was a big reason for the spore-like multiplication of sants and deras. 'Someone might be working in a dera, but cannot become its leader or make a name of his own,' a businessperson in the town of Moga said. 'So, he either splits the dera, or starts one of his own. The new leader usually gets someone, perhaps a follower of the original dera, to back him financially. They do a few functions to which local leaders are invited, and thus the forging of bonds begins.' In a nearby village called Barauli, three or four new deras had come up, he said. 'People are going there because they feel the work will get done.'

All this was inevitable, said Bains. 'When formal institutions fail, informal ones come up. Even in a dictatorship, informal channels will work. There is always networking in society.' In a sense, an old pattern was perpetuating itself. As Sekhon said, 'Every system has patronised the deras, be it the centre, the militants or the state.' Larger deras marketed themselves aggressively. They ran schools and health camps, offered subsidised food in canteens—not like the langars of gurudwaras, but colas and chowmein—drawing people in with novelty.

Apart from the nexus between deras and politicians, economic insecurity was also pushing people towards the supernatural, be it the deras, mazaars, Shani or self-attested godmen, according to Kali. 'I am ailing. I am broken. The book [the Guru Granth Sahib] doesn't give me solace. I want a remedy for the specific things ailing me. I want a human to hear me and respond to me. I want someone to put their hand on my head and tell me everything will be fine. Human touch!'

I had heard a similar explanation in Odisha. 'Physical poverty and distress has a psychological and social effect on people,' a medical professional there had said. 'This belief in babas springs from there, be it Radhe Maa or Sarathi Baba. People live in the hope that the guru will change the condition of their lives—an illness they cannot cure on their own, lack of money, whatever.' Baba Deep Singh's gurudwara was another case in point. People went there because, in Kali's words, 'there is a force there. The force of a martyr.'

Ronki Ram, a dean at Panjab University who has studied the Ravidasia movement to conceptualise the rise of religions, was also seeing religiosity rise across the state. 'People are living on the edge.

When things go wrong, some turn to Sikhism, others to the deras. Some read the Guru Granth Sahib, others pin their faith on books written by Valmiki. Between them, religion is growing.'

All this, he said, was playing out in the absence of development. 'In their understanding of causes, people are guided more by religion than rationality. That is because the central logic running through the people is religion. Development is to be received through religion, not through technical means.' A religious society, Ram implied, would try to solve even technical problems through religion.

In the absence of people like Paash, who broadened people's understanding of the processes shaping their lives, societies, like Punjab's cotton farmers, fall back on what they know.

'Where will this response take Punjab?' I asked Ram.

'A rise in religiosity can give rise to new confrontations. People get angry not because their survival is in danger but because they think they are discriminated against due to their religion. If they save their religion, they think, they will save themselves.'

A likely outcome of underdevelopment, listening to him, seemed to be a rise in sectarian strife.

Close to a year had passed since *Ear to the Ground* had started. With only three states under my belt, I was running tremendously late. I had also found a question much larger than the one I had started out with. Democracy was not working well in any of these states. Each was failing to deliver health, education and justice. This is a key feature of Indian democracy. As Amartya Sen and Jean Drèze write in *An Uncertain Glory*:

> When it comes to catastrophic calamities—with the problems in the limelight for all to see—democracy tends to generate a basic accountability that has been important in the prevention of disasters like famines in India. ... That affirmative recognition leads to a more demanding enquiry: to what extent has the

reach of accountability been extended to cover other kinds of
problems of deprivation and disparity, which may not be as
drastic as famines, but which are still extremely important in
the lives of ordinary Indians? At an immediate level the answer
seems to be clear and deeply disappointing. The kind of failures
we have been discussing ... in the delivery of school education,
or in providing elementary health care to all, or in running a
responsible and efficacious system of public services, have not
received ready solutions through the practice of democracy.[57]

In all three states, administrative incapacity and low budgetary
support had been trotted out as explanations. These, however, were
superficial answers. If its politicians had not annexed road building,
Mizoram's state revenues would have been higher. If Odisha had
retained more of the revenue from the iron ore boom, it could have
spent more on teachers. Had Punjab mopped up revenues from liquor
and stone crushing, it could have had more than one cardiologist for the
entire state. Each of these were choices made, not by the bureaucracy,
but the political leadership. In all three states, political parties, voted to
power to find solutions to the problems facing these states, had made
choices that helped them grow at the cost of their people.

Neither Odisha nor Punjab tolerated dissent. Both states also
showed a concentration of political power. Odisha has been ruled by
Naveen Patnaik for twenty years as this book goes to press in 2020. The
Badals controlled Punjab. In all three states, democratic institutions
were weakening. In Mizoram, neither the state anti-corruption bureau
nor courts heeded the charges against Lalthanzara. Odisha saw little
systemic challenge to the under-collection of mining revenues and the
speculation that followed. In Punjab, the insidious innovation of the
halka in-charge went unchallenged. In all three states, foregone revenue
co-existed with non-productive populism. A small elite close to the
political power gained far more than others.

From Tamil Nadu onwards, I would try to understand the mechanics
underpinning these changes.

4

The State That Embraced
Messianic Populism

Have you heard of Divya and Ilavarasan?

She was a twenty-year-old nursing student. He was three years older, a first-year college student learning about computers. Both lived in Tamil Nadu's Dharmapuri district. She in a village called Naickenkottai. He in a nearby dalit settlement called Natham Colony. In 2011, they fell in love. They had met, said one news report, during bus rides to college.[1] Their romance deepened, added another, over furtive meetings at juice shops.[2] It would have been easy to ascertain these elementary facts of their fledgling relationship when I visited in 2016 if not for one thing. E. Ilavarasan was no more. N. Divya was back at Naickenkottai and went to college but did not meet many people.[3]

Theirs was a love story plundered by opportunists. He was a dalit. She was a vanniyar. In India's pernicious caste complex of graded hierarchy, dalits are treated as inferior to vanniyars, a dominant caste in Tamil Nadu. Wanting to be together but fearing opposition from Divya's community, the couple ran away to the neighbouring Andhra Pradesh and got married in 2012. Upon their return, while their families acquiesced to the union, members of the vanniyar community did not. An ultimatum was issued to Natham Colony, telling its people to return Divya. She refused to go back.

The same day, her father hanged himself. Within an hour, about 2,000 vanniyars descended on Natham Colony and two other dalit colonies nearby, Anna Nagar and Konampatti, ransacking and setting ablaze over 300 houses. No lives were lost, but household assets like motorcycles, televisions and refrigerators were incinerated. As were education certificates.

The couple and Ilavarasan's family went on the run. Divya's mother filed a court petition alleging her daughter was in illegal custody. Ilavarasan's college told him he could not study there any longer.[4] A job he was hoping for in the state police was stayed as well. On being told her mother was unwell, Divya went home and never returned. In the next court hearing, lawyers and functionaries of the Pattali Makkal Katchi (PMK), a party that claims to represent vanniyars, accompanied her and her mother to the court. Unable to speak to her, Ilavarasan filed a court petition saying his wife was not free.

Ilavarasan spent the next night, 3 July 2013, with friends, planning to leave the next day for Chittoor in Andhra Pradesh to look for a job. The following morning, he left after getting a call from someone unknown. Later that day, his body was found on the rail tracks. Post-mortem reports were contradictory. The police closed the case as death by suicide. His parents and lawyers and at least one doctor who performed the autopsy disagreed, alleging foul play.[5]

If religiosity was rising in Punjab, caste identities were intensifying in Tamil Nadu. Along the way, as the story of Divya and Ilavarasan showed, the nature of caste violence was also changing in the state.[6]

Till three decades ago, attacks on dalits were connected to disputes over land, farm work and access to local resources. These could be brutal. In 1968, forty-four dalits were burnt alive in a village called Kilvenmani in Nagapattinam district after they asked for higher wages for farm work. On the other hand, so-called honour killings—families killing their own for crossing caste lines in pursuit of love—were rare. Inter-caste marriages were being accepted. Even Natham Colony had inter-caste couples—dalit men married to vanniyar women—living in the settlement when the Divya-Ilavarasan relationship became political fodder.[7]

By 2016, all this was upended. A fact-finding team that visited Natham Colony after the attack only found arson. 'Nowhere had we heard of anybody being hit by the mob. It had clearly targeted property of Dalits, particularly the symbols of their prosperity like motorbike, cycles, refrigerator, almirahs, and furniture.'[8] Honour killings, however, were spiking. 'They have been especially on the rise since 2006,' said Kathir Vincent Raj, founder of a Madurai-based dalit rights NGO called Evidence.

There were other signs of intensifying caste identities. Since 2000, parties vying to represent single castes had mushroomed in Tamil Nadu.[9] Around 2005, steel cages began coming up around statues of leaders—be it Dr Bhimrao Ambedkar or the first dravidian chief minister of Tamil Nadu, C.N. Annadurai—after repeated incidents of desecration by other caste groups. In some places, followers of the leaders erected these cages. Elsewhere, local police, wanting to minimise riotous assembly, got the iron-work done.[10]

In such developments, the causality is usually traced to dalit assertion and reactive pushbacks by dominant castes like thevars, vanniyars and gounders. This is an incomplete explanation. Tamil Nadu's rich anti-caste social reform legacy, its history of industrialisation and migration, and the political assertion of dalits had gradually yielded varying degrees of dalit autonomy since Independence. In contrast, the changes listed above—defacing of statues, rise of caste-based parties, spike in honour killings, vandalism of assets—were all relatively recent, starting around the year 2000.

———

Both the dominant parties in Tamil Nadu, the Dravida Munnetra Kazhagam (DMK) and All India Anna Dravida Munnetra Kazhagam (AIADMK), are offshoots of the Self-Respect Movement started by E.V. Ramasamy, popularly known as Periyar. As the historian V. Geetha writes:

> In the 1930s and 1940s, Periyar pointed to the three types of prejudices that one had to oppose, to build an equal, self-respecting and just society: of caste, religion and the nation.

In some instances, Periyar added a fourth and fifth prejudice: to do with language; and with the set of ideas which justified the subordination of women, for instance, the doctrine of compulsory chastity, which kept women bound to unhappy marriages, and prevented them from exercising their emotional and sexual rights.[11]

Like M.K. Gandhi, who wanted the Congress to stay out of politics, Periyar too wanted the Self-Respect Movement to avoid electoral politics and focus on social reform, which resulted in his follower Annadurai breaking away to create the DMK. The party continued to draw its ideology from the Self-Respect Movement and famously spread its message through cinema. Movies like *Parasakthi*, with Sivaji Ganesan in the lead, attacked obscurantism and Hindu customs; sought to create an association between the protagonist and the party; and espoused pro-poor, anti-landlord, anti-Aryan and pro-Tamil values.

In 1969, when Annadurai passed away, M. Karunanidhi stepped in. The party split in 1972 due to the personal rivalry between him and M.G. Ramachandran (M.G.R), a popular film star and politician, and AIADMK was born. In 1987, after the death of M.G.R, the redoubtable J. Jayalalithaa, also a film actor, took charge of the AIADMK. She ran the party with an iron hand till she passed away in December 2016. As for Karunanidhi, he headed the DMK till his death in August 2018. Between them, these two parties have run the state for fifty unbroken years.

In other words, caste identities had intensified in a state led by political parties whose ideology sought to obliterate caste.

———

The three acres around Sambath's house lay fallow. Till 2008, the farmer, a man in his fifties, used to sow right up to the house. But when I met him in 2016 in Mahashivanendal village near the town of Shivagangai, his fields were all barren brown earth with their fringes overtaken by *Prosopis juliflora*, an invasive species rapidly spreading across India.

He was not the only one with untilled fields that rabi season. On the road from Shivagangai to Mahashivanendal, more farms lay fallow than under cultivation. As in Punjab, the rains had become unpredictable. Lying to the south of the Cauvery delta, these villages used to get soaked by both the southwest (June to September) and the northeast (October to December) monsoons. The first to vanish around 1995 was the southwest monsoon. Now, the northeast, which supplied Tamil Nadu with 70 per cent of its rainfall, had changed too. It used to, said Sambath, rain every day between September and November. 'In the last seven years, it has rained every two days. In the last two years, things are especially bad. There has been no rain.'

Annasamy Narayanamoorthy, the head of the Department of Economics and Rural Development at Alagappa University in nearby Karaikkudi, also alluded to changes in the northeast monsoon. 'It used to rain for seventy-five to eighty days. Now, it rains for no more than forty days.' He was also seeing another change. 'Unless there's a cyclone over the Bay of Bengal, we don't get rains here.' The seas off Tamil Nadu have been warming at a rising pace. Between 1961 and 1976, the average annual sea surface temperature changed from 27.7°C to 28°C. But the same 0.3°C rise happened in less than ten years between 1997 and 2005, when the temperature rose from to 28.7°C to 29°C. This increase, I found, was not only affecting fish behaviour* but also changing rainfall patterns and triggering more cyclones.

---

* Threadfin breams were spawning later in the year. Oil sardines were moving north away from the tropics, which were growing warmer, and were now found in increasing numbers at 6° latitude further north than before, moving from 14°N to 20°N, as researcher Nagraj Adve observed. According to him, this implied that oil sardines had extended their range northward by over 650 kilometres in less than thirty years, or over 20 kilometres a year. Other taxa were moving into deeper waters too. Caught mostly at or near the surface earlier, mackerel were now being caught at depths of 50 to 100 metres. See: Nagraj Adve, 'Moving Home', *Economic and Political Weekly* (27 September 2014), epw.in/journal/2014/39/insight/moving-home.html.

In this way, rising sea surface temperatures combined with industrial pollution and overfishing to create a livelihood crisis for the fishing communities. As previously caught fish became rarer, fisherpeople were netting what they

Till the 2000s, Sambath used to grow two crops a year—either groundnuts or pulses during the southwest monsoon and paddy during the northeast. By 2016, farmers like him were not sowing in the first season and saw yields dropping from the second. 'At one time, I would get eighty koni [one koni is sixty-six kilos] per acre. Now, I get twenty-five.'[12]

Two other factors were adding to his woes. Paddy prices were low. 'One kilo of raw rice should fetch Rs 16. But the government doesn't buy, and so private traders buy at Rs 12.' At the same time, inputs like urea and labour had gotten costlier. Selling eighty konis per acre at Rs 16 a kilo, he used to make Rs 2.5 lakh from paddy alone. What he now made was Rs 60,000, and retained just half of that after accounting for costs.

The heat accumulated during the day was yet to dissipate. We stood chatting outside his 'Amma House', a modest-sized pucca building with a small veranda, built by the state government. On the front wall, the state had plastered what looked like a tile with the then chief minister Jayalalithaa's image. She looked on as we chatted.

Sambath was a synecdoche. According to the NSSO's data for Tamil Nadu, while farmers' gross incomes climbed from Rs 24,864 in 2002–2003 to Rs 83,760 in 2012–2013, their profitability fell for the same period.[13] 'In the 1970s, you could invest Rs 2,000 and get back Rs 3,000,' Narayanamoorthy said. 'Now, you invest Rs 40,000 and you might get back Rs 43,000.' This is why, he told me, farmers were giving up on agriculture.

---

earlier discarded as by-catch. With smaller catches of mostly low-value fish, they spent more per fishing trip. Their incomes were low and erratic, pushing them to overfish. Nets were so fine even fishlings could not get out, pushing both fish species and their own livelihoods towards extinction. When the gap between income and expenditure got too wide, fisherpeople borrowed, turning not to formal institutions but to informal credit like thandal and kanduvatti that cost as much as 5 per cent–6 per cent a month. See: M. Rajshekhar, 'Why Tamil Nadu's Fisherfolk Can No Longer Find Fish', *Scroll.in* (8 July 2017), scroll.in/article/808960/why-tamil-nadus-fisherfolk-can-no-longer-find-fish.

With that came the loss of another income—livestock. Sambath used to have over fifty goats. He had sold them all in the last two years. Others in Mahashivanendal had sold off their livestock too. Narayanamoorthy explained this: 'When agriculture fails, livestock fails too. Without crop residue, you cannot keep buffaloes. Income dwindles—none from agriculture, none from livestock. All you're left with is labour.' Indeed, when I visited, this village of dominant-caste yadava and thevar families lived off MGNREGA and industrial wage-work in towns like Coimbatore and Tirupur. Of the fifty families in the village, as many as forty had members working outside. Families were also borrowing more, mostly from informal sources, at rates as high as 6 per cent–7 per cent a month. That was the other big change in rural Tamil Nadu. Its most profitable occupation now was moneylending.*

---

* Even as the need for financial support rose, the Self Help Group (SHG) programme—in which NGOs band women into groups, get them bank loans and monitor repayment—was stopped in the state after Jayalalithaa came back as chief minister in 2011. In the run-up to the elections, on the demand of the NGOs to write off women's loans, M.K. Stalin of the previous DMK government had acquiesced. Once she came to power, recognising the muscle power of these NGOs, Jayalalithaa nationalised the SHG programme and turfed out the NGOs. In the earlier model, the organisations had ensured repayment. Now, with the state government unwilling to provide similar comfort, bank loans to SHGs shrank.

To fill this void, not only did formal lenders, like microfinance institutions (MFIs), scale up, but also locally affluent people—those with children working abroad, the landed elite and those with government jobs—became informal lenders. Attracted by the high returns, new communities, like the dominant caste of nadars in southern Tamil Nadu, entered moneylending. Yet others borrowed from banks and lent further. By 2016, households in the state were both borrowing and lending. A person might borrow at 3 per cent and lend to another at 4 per cent.

It is hard to say how much debt households accrued. NSSO data suggests that, around 2013, the gross annual income of rural families was Rs 83,760. Their outstanding debt was Rs 115,420. The amount left for repaying loans after meeting expenses was a fraction of that. To pay off their debt, some migrated seeking work. In Thagatti panchayat of Krishnagiri, one of the poorer districts of Tamil Nadu, families put up ration cards as collateral. Others became bonded labour.

As for Sambath, he managed with the money his son sent from Dubai and the Rs 900 he got each month as pension from a local factory he used to worked at. It was nowhere near enough. He looked at his 100cc motorcycle and laughed at how little he used it now. 'When I last went to the town, I got the motorcycle filled with petrol for Rs 50. I have not used it since,' he said.

———

But how is any of this connected to Divya and Ilavarasan?

Since 1991, Tamil Nadu, like the rest of India, has seen extraordinary change. Industrial jobs, driven by liberalisation, offered a new way out of villages. As the state urbanised, real estate construction boomed. So did farmland prices, putting more money into rural areas than any government programme.[14] Between rising incomes and a boom in the entertainment industry, consumerism and aspirations increased. To capitalise on these changes, each caste group responded differently.

Erstwhile village elite moved to cities. Vanniyars, buying out the land of those leaving, sought to replace them in central Tamil Nadu. Gounders, another dominant caste in regions around Coimbatore, forayed into manufacturing. Arundhatiyars, a dalit sub-caste in northern and western parts of the state, turned to industrial work. Parayars, another dalit sub-caste spread across both Tamil Nadu and Kerala, moved out of villages. 'They used education and urban employment as [their] weapons,' said S. Anandhi, a professor at Madras Institute of Development Studies.

Another response, however, was to spend more, for consumption suggests credit-worthiness and makes it possible to borrow more. Moneylending slowly became the most profitable activity in the state.

Signs of over-borrowing were visible. Lenders hedged by giving small loans. Borrowers defaulted on loans from banks, which could not harass clients the way the informal economy lenders or MFIs could. Sambath, for instance, had not made his house loan repayments for the last eighteen months. See: M. Rajshekhar, 'A Tsunami of Debt Is Building Up in Tamil Nadu—and No One Knows Where It Is Headed', *Scroll.in* (2 August 2017), scroll.in/article/810138/a-tsunami-of-debt-is-building-up-in-tamil-nadu-and-no-one-knows-where-it-is-headed.

These gambits yielded unequal results. The farm crisis thwarted the vanniyars' hopes of upward mobility. Gounders struggled as the state's manufacturing clusters slipped into trouble. The apparel-making town of Tirupur, for instance, was forced to import cotton at higher prices from states like Gujarat and Maharashtra because local farmers, given a worsening shortage of farm labour, switched from the labour-intensive cotton to plantation crops. In Coimbatore, the farm crisis caused the groundwater pump manufacturing industry to slow down. Other small and medium units were hit by power shortages. In contrast, dalits, who fled villages for education, construction or industrial wage-work, saw their conditions improve. Even in villages, they demanded higher wages or stopped working in the fields entirely.

In Natham Colony and Naickenkottai, when I asked dalits and vanniyars about their livelihoods, the answers were strikingly similar. 'Most people don't work in the village,' said Sasikala, who had moved to the dalit settlement after her marriage. 'They work in Coimbatore or Bangalore, mostly in construction.' The fact-finding team that visited the area after the riots also reported that most men worked in construction or scrap dealing. The women worked in the village. A family with two working members, estimated Sasikala, would earn about Rs 7,000 every month.

Later that evening, when we met outside a school on the main road, panchayat president Chinnaswamy, from the vanniyar community, said that agriculture was loss-making and that people in his village too worked as labour in Bangalore and Coimbatore. 'We get Rs 300 a day and work six days a week.' A monthly income of about Rs 8,100.

This newfound equivalence between dalits and dominant castes resulted in heightening caste identities. 'If we don't have the material resources to assert our power, what do we fall back on? The cultural idea of a caste,' said Anandhi. According to her, with little in terms of income difference, dominant castes in the state were holding on to cultural differences. This is what the novelist Desraj Kali had said in Punjab, that people drew arrogance from their caste.

Hardwired into this response was a sense of injury. Chinnaswamy and his friends insisted that dalits were doing better than them. A young man with him said, 'Most of them are working with the government, in the electricity board, as police and clerks. We aren't getting those jobs. We have to work in Bangalore or Coimbatore as contract labour.' But this was not true—most dalits in Natham Colony too worked as labour in these cities.

Nonetheless, this misguided sense of having fallen behind fuelled demands for more reservations in government jobs and colleges. As Chinnaswamy said that evening, 'Us vanniyars are MBCs. We get 20 per cent reservation. But there are 108 MBCs in all and we have to share with them. In contrast, pallars and parayars [who fall under scheduled castes/scheduled tribes, or SC/ST, category] get 16 per cent reservations, but they are just two communities.'

Neither were there enough government jobs nor did a college degree guarantee employment. Yet, Chinnaswamy and his friends did not ask for higher farm prices, cheaper credit or predictable power supply, measures that might have an actual and positive impact on farming and their lives. Did these communities see no future in agriculture or were they tailoring their demands to what they thought the state could provide? If the latter, were these shrunken expectations engendered by the dravidian parties? The complexity of the livelihood crisis notwithstanding, their responses were limited to political gestures, like greater reservations.[15]

Even as the community struggled, a political battle to represent it intensified. Till 2016, the two dravidian parties, while publicly opposed to caste, had almost always chosen poll candidates from the dominant community in each constituency. Following gounders and thevars, who already had single-caste parties, in 2012, the PMK, which was founded in 1989, started refocusing on the vanniyars.

Instead of focusing on the precarity of the community, the party too focused on dalits as the common enemy and used controversies like inter-caste love affairs to position itself as defenders of the community.

This template was first articulated by S. Ramadoss, the party's founder, in 2012.[16] He made an infamous speech accusing dalit youngsters of 'wearing jeans, T-shirts and fancy sunglasses' to lure girls from other castes with their 'bogus professions of love'.[17] This fuelled hysteria. Lynchings accelerated. Parents, as Vincent Raj found in a college in the district of Dindigul, began getting their girls married before sending them to college. Of the 1,200 girls in the first year, 230 were married. 'This was to ensure the girl wouldn't fall in love,' he said.

As the number of caste-based parties rose, a competitive whipping up of passions followed. Parties became more and more hard line. Some of them, said P.V. Srividya, a reporter with the *Hindu* in Krishnagiri district in the state, maintained cadres that picked up inter-caste newlyweds and forced them to break up. Even at the community level, one leader's request for forgiveness got drowned out by another's demand for ostracism and a third's insistence on yet more punitive treatment.

Put it all together and the reason for why Divya and Ilavarasan's romance was crushed becomes clear. The recent economic equivalence; the dominant castes falling back on their identity to feel superior; inter-caste marriages, once seen as family affairs, becoming supra-local events where the honour of the community was at stake; local leaders, vying to upstage rivals, ratcheting up self-serving rhetoric—all these waves had crashed against these two youngsters just starting their lives.

It was a grim lesson in the persistence of caste. As Father Jeyapathy, the principal of Loyola College in Chennai, told me, 'Unless you address old inequities, caste lies low but comes back.' This echoes human rights activist K. Balagopal's words: 'Caste will undoubtedly be the last of the iniquitous institutions to die out in this country. It will outlast everything else.'[18]

If annihilation of caste was one objective of the Self-Respect Movement, welfarism was another. In healthcare and education, under the dravidian parties, Tamil Nadu outperformed almost all states in India—showing persuasively that the Indian State, if it wants, can

indeed deliver world-class results. Hearing of decay in both these
sectors, I turned there next.

———

It was not going to be an easy delivery. Around March 2014, when
nineteen-year-old Soumya Ramakrishnan became pregnant, she
weighed just thirty-six kilos. The hamlet she lived in, Yerumuttinapalli
in Krishnagiri district's Anchetty panchayat, was close to Tamil
Nadu's border with Karnataka. Hilly and forested, with a large adivasi
population now separated from the forests that once supported them,
this continued to be one of the poorest parts of the state. The primary
source of food for Soumya's family was the local ration shop, from
which they got thirty-five kilos of rice, a litre of cooking oil and a kilo of
pulses. Vegetables and milk being too expensive, most days, her family
supplemented their diet with ragi mudde, dumplings made of coarse
cereal.

It was a meagre diet for a woman who needed to feed not only
herself but also the embryo inside her. Soumya stayed anaemic
through the pregnancy, her haemoglobin count hovering around 9.5,
against the required 12.5. Her baby, weighed at 1.7 kilos at the primary
health centre (PHC) at Anchetty where Soumya delivered—the local
health sub-centre closer home was not functioning—was 0.8 kilos
underweight. 'The baby almost never cried. Just twice since birth,' said
a middle-aged woman living in the same mud-walled neighbourhood
as Soumya. 'It would not suckle. It needed to be spoon-fed.'

The baby's health deteriorated over the next thirty days. A small-
boned woman, with dark eyes and narrow, slumping shoulders, clad
in a purple, black and yellow nightgown, Soumya's answers, when they
came, were stumbling and hesitant. She was too waif-like to even be
twenty. The baby was taken back to the PHC, was referred from there
to the district hospital in Hosur, and then referred again to the medical
college in the neighbouring district of Dharmapuri. After four days
there, the newborn died.

I met Soumya while trying to understand a perplexing pattern in Tamil Nadu's health numbers. On some fronts, there was steady improvement. Nearly all babies born in the state were delivered in clinics. Institutional deliveries climbed from 87 per cent in 2002–2004 to 98.9 per cent in 2012–2013. On a set of other fronts like infant mortality rate (IMR) and maternal mortality rate (MMR), the state's numbers were plateauing. On a third set of health indicators, the state's numbers had worsened: the number of pregnant women who got antenatal care fell from 98.8 per cent in 2002 to 90.7 per cent in 2013. The number of children who got full vaccination fell from 81.8 per cent in 2007–2008 to 69.7 per cent in 2015–2016.[*] How could the same department deliver three starkly different outcomes simultaneously?[19]

In development circles, IMR and MMR are used as proxies for a population's well-being. In Tamil Nadu, as in most of India, MMR had fallen mainly due to institutional deliveries. As for IMR, it too had fallen because of this, alongside improvements in care for diarrhoea and respiratory infections. In public health circles, this focus on deliveries in well-equipped clinics is seen as a bureaucratic shortcut. 'States should work on overall development and see if the results show up as an improvement in MMR and IMR,' said healthcare researcher Rakhal Gaitonde.

The state, however, was focusing on reducing IMR and MMR numbers to suggest wider improvements in health. By 2016, this approach had hit the law of diminishing returns. With institutional deliveries at 98.9 per cent, future reductions in IMR and MMR had to come from remedying more fundamental causes—poverty, and caste and gender discrimination.

Nutrient intake of the poorest families was going down across India.[20] In Tamil Nadu, the public distribution system (PDS), essential to

---

[*] A child is considered fully vaccinated on receiving bacille Calmette-Guérin (BCG) against meningitis and TB, three doses of pentavalent against multiple diseases, three doses of oral polio vaccine and one dose of measles vaccine.

address under-nourishment, was plagued with not only an incomplete selection of nutrients but also caste discrimination. In a village called Kalimangalam near Coimbatore, a group of adivasi women told me that they got twenty kilos of rice and less than a kilo of dal from their ration shop. P. Selvaraj, a farmer from the locally dominant gounder community in the same village, gave a different answer. 'Rice, twenty kilos. Kerosene, three litres. Tur dal, one kilo. Urad dal, one kilo. Palm oil, one litre. Wheat, eight kilos. Sugar, two kilos if there are three people in the family and three kilos if there are more.' Repeating this question in subsequent travels, including in Natham Colony, I got the same unjust pattern.

Such biases also existed in sanitation programmes and anganwadis, which have to provide at least one healthy meal daily to children below six.[21] Along Coimbatore's Variety Hall Road, a slum largely home to dalits had no more than two functional public toilets for its over 700 residents. Dravidian parties, by choosing electoral candidates from the local dominant caste, had institutionalised a locally majoritarian bias in every constituency over the years.

Added to this caste bias were gender asymmetries. In 2015–2016, the National Family Health Survey found 55.1 per cent of women between fifteen and forty-nine years of age in the state to be anaemic, higher than the national average.* The corresponding number for men stood at 20 per cent. The historian Geetha attributed this gap to food-sharing arrangements within households, which gave preference to male members. Women also faced the pressure of repeated pregnancies till they birthed a son, she said.

Addressing such challenges, all hardwired into society, was not easy. Yet, even as the residual problem had gained in complexity, the state's once-impressive health infrastructure had weakened.

Understaffing was one cause. Going by state government numbers, the forested, hilly block of Thally, where Soumya's village was located,

---

* The equivalent numbers for India for the same period stood at 53.1 per cent for women and 22.7 per cent for men.

should have been thickly dotted with health workers. There should have been a qualified nurse at the local health sub-centre for every 5,000 people, and a PHC staffed with two doctors and three staff nurses, open between nine in the morning and four in the evening, for every 35,000–50,000 people. Above these, there should have been block and district hospitals. Travelling around the block, I found that twenty of the thirty-six health sub-centres in Thally did not have nurses. In Urigam, one of the larger villages in the block, the PHC was closed. A month later, when I crossed it again, the centre was open but only a nurse and compounder were around.[22]

The people of Thally had to travel to the taluka hospital in the nearby town of Denkanikottai. Serving a population of 1.64 lakh people, it got 200 to 300 patients every day and did not have enough staff to tackle emergencies. Medical staff reached at nine in the morning but left by one in the afternoon, said a paediatrician there. 'After that, only one doctor is on duty.' Between 50 and 80 patients visited in the afternoon, whom the doctor examined between three and five in the afternoon. That is 25 to 40 patients per hour; anywhere between 90 and 144 seconds for consultation, diagnosis and prescribing treatment.

A former health secretary of the state in the Tamil Nadu administration, who had worked in its Health and Family Welfare Department, said that a chunk of health workers got themselves transferred closer home and attributed this to the rising clout of employee unions. As these unions comprised people from dominant castes, political parties needed their support during elections. Caste played a role even in the staffing.

The rot ran deeper yet. While Health Department officials in the state claimed that Tamil Nadu performed better than other states because doctors headed the directorates under the department— rather than officials of the Indian Administrative Service (IAS)—this had a flip side. 'The state created a professional healthcare system but also pushed out other skills, especially at the lower end of the spectrum, like working with communities, local governments, ASHAs, health workers, etc., in favour of an excessive reliance on doctors. High-end skills relating to healthcare financing, health economics, regulation, etc., are also under-represented,' said T. Sundararaman, a former head of the National State Health Resource Centre, an advisory arm of the National Rural Health Mission.

Between 2006 and 2016, Tamil Nadu's public health service had not just concentrated healthcare services at the PHCs. After three children died in 2008–2009 from measles contracted during vaccination, the Health Department also moved immunisation from health sub-centres to PHCs. As for institutional deliveries, earlier, women went to health sub-centres whose nurses were trained midwives. Subsequently, the department moved child births to PHCs, contending they were better equipped. In the process, it 'missed the simple fact that the woman may go into labour at any time of night,' said Srividya.

Parallelly, the department also became more selective about the services it would offer. As it focused more and more on IMR and MMR reductions, the result was Kafkaesque. Auxiliary nurse midwifes— village-level health workers who are the first point of contact between the community and the health system—spent more time updating the state's PICME (Pregnancy Infant Cohort Monitoring and Evaluation) software—which collates real-time information about pregnant mothers and newborns across the state—than on home visits. Parents were forced to travel to vaccination sites, which pushed down the immunisation numbers. PHCs accepted only 10 per cent of morbidity cases and turned the others away, said Sundararaman. Taluka hospitals too, struggling with understaffing, told people with trickier cases to go elsewhere.

A senior official in the state's Health Department in Chennai claimed everything was fine. Asked about understaffing in Krishnagiri, he said the department ran three mobile clinics that travelled to remote hamlets, and that it audited the death of every mother and child. Because of these measures, he said, IMR and MMR in the district were close to the state average. While he was right about government data showing no difference between Krishnagiri and other districts, the reasons were not what he claimed.

In Malhalli, another village in Krishnagiri, several women did not have Mother Child Protection (MCP) cards, which register pregnant women into the healthcare system and help with consequent observation. The former health secretary said, 'We are not good at capturing deaths during early pregnancies due to complications; of women not in the MCP cards due to carelessness or weak data collection; deaths of migrants without ration cards; and of unmarried women trying to keep their pregnancy a secret.' IMR was even harder to capture. Some private hospitals in the state, a mid-ranking official in the state Health Department told me, again on the condition of anonymity, were reporting infant mortalities as stillborn to escape government scrutiny. 'The norm is that stillborn babies are half of IMR. But our numbers say the number of stillborn babies is equal to IMR.'

According to Gaitonde, Tamil Nadu had incomplete data on the wider health of its population. 'Most of the focus is on immunisation, deliveries and antenatal care. On diseases like chikungunya and dengue, there is a complete breakdown of surveillance.' Complicating matters, Tamil Nadu's Health Department was producing data in isolation. Rival datasets, against which its numbers could be tested, were not being created. While carrying out surveys as part of a health rights awareness project, Gaitonde's team found that only some of the healthcare needs of 40 per cent of the people in the state were being met. The state government stopped the project's funding, he said.[*]

Not only was the state Health Department missing some of the morbidities due to its overweening focus on reproductive and child health but also was letting the most vulnerable fall through even within that narrow net. Its response, instead of introducing systemic corrections to tackle deeper causes for poor health, was to polish a selective handful of metrics to suggest wider gains in public health. It was also using what the former health secretary called 'decorative programmes'—schemes like Amma Canteens that served subsidised

---

[*] I sent questions over email and SMS to J. Radhakrishnan, principal secretary to the state government for health. He did not respond.

meals or Amma Baby Care Kits that went to every newborn, buffing up the image of the chief minister.

Soumya's baby died from more than just poverty. Along with it, caste and gender discrimination had left the mother anaemic. The local ration shop had not worked well. Her weak condition, right through the pregnancy, even assuming it was spotted by the state's health management software, had gone uncorrected. Although the delivery was institutional, it was not at the nearby health sub-centre but at the PHC farther away. Subsequently, however, there was little succour. Her sickly infant was referred up to successive hospitals that failed to save it.

———

Between 2010 and 2016, the percentage of students passing Tamil Nadu's tenth standard state board exams rose from the mid-eighties to the mid-nineties. The number of students scoring a perfect hundred rose as well. In the twelfth standard too, overall pass percentage rose from 85 to 91, and average marks scored by students went up, along with centums.

These numbers, however, clashed with India's National Achievement Survey (NAS), conducted by the centre's National Council of Educational Research and Training (NCERT), which track learning outcomes across the country. The 2015 NAS assessment of tenth standard students placed Tamil Nadu close to the bottom in every subject. The report card for the state said, 'Average performance of students in the state was significantly lower than the national average in all five subjects—English, Mathematics, Science, Social Science and (Modern Indian Language)—Tamil.'[23]

When I met her, the then education secretary Sabitha Dayashankar dismissed the NAS data. 'NCERT questions are based on the CBSE [Central Board of Secondary Education] pattern. Our children will not be able to understand.' Later, she added, 'We don't know why NCERT is conducting these assessments. The Government of India should stop these and just fund us properly.'

These were extraordinary answers. Can science or mathematics be taught so uniquely that students cannot comprehend a question asked by a rival school board? How useful is such an education? Centralised evaluations are an accepted part of pedagogy. Not only do they test whether students understand concepts and utilise them but also provide an independent assessment of outcomes. Without them, all we have is states appraising their own work.

What I found here was a structural flaw and a government that, instead of correcting it, was boosting its own results by manipulating exam results.[24]

By 2005, Tamil Nadu had three different schooling systems—government schools, matriculation schools and CBSE schools. Each differed in important ways. Government schools followed the state syllabus and taught in Tamil. CBSE schools followed their countrywide curriculum and taught in English. Matriculation schools, the fastest-growing segment of the state's school sector, set their own syllabus, also in English, and held their own examinations. They had another unusual edge: 'What is taught in sixth standard in a school elsewhere is taught in a matriculation school's fourth standard,' a former official at the Directorate of Government Examinations told me. The resulting sales pitch, that matriculation schools were better than the state board schools, resonated with parents.

This was an unfair system. Children in government schools, most of whom hailed from poor or more vulnerable communities, like dalits or scheduled tribes, got lower-quality education than the ones in matriculation schools. Students in the latter, however, received an education weaker than that of their peers in CBSE schools.

Around 2008–2009, under the DMK, this system finally saw an overhaul. Working under the DMK's education minister Thangam Thennarasu, a group of government officials and educationists created a common syllabus for government and matriculation schools. Rote learning went out and activity-based learning came in. At the same time, with the passage of the Right to Education Act, 2009, the state scrapped exams till the ninth standard, while the state board retained the responsibility of conducting exams in the tenth and twelfth standards. The test-based evaluation system was revamped as well.

Matriculation schools opposed this move. The common syllabus meant they could no longer set their own curricula, an important differentiator between them and the state schools. Opposition also came from teachers. Some felt their schools were being dragged down to the level of government schools. Both matriculation schools and the teachers' lobby were powerful forces. 'Several of Tamil Nadu's top politicians and bureaucrats own matriculation schools,' Thennarasu said. Many of the teachers belonged to local caste associations.

The onus for making sure the new system worked passed to the AIADMK government, which was voted into power in 2011. 'There should be a constant review to ensure adherence to the new system,' said Thennarasu. 'I have my doubts if this is happening.' Such programmes were seen as something brought in by the previous government, he added.

Compounding matters, pressure to show dramatic improvements in education delivery rose under the AIADMK government. Till 1995, state pass percentages hovered around 60 or 70, said a consultant working with the state education department. And then, they started increasing. 'The difference is that, during the DMK [government's regime], these numbers would rise gradually—from 75.2 to 75.5, say—just to show there is no decline.' But, in the past five years, the consultant said, 'pass percentages have increased like anything. Out of every 100 students, 95 are passing.'[25]

Bureaucrats were trying to make Chief Minister Jayalalithaa look good. College managements too had to be pleased. The former official at the Directorate of Government Examinations said, 'If I declare 75 per cent as the pass percentage, I take 2 lakh students out of the college education market. That is the other lobby working here.'

By 2016, Tamil Nadu was handing out a 'slow learners' kit' a few months before the state board examinations. A hundred and fifty pages long, it contained key questions from all five subjects. 'Most of the questions [in the exam] are repeated from this,' said Thennarasu.

'The pattern doesn't change. If students still don't manage to pass, at 40 marks, the [AIADMK] government does moderation.' The term 'moderation' was academic bureaucracy's newspeak for manipulating exam results to make students pass. The former bureaucrat in the Directorate of Government Examinations corroborated Thennarasu's claim. 'We have a programme,' he told me. 'We tell it the targeted pass percentage, and it allots marks accordingly.'

This extraordinary claim was supported by numbers. Out of the total of 1,023,566 students who sat for the tenth standard board exams in 2016, the percentage of students who passed in four subjects— English, mathematics, science and social sciences—was exactly the same: 92.6. In 2015 too, the percentage of students who passed across the four subjects remained the same: 91.9. Such congruence is highly improbable.*

Before 2011, Tamil Nadu's education system was uneven. Students in rural, matriculation and CBSE schools got starkly dissimilar education. What the state had by 2016 was worse—a greased slide that passed students along to the next class without testing what they knew. Under the Right to Education Act, students cannot be failed till the eighth standard. But in Tamil Nadu, fearing a bad reputation, schools gave them the passing score in ninth standard too. Given the state's efforts, it was hard for students to fail in the tenth exams. The eleventh standard was but a formality, an IAS officer in the state told me. 'If a child is faring poorly, he or she is merely urged to transfer to another school.' In twelfth too, the state tried to pass as many as possible. College admissions were based not on entrance exams but on the marks students scored in their twelfth board exams. The students were effectively tested for the first time only in the first year of college.

'As kids pass without exams, the burden of incomprehension keeps rising,' the consultant said. This showed clearly in the NAS surveys. The third round of the survey, conducted between November 2010

---

* I sent questions about these aberrations over email and SMS to Dayashankar. She did not respond.

and March 2011, placed fifth standard students in Tamil Nadu close to the top. After a few more years of schooling, those students, when in class ten, completely squandered that lead and were stuck at the bottom along with states like Gujarat and Punjab. When an engineering college in Coimbatore administered a test to a new batch of students, 40 per cent of them failed. 'They had all scored between 90 per cent and 100 per cent in their boards,' a senior college official said.

———

In Mizoram, Odisha and Punjab, I had traced back the failure to deliver health and education to underfunding and administrative incapacity. What I saw in Tamil Nadu was different. Here, a functional administration had begun ignoring systemic improvements in favour of ploys that made the elected political party look good at the cost of the state's people.

Towards the end of the Punjab stint, I spoke to the economist Abhijit Sen, who said that India's political parties maintained their party cadres through the construction sector. Tamil Nadu was a good place to study that. The state saw mining of beach sand, river sand and granite on a large scale. Scams continued to be flagged in each. I chose river sand mining for a closer look.

———

V. Chandrasekhar's shirt was so white, detergent advertisements came to mind. The creases in the starched white veshti around his legs were like the edge of a knife. He was tall and lean, clean-shaven, with oiled, carefully combed-back hair. At first glance, he looked like another middle-class householder in the state, but he was much more than that. From 2006, this resident of Bahour, a village twenty kilometres to the south of Puducherry, had waged a lonely, dangerous battle to save the local river, the Thenpennaiyar, from sand miners.

It was a battle he stumbled into. In the 1980s, when sand miners arrived, his village did not pay much attention. Sand had always been mined. People building houses would take a cartload or two from the Thenpennaiyar, flowing less than two kilometres to the south. Transporters, mining sand for the cities, would pay a small amount to the panchayat and lug back a trailer load or so. Against these puny subtractions, the riverbed, broadening as it neared the Bay of Bengal and luxuriantly carpeted with sand, seemed vast and inexhaustible.

Big mistake. By the late 1980s, real estate development in Tamil Nadu built up a head of steam, and the demand for sand rose. By 2005, miners had trucked away so much sand that the riverbed fell by thirty feet. In tandem, local wells dried out—it is sand that holds the river water long enough for it to percolate into aquifers. As groundwater levels fell, sea water seeped into the spaces vacated by freshwater aquifers. Wells and shallow borewells turned saline.

Chandrasekhar tried to mobilise his fellow villagers but failed. He went to local political parties, bureaucrats and police officials, but they did not step in either. He sensed a win in 2010 when the Madras High Court stayed sand mining on the Thenpennaiyar, but the state government did not implement the order. After two more years of work, Chandrasekhar managed another favourable order from the National Green Tribunal in Chennai. This was not implemented either. After a second petition resulted in the court blasting the local officials, the region's subdivisional magistrate began enforcing the court's order. The official was transferred out. In all, sand mining stopped for just a month.[26]

Others opposing sand mining in the state had similar tales. A lot of struggle, a rare glimpse of victory, but no durable wins. This industry was impregnable to even court orders.

As in Bahour, sand mining was an unorganised activity across Tamil Nadu into the 1980s. As urbanisation picked up and demand for sand rose, micro-level politicians, like councillors, and panchayat members and secretaries, all belonging to political parties, took over the trade. Their dominion, however, did not last long. As demand for sand rose, so did quarrels between these local leaders. In the process, district-level political leaders, who had to adjudicate these disputes, realised that sand, like liquor, was rather profitable and moved in.[27]

These district-level politicians, along with transporters, bought mining permits for government-approved sites along a river's course at auctions conducted by district authorities. Then, as politicians began backing contractors, some yards went to the DMK and others to the AIADMK. Things went on like this till the early 1990s, after which, district politicians lost control to a small group of sand miners. This happened twice, a researcher who had studied sand mining told me.[28]

First, when the state government inserted a clause in the Tamil Nadu Minor Mineral Concession Rules, 1959, which allowed it to grant mining leases without an auction. As I reported:

> The state, ruled at the time by the AIADMK, used this clause to give an exclusive right to mine on one sand quarry on the Palar river to a contractor named O Arumugasamy. Simultaneously ... all other sandpits in the vicinity were shuttered.
>
> This model was replicated across the state. A report by a citizens' committee on illegal sand mining in Karur district quotes a 2001 order of the Madras High Court which said as many as 35 leases were granted using this clause. Most of these ... went to Arumugasamy.[29]

It is not clear how and why Arumugasamy was chosen.* Clearer, however, were the consequences of this switch. Rival political parties lost access to sand mining revenues. Inside the AIADMK too, local leaders lost an independent source of funds, which increased their dependence on the high command.

This arrangement of mining contractors replacing district leaders continued even after the AIADMK was voted out. In some cases, contractors close to the AIADMK were replaced by those nearer to

---

* I emailed questions about this policy change to the office of the then chief minister Jayalalithaa, who also headed the state when this shift took place; to K.N. Venkatramanan, principal secretary to the chief minister in 2016; and to Arumugasamy. I called their offices, informing them about the emails. A local reporter informed Arumugasamy about my questionnaire over the phone. None of them responded.

the DMK, which formed the next government. In others, existing contractors tapped people close to the new leadership and asked them to take the contracts, offering to do all the work.

Things continued like this till 2003. Then, the mechanism of how the sand miners were chosen changed. A 2001 high court order—in response to a public interest litigation (PIL) detailing how sand miners were using heavy earthmoving equipment, mining outside allotted quarries and driving vehicles on the riverbed—squashed all leases granted without an auction. In response, in 2003, the state government under the AIADMK brought sand mining under its purview and allowed only the state PWD to mine sand. But, the department was permitted to outsource the loading and transport of sand by trucks to contractors. Predictably, it was the contractors who once again ran the show, illegally stockpiling and selling the sand. A team of the People's Union of Civil Liberties, after a fact-finding trip along the Palar and Cheyyar basins, reported, 'Total absence of any official of government at the quarry sites or stockyards. Locals also report that officials are seldom to be seen in the mining sites.'[30]

The only thing that changed in reality was the legal basis for appointing contractors: these were no longer discretionary allocations by the party high command. Despite contracts now being allotted by the PWD, Arumugasamy continued to do most of the mining. Between 2003 and 2006, of the forty or so leases given out in the entire state, most went to him and his benamis.[31] In 2006, when Tamil Nadu brought the DMK back to power, Arumugasamy's empire shrank once more to the river Palar. Five years later, when the AIADMK won again, leases returned to him. But, when the party got to know that he had taken an AIADMK district member as his partner, 'the district official was fired and Arumugasamy's contract was cancelled,' said the researcher. Sekar Reddy, another businessperson also known to the senior leaders in the AIADMK, replaced him.

By 2016, the industry's scale dwarfed the imagination. Stepping on to a sand quarry on the Thenpennaiyar riverbank, the first thing I saw was a ten-wheeled tipper. Moving slowly along, it ground to a halt behind thirty or so similar trucks. Beyond them lay a vast, empty space—the dry summer riverbed of the river, which looked as though a giant tractor had ploughed it. There were long trenches as deep as seven metres, separated by ridges wide enough for tippers to move on. There was a scab of dark earth at the bottom of one trench. So much sand had been scraped away that the riverbed's clay base stood exposed. The ridges were all that was left of the original riverbed. There were more queues of trucks, and at the head of each was an excavator. The arm of the machine dipped into a trench, dug out a shovelful of sand and poured it into the tipper waiting alongside. As the tipper filled up, it moved away, and another tipper took its place. I was hard-pressed to tell where this quarry ended. As I wrote:

> According to locals, anywhere between 2,500–3,000 tipper-loads of sand leave from here each day. With each tipper designed to carry 20 tons, that's 50,000 tons of sand a day. This quarry in Villupuram district, about an hour from Pondicherry, is a good introduction to the daunting scale of sand mining in Tamil Nadu. The Thenpennaiyar enters this part of northern Tamil Nadu from Karnataka and flows through the district for about 100 kilometres before entering the neighbouring district of Cuddalore. In this stretch, said locals, there are two more quarries of similar size. And that's just one river in one district.[32]

In an investigation into illegal mining in Tamil Nadu for *Frontline* in 2015, the veteran journalist Ilangovan Rajasekaran reported that sand was being mined in most major rivers in the state—Cauvery, Palar, Vellar, Thenpennaiyar and Amaravati in north and central Tamil Nadu, Vaigai in the south and Bhavani in the west, among others. Miners 'have not spared even the tributaries of these rivers and also streams'.[33]

Despite the clear environmental costs of groundwater levels collapsing across the state and wells in coastal areas turning saline, responding to a PIL filed by the Cauvery Neervala Athara Pathukappu Sangam, a non-profit in Erode, the government argued that sand mining did not need an environment clearance since quarrying was done scientifically by the PWD. When the court insisted on an environmental impact assessment, the government rushed an environmental clearance through in just three months; these usually take at least a year.

There were also economic and political costs. In 2013, as the *Times of India* reported, a unit of sand was to be sold at Rs 950. Of this, loading contractors were supposed to get Rs 220.[34] In other words, the state was to get 77 per cent of the sand's value. But, as in Punjab, a secondary market with a politically connected intermediary was created. Those buying sand paid Rs 4,000 or more per unit at the illegal sand miners' private depots, who retained most of this cash.[35]

By 2016, the industry was said to have anywhere between 50,000 to 100,000 trucks in service.[36] Even conservative calculations of foregone revenue yielded eye-popping numbers. If 50,000 trucks made one trip a day, carrying 6 tonnes at a time—some of the tippers I saw at Villupuram were 20-tonners—that added up to 300,000 tonnes of sand a day. If the industry worked 200 days a year, accounting for rains and non-work days, 6 crore tonnes of sand would have been mined in 2016. At Rs 4,000 a tonne, annual sand sales added up to Rs 24,000 crore.

In contrast, Tamil Nadu's budget estimates for 2014–2015 pegged incomes from sand quarries at Rs 216.82 crore. The previous year, it had stood even lower at Rs 133.37 crore. The estimated size of the state budget in 2014–2015 was Rs 91,835 crore. If the state had captured 77 per cent of river sand sales, it might have had another Rs 18,480 crore to spend. Per usual, questions I sent to the state government asking for its response to these numbers went unanswered.

The economic costs surpassed foregone revenue. Not only did Tamil Nadu's construction and real estate industry pay inflated rates for sand, but also the state lost money repairing the damage wreaked by miners. So much sand was trucked away from the Amaravathi that it began flowing twenty feet lower. Irrigation canals fed by the river ran dry— the river now flowed below the canals' mouths. The government had to build a barrage to raise the water level high enough for the canals to function.[37] Also, when groundwater levels fell, farmers needed larger, costlier pumps, bringing along changes in cropping patterns, dipping income levels, migration and more.

There were political costs as well. Over the years, the role of money, as cash given to voters and funds spent on campaigning, had gone up in Tamil Nadu's elections.[38] This was the state's notorious 'Thirumangalam formula'. In 2009, M.K. Alagiri of the DMK was said to have paid, according to the US Embassy cables leaked by Wikileaks, as much as Rs 5,000 per voter in the Thirumangalam assembly by-election.[39] The biggest spenders were the DMK and the AIADMK.

The arithmetic here is instructive. If we assume that the ruling AIADMK paid half of the 5 crore voters in the state, as of 2016, Rs 1,000 each, it works out to an outlay of Rs 2,500 crore once every five years. In contrast, the value of sand being extracted stood roughly at Rs 1.2 lakh crore over a five-year period. Even if we assume that some portion of the illegal profits from sand mining were used to buy votes, where did the rest go? A part went to the party cadre. 'Village councilors are reported to receive Rs. 10,000 monthly, panchayat presidents Rs 1 lakh, and MLAs Rs 5 lakh,' write Harriss-White and J. Jeyaranjan.[40] This was also echoed by state politicians like K. Kaliyan of the Communist Party of India (Marxist). The rest was shared between, write Harriss-White and Jeyaranjan, the sand miner and 'his contractors, politicians, the bureaucracy, police, and derived markets of fixers.'[41]

Much of this money, of course, remained unaccounted for. The AIADMK's annual report for the financial year 2013–2014, for instance, declared an annual income of Rs 38.47 crore.[42]

Access to these funds gave both the parties an advantage over smaller rivals. 'I'm not able to spend Rs 2 lakh per constituency while others are spending Rs 10 crore,' said a senior leader of Viduthalai Chiruthaigal Katchi (VCK), one of the major dalit parties in the state. 'In the 2011 polls, an old woman threw my leaflet in my face. She said, "Give me Rs 1,000, and I will vote for you."'[43]

It was a sign of disillusionment. 'There was also the growing feeling that the politician was venal and in the political game only for personal gains, hence the total disenchantment with ideological promises and focus on individual gains,' writes former bureaucrat S. Narayan in *The Dravidian Years*.[44] So, parties like the VCK had to tie up with the dravidian ones. This nobbled their capacity to challenge the hegemony of the dominant castes.

———

Like the Dongria Kondhs, villagers in Tamil Nadu should have opposed sand mining, which threatened their way of living. But, as Chandrasekhar found, opposition stayed low. This was partly due to blandishments. When sand miners first got to the district of Villupuram, they gave money to build temples to villages and asked for permission to mine. In 2015, they also gave Rs 4,700 per ration card to villagers near the quarries. Till two years before that, they had only paid panchayat leaders, and then the villagers insisted on getting paid too.[45]

There was also violence to contend with. Officials and locals opposing the trade had been killed by sand miners.[46] The state government had its own brand of coercion. In 2014, in Kalathur village on the banks of the Palar, police charged women protesting against sand mining with rioting, possession of deadly weapons, preventing officials from discharging duty and criminal intimidation.[47] 'The police is an instrument of the state,' said Chandrasekhar.

But it was not just a case of villagers being paid off. The milieu in which sand mining rose was one where rainfall was declining, industrialisation was accelerating, and members from rural families were migrating out. In these conditions, even as sand mining entered, villagers bullish about finding jobs in the state's industrial clusters were indifferent. Those staying on in villages found employment in mining. Caste entered the dynamic too. In Villupuram, for instance, miners mostly employed dalits. This made it impossible for the villages to present a united front.

In the absence of a groundswell, the few isolated voices expressing alarm needed support. For activists like Chandrasekhar, rival political parties were the next port of call. But miners funded them too.

Local officials, taking their orders from the state government, stayed unresponsive as well. They too were not immune to the violence and threat to life.

The media's coverage was circumscribed. It covered protests, attacks on protesters, ecological damage, court rulings and, eventually, with Rajasekaran's reports, losses to the state exchequer. But it stayed silent on the webs of payments that extended outwards from people like Arumugasamy, all the way up to the ruling government, bolstering their impunity. The AIADMK's taste for defamation suits was one reason that held the media back. As the *News Minute* reported, between 2012 and 2015 alone, the state government filed seventy-five criminal defamation cases against the media.[48] These carried the risk of a two-year imprisonment and/or a fine. Newspapers, hence, did very few investigations.

Some television news channels, as in Odisha, were owned by political parties and acted as their mouthpieces. 'They didn't get into critical points,' said a former editor of Puthiya Thalaimurai, an independent TV channel. As for independent news channels, only those with deep pockets could survive the TV news business. However, those who ran them had multiple business interests. Puthiya Thalaimurai, for instance, was owned by the SRM group, a Rs 1,000 crore education, transport, hotels and construction group. This made them vulnerable to government action.[49]

The judiciary, on the other hand, took government submissions at face value and dismissed petitions. Court-appointed fact-finding committees were outsmarted by miners. 'Even if the high court orders a surprise inspection,' a Madurai-based lawyer told me, 'it takes two to three days for the committee to reach, and in that time, they get tipped off and fill the trenches in.' Miners also took advantage of delays in hearings to expedite mining, which is what happened with the Amaravathi. During an adjournment in court hearings, miners removed twenty-one feet of sand in just three months along a ten-kilometre stretch of the river.[50] Alternately, as Chandrasekhar found, the state government ignored court orders.

For bureaucrats, said Thennarasu, the cost of disobeying politicians was greater than disobeying the judiciary. This was new. 'In the last ten to twenty years, the state has lost all fear of the judiciary.'

There could yet be a silver lining in all this. By 2016, Tamil Nadu was seeing more protests than before. Given slowing industrial clusters, some workers returned home only to find their farms hit by sand mining. Chandrasekhar too saw a glimmer of hope. 'People are more aware now,' he said, 'due to problems with drinking water, irrigation, agriculture. They support me much more than before.'

———

On some days, Tamil Nadu seemed like an archetypal strong State. The singer-activist Kovan was arrested in 2015 for mocking Jayalalithaa in a song about liquor shops in the state. Fisherpeople protesting against the Kudankulam nuclear plant were charged en masse with sedition in 2011 and 2012. With sand mining too, the state remained unmoved by protest. Other days, however, it seemed like an indecisive State fearful of attracting the ire of its people. Take its response to alarmingly depleting groundwater reserves across the state.

Despite a deepening water crisis,* the state junked the Tamil Nadu Groundwater (Development and Management) Act, a decade after it was passed in 2003.[51] Meant to help the state use the resource more sustainably, it was never implemented. 'If the Act in the present form was implemented and groundwater was not allowed to be tapped, it would have led to a public outcry,' the government said at the time.[52] A 'senior official' also told the *Hindu* that the state government would soon come out with a 'comprehensive and workable law'.[53]

---

* Just 170 kilometres long, the Noyyal, a minor tributary to the Cauvery that I travelled down, was replete with water conflicts—between villagers; between villagers and industrial plants; between villages and cities like Coimbatore and Tirupur; between villagers and ashrams (and educational institutions) they accused of land grabs and blocking tributaries. See: M. Rajshekhar, 'How a River in Tamil Nadu Turned into a Sewage Canal', *Scroll.in* (29 August 2016), scroll.in/article/812450/how-a-river-in-tamil-nadu-turned-into-a-sewage-canal.

That was in 2013. By 2016, people were still waiting. By 2019, Tamil Nadu had the highest number of blocks with over-exploited groundwater in the country. That year, borewells ran dry. Families stuck buckets under air-conditioners to collect drips of condensation. There was talk of trucking water in from the Hogenakkal falls near the state's border with Karnataka, as far as 400 kilometres away from Chennai.

Strong State? Weak State? A predatory State fearful of losing its grip?

Elsewhere in India, larger regressions continued. In January 2016, a month before I reached Chennai, PhD scholar Rohith Vemula died by suicide after facing caste discrimination by the authorities of Hyderabad Central University. Letters from the central minister for Human Resources Development to the university vice chancellor, demanding action against him and four other students for allegedly assaulting a student from the BJP-backed Akhil Bharatiya Vidyarthi Parishad (ABVP), had resulted in his suspension.[54]

A month later, Jawaharlal Nehru University student leader Kanhaiya Kumar was arrested in an alleged case of sedition. Three days later, when he was brought to the Patiala House court, a group of lawyers attacked him and his fellow students, professors and journalists.[55] Kumar was again beaten up inside the court complex by some of the lawyers two days later.[56] That month, the Bastar police coerced my colleague Malini Subramaniam and the Jagdalpur Legal Aid Group, a group of idealistic lawyers working with adivasis, into leaving the district.[57] Around the same time, two people threw an acid-like liquid on adivasi rights activist Soni Sori in Dantewada, leaving her face blackened, her eyes burning.[58]

A sentence in botanist Madhu Ramnath's account in *Woodsmoke and Leafcups* of the thirty years he spent with Bastar's Durva adivasis reverberated deeply: 'The three qualities of the Sarkar: To beg, to frighten and to make the heart ache.'[59]

In the face of such a State, what does it take to rouse societies?

In Tamil Nadu, despite a worsening water crisis and weakening delivery of healthcare and education, the people were quiet. Societies can, indeed, correct their course. In the past, the subcontinent united around the demand for independence. But how does that coalescing around a common purpose happen? Do we need charismatic leaders to articulate those visions? Don't movements throw up their own leaders? Father Jeyapathy had one part of the answer for why common purpose eludes people: the erosion of folklore. 'How do people develop on the ground? Folk is one way to understand what is happening. It came out of the lived experiences of people. When you did not have TV, etc., people had leisure: they designed their own games, their own stories. But now, they are not connected to their own experiences or communicating it. What we have now is a mass media culture. One which generates the images that form the consciousness of the country. What that means is that you are not connected to what is happening to people.'

This is what Sumail Singh Sidhu had said about Paash. The poet had tried to impregnate the people's language with complex ideas, making it possible for them to comprehend the forces that acted on them and understand that they were not alone.

People with fewer resources, and thus fewer choices, can compensate for their individual weaknesses by closing ranks and engaging in collective action. But civil society institutions for collective action, like labour unions, have now ceded to more subservient structures.

Post liberalisation, trying to stay competitive, companies across India reduced permanent staff. For this, they relied on informal economy labour contractors at first. And then came the formal economy actors—manpower supply companies. These, the academic M. Vijayabaskar at the Madras Institute of Development Studies said, might have as many as 60,000 workers on their rolls, who are sent to the clients' locations. In the old regime, most workers led bleak lives—low salaries, no job security, no safety nets for accidents or retirement. Although people working with manpower supply companies do get employee benefits like contributions to their public provident fund (PPF), they continue to have little control over their income or career. There is little demand for older workers. Once laid off, even those in their late twenties or early thirties struggle to find jobs. When redeployed from one firm to another, they do not get the same pay as before. With one firm hiring them for assembly-line work and the other for gardening, there is little scope for acquiring work skills either. Yet, precarity is not the only cost of increasingly insecure employment.*

This change in the labour economy also affected society's capacity to think for itself, the Hosur-based novelist Aadhavan Deetchanya told me. In 1973, Hosur, abutting Tamil Nadu's border with Karnataka, was chosen as the site for the state's second industrial cluster. Through the 1970s, a diverse clutch of companies, producing everything from trucks to garments and medicines, set up factories here. In those early years, it was a relatively equal town. 'When the workers were bachelors, they lived together in the same room. They cooked together. In the first week of the month, they would eat mutton, and then move to chicken, then fish and then, by the end of the month, beef.'

'Because it was the cheapest?'

'Because it was the cheapest. There was no taboo. This was partly due to the bachelor life. And partly due to the lack of permanent jobs. We see the 1980s as an age of direct employment. But it was also a time when companies hired workers as apprentices or pre-trainees—non-permanent staff. A vacuum cleaner company, for instance, used to employ people for 179 days, lay them off and then hire them back again. All this resulted in worker struggles. The culture that was created in the process was egalitarian.' This intermixing was not based on Periyar's

---

* As in Odisha's debt-induced migration market, politicians operated in Tamil Nadu's manpower supply sector too. One of the biggest companies here, Upshot, was started in 2010 by the DMK MLA M. Varalakshmi and her husband. As competition intensified between manpower supply companies, these firms increasingly recruited migrant workers, who worked out cheaper. This accelerated migration from north India to the south and added to the job crisis in Tamil Nadu. In my first month in the state, people I interviewed told me that employment in industrial clusters was a source of caste emancipation. That epoch seemed to be ending.

ideology, but on their living conditions. But, as workers got married, they again behaved in line with their caste identity.

Hosur too failed to live up to its initial promise. With liberalisation, local sub-contracting shrank. Units began to close. Workers, seen till then in uniforms, began selling fruits at the bus stand.

Disillusioned by the trade unions' inability to staunch job losses, workers went into self-preservation mode. 'We used to screen Anand Patwardhan's films. *Ram ke Naam* was screened here. A thousand people would come and see those.' Those screenings had stopped, Deetchanya told me. 'When a person wants to do something for a cause beyond the family, the first thought that strikes you is that some money will go out of your pocket. The rationale for disengagement with things that don't affect you starts from there—"What else can I do with that money?" People get more self-centred,' Deetchanya said.

Large processes subsequently played out in the town without much opposition. Communalism reared its head—Hosur was affected by right-wing politics in nearby Karnataka. As the manufacturing boom ended, a new boom of real estate replaced it. At each stage, the town saw the ratio between winners and losers skew further. When the manufacturing industry came up, migrant workers gained more than the local communities. When the real estate boom began, workers and factory owners lost, and a small handful of politicians gained—most land in the town was now owned by them.

Trade unions used to be a mobilising force, Deetchanya said. 'They made this town liveable. Hosur was seen as a good-for-nothing town, a place where people just came for work. Trade unions created a townwide sense of working-class solidarity. They gave it soul.' As unions shuttered in the 1990s and manpower supply companies came in, people turned more inwards, and Hosur's capacity to engage with these changes shrank. 'What are the social institutions in Hosur? There's no ideology, no political idea. This is what happens when a society has been sedated. Earlier, whenever we organised a writers' conclave, we would meet a thousand people and collect Rs 100 from each. And then, it became about meeting ten people to get Rs 10,000 each. And now, we need to find two people who can give us Rs 50,000 each. We are moving from the realm of readers to that of sponsors.'

What happens in the absence of progressive mediating organisations? In January 2017, Tamil Nadu boiled over in protest when the Supreme Court banned the rural bull-taming sport of jallikattu. Anywhere between half a million and a million gathered in Chennai alone. One reason was Tamil pride. For far too long, state politicians had blamed the centre and adjoining states for its problems like water scarcity. Now, jallikattu was presented as a similar assault on the state by the Delhi sultanate. Apart from this, the protests also gave people a chance to express a range of frustrations. Lacking critiques of the suboptimality, however, the protests yielded little. The powers conceded on jallikattu. Everything else stayed the same.

———

I slowly started to see political parties not as emissaries of regional, religious or caste-class interests but as self-interested institutions that sourced electoral power from their constituencies. In state after state, political parties seemed to share four traits: they were extractive, dominant, centralised and clientelist.

Extractive political institutions divert wealth from the larger society to benefit themselves. In India, parties siphon money from government programmes; extract rents from companies; hand over old commons, like public sector companies and mineral reserves, and new commons, like welfare payments and tollbooth collections, to entities related to politicians or private parties in return for bribes; sell government jobs; extract rents for favourable policy decisions; and formulate policy that favours private firms likely to share the kickbacks. As for the parties out of power, they make money through other means, like selling Rajya Sabha seats.[60]

In an essay titled 'Where Indian Democracy Went Wrong', the senior journalist Prem Shankar Jha attributes this drift to the financials of political parties.[61] India's founders, he writes, failed to create a system for funding democratic politics that would insulate it from vested interests. The country should have had State funding for elections, but it instead followed the British model in which candidates use their own funds. But, unlike the average British constituency which is 375 square kilometres in size and has 60,000 voters, its counterpart in India spans 6,000 square kilometres on an average and even in 1951, had 300,000 voters. Canvassing is bound to be costlier.*

This could have been corrected, writes Jha, with a constitutional amendment, but in 1968, Indira Gandhi took India in the opposite direction by banning company donations to political parties. The Congress had just lost elections in seven major states and come close to losing nationally. Voters had turned to new parties like Swatantra and Bharatiya Jana Sangh, the forerunner of the BJP. Gandhi intended to deprive this rising challenge of funds. Through the new decree, parties were forced to 'replace a relatively small, and stable, cadre of large donors with a much larger number of widely dispersed donors who were prepared to contribute small sums in cash'. Some parties shut shop. Even the Congress, despite being in power, struggled to raise funds. 'Over time, the sheer difficulty of doing this every few years, has made [parties] extremely reluctant to disturb a financing network once it [has] been established.'

Even after that funding ban was lifted by Rajiv Gandhi, India's political parties continued to run on undeclared funds from the caste-class networks that had emerged to fund them. Slowly, these networks grew into independent power centres and accelerated India's move towards dynastic politics and centralisation of political power. When leaders look for individuals to manage these unaccounted funds central to running parties and campaigns, writes political scientist K.C. Suri in a research paper titled 'Parties Under Pressure', they inevitably turn

---

* In 2014, I met a Shiv Sena MLA in Pune. His campaign had cost him Rs 5 crore. 'If I contest the next time, I will have to spend Rs 10 crore,' he said. In other words, he would have to make at least Rs 15 crore as MLA, that is Rs 3 crore each year or Rs 25 lakh every month. Since then, every time I see crummy public infrastructure, I recall that chat.

toward family members, who are unlikely to oust them.[62] Indeed, almost all parties in India are run by one or two people at the top.

The Congress gets much flak for sticking, limpet-like, to the Gandhis. But other parties are no different. In 2014, the AIADMK announced that Jayalalithaa was elected unopposed because 'no one except her filed the nomination papers'. The previous year, the Shiv Sena declared that all party officials were elected unopposed 'as the number of forms ... received equaled the number of posts'.[63] Even in the BJP, democratic processes exist mainly as ritual, senior journalist Nilanjan Mukhopadhyay wrote in the *Economic Times*. 'The chief's selection is "settled" behind closed doors by a handful of leaders. Any opposition is put down forcefully'.[64]

Parties create a system of clientelism by doling out benefits to supporters in exchange for votes—jobs (Mizoram's autonomous district councils), cash payments and freebies (Odisha, Tamil Nadu) and, as academic Ward Berenschot shows in *Riot Politics*, access to State services.[65] When the State is unhelpful, citizens need intermediaries to intervene on their behalf. In Berenschot's study site in Ahmedabad, textile industry trade unions used to be such an intermediary. They, however, withered away, leaving political parties and their workers as the sole intermediaries in play.

This is far from unique to India. In its early decades, the USA suffered from it too. Where State capacity is weak, politicians find it hard to achieve policy goals and are more likely to rely on clientelism. For the same reason, people too evaluate candidates on their capacity to deliver these goods, given the limited capacity of the State to provide essential services. 'The most modern bureaucracies were those established by authoritarian states in their pursuit of national security,' writes Francis Fukuyama.[66] In contrast, countries that democratised early, before they developed modern administrations, found themselves saddled with clientelism.

Finally, think of as many public institutions in India as you can. Bureaucracies, state pollution control boards, the CBI, the media, human rights commissions, the judiciary, public and private sector companies, cooperatives, banks, panchayats, zilla parishads, municipal corporations and political parties. Now, slot these bodies into those that retain their independence and the ones that do not, an exercise from systems theory. A strong system takes over weaker ones and works them to its gain. Going by that frame, political parties are the most dominant public institutions in India right now. They control, directly or indirectly, almost all the others listed earlier.

———

These four traits, singly and together, torpedo the capacity of political parties in the country to serve as the primary problem-solving agents in a democracy.

Take extractiveness. Unlike voters who have to wait for the next election, funding networks can drop support faster, making parties more responsive to funders than the people.

Relying on clientelism for votes—and in the absence of a public demand to quell the practice[67]—parties care less about improving State capacity.[68] While the State is supposed to serve everyone, clientelism allows parties to ignore communities that do not support them. Berenschot cites the example of Shailesh Makwana, a BJP leader accused of murder in the 2002 Gujarat riots and who subsequently became an MLA. Makwana financed only one project in a Muslim chawl in two years, even though Muslims constituted about 40 per cent of his constituency. As Berenschot writes, 'The message "I am your man" can be made much more convincing with an accompanying "and I am not their man".'[69]

Centralisation removes checks and balances within parties and makes the top leadership unaccountable. A rising trend of chief ministers marginalising MLAs and instead working with hand-picked bureaucrats adds to the unaccountability. In *Chasing His Father's Dreams*, Biswajit Mohanty shows what little say MLAs have in running Odisha: 'The chief minister's office on the third floor of the secretariat building oozes an aura of all-pervasive authority due to an extraordinary centralization of power. ... Babus and politicians talk about this floor in hushed tones. ... Consequently, when Third Floor Bureaucrats advise ministers to sign files without comment, they do.' Ministers, he goes on, are 'also scared to issue written orders for even inconsequential favours. In fact, they rarely expressed their views, so scared were they of Naveen's reaction.'[70]

In Tamil Nadu too, when Jayalalithaa was the chief minister, a senior bureaucrat told me, a clique was running the state.* 'This is a black box. We do not know how decisions get made.'[71] The consequences extend beyond opacity. When bureaucrats are chosen for their loyalty, India sees what retired Gujarat police official R.B. Sreekumar called 'anticipatory sycophancy' in an interview to me. In Tamil Nadu, bureaucrats launched schemes to boost Jayalalithaa's image. In other states, their peers looked away or helped the ruling party make money.

When bureaucrats, not MLAs, define government priorities and responses, administrative concerns like fiscal conservatism replace public needs. 'A bureaucrat who is overpaid and under pressure from politicians, plus worried about the State's fiscal situation, will not want to extend the State,' said Abhijit Sen. In such a construct, keeping staff costs low becomes a greater imperative than development.[†]

Such a State is happier with fixed investments, like new buildings, than running investments, like salaries. This also fits into the

---

* This inner circle comprised Sheela Balakrishnan, adviser to the government, principal secretary K. N. Venkatramanan and director general of police K. Ramanujam. The terms of all three were extended. See: V. Prem Shanker, 'Jaya's Three Commanders: Jayalalithaa's Trusted Aides on Whom She Banks for Her Decisions', *Economic Times* (1 August 2014), economictimes.indiatimes.com/news/politics-and-nation/jayas-three-commanders-jayalalithaas-trusted-aides-on-whom-she-banks-for-her-decisions/articleshow/39384756.cms.

† This is one reason why governments, instead of hiring people to monitor implementation of welfare programmes, opt for tech-fixes like Aadhaar. See: M. Rajshekhar, 'Aadhaar Shows India's Governance Is Susceptible to Poorly Tested Ideas Pushed by Powerful People', *Scroll.in* (27 December 2016), scroll.in/article/825103/aadhaar-shows-indias-governance-is-susceptible-to-poorly-tested-ideas-pushed-by-powerful-people.

politicians' interests. More money is made in construction than in appointments.[72] In states like Odisha, there were well-built PHCs, constructed with the centre's money, with an ambulance parked outside. But there was little staff. Even when the state did hire, it did so on a contractual basis. This resulted in a workforce with starkly different pay scales for the same role, which spawned its own discontent. Such a system creates Kafkaesque outcomes. Leaders use populism to retain power: free bicycles for students but no teachers and compensation when a family member dies but no doctors.

Dominance makes political parties even less accountable as external checks and balances wither away as well. As Todorov writes in *The Inner Enemies of Democracy*, 'Democracy is characterized not only by the mode of institution of its power, or by the goal of its actions, but also by the manner in which power is exercised. The key word here is pluralism, because it is deemed that all powers, however legitimate, should not be handled by the same people or concentrated in the same institutions.'[73]

This decay in India's political parties is a problem. At the best of times, they have a tough task. Issues facing the country are multivariate, and many are such that a state or even the country cannot resolve them on its own. Compounding matters, parties have to find answers while operating under constraints like limited financial capacity. Corrupting political parties, these four traits further diminish India's prospects of resolving challenges.

5

The Absent State

On the day India celebrated Holi, Bajitpur, a village fifteen kilometres to the north of Chhapra in Bihar, saw a murder. The specific details were tragic but far from uncommon. Around half past six that evening in March 2017, after taking a bath, twenty-two-year-old Mohammad Shamsher was sitting outside his house in the village's Muslim tola, or settlement, when he was dragged into the adjoining Hindu locality and stabbed. Rushed first to the government hospital in Chhapra, he died while being moved to the Patna Medical College and Hospital.[1]

Events before and after his stabbing, however, were anything but quotidian. At eight that evening, even as the residents awaited updates, members of the Bajrang Dal, the brawn of the Sangh Parivar, clogged the narrow lane that led into the tola. When I visited two days after the murder, Mohammad Manu, roughly the same age as Shamsher, told me what happened next. 'They were on bikes, carrying swords, shouting slogans like "Attack! Set fire! Break the mosque! Slash the Muslims, these children of Babur!"'

It was the Bajrang Dal's fourth visit in as many years. Its members first showed up in 2013 when some local Hindus wanted to build a temple on government land near the village qabristan, the Muslim graveyard. I learnt this from Manu and about fifteen others—teenagers and men in their early twenties—sitting on the crudely finished brick-and-cement steps leading into their small local mosque. The Bajrang Dal came back when a Muslim boy, whose mother was unwell, objected to the temple playing bhajans loudly. Then the group returned the day the neighbouring town of Garkha saw a religious procession. 'That day,' said Manu, 'about ten motorcycles, each with two riders, swords in their hands, rode down our gali yelling anti-Muslim slogans.' And they came again the night Shamsher died. This time around, the posse could not enter because of police presence. They stood in the lane, shouting out their threats. A terrifying night followed. 'We had the police in front of us and the Bajrang Dal facing them.'

In this tiny tola of no more than twenty-five houses, all pressed up against each other with the mosque in the middle, the air was heavy with apprehension. Its vulnerability was evident. No house here could afford to coat its brick walls with plaster. The mosque too stood unfinished. All around it were larger Hindu villages. 'On the night of the murder and the day after that, no one could eat. Only the children did,' Mohammad Sayeed, Shamsher's uncle, told me. 'Everyone is worried.'

What happened that evening? Sayeed and the young men at the mosque insisted that the dispute that claimed Shamsher was not 'Hindu-Muslim' in nature. I got the same answer in the Hindu quarters of Bajitpur. Yet, the Bajrang Dal had landed up.

Bajitpur illustrated a larger pattern. Chhapra, the crowded, unkempt headquarters of Saran district, had also been seeing a spike in communal tensions since 2014.

Jilani Mobin, the son of a much-respected zilla head with the Rashtriya Janata Dal (RJD)—the late Balaghul Mobin who had died the previous year—was lying on a divan in the small living room of his house, talking to visitors, when I reached his place crossing narrow lanes filled with puddles of sewage. He looked sleep-deprived. The Bajitpur case had kept him up late the previous night.

He had stepped into his father's shoes at a tough time. 'Since 2014, even everyday events have acquired communal hues. Recently, a Muslim boy killed a monkey that had been biting passers-by,' he told me. 'A village headman began saying, "Hanuman has been killed," and a mob quickly took shape.' According to him, Chhapra was seeing two to three such attempts to inflame tensions every month. After each incident, Bajrang Dal volunteers would swiftly converge on the town. 'They come within an hour. There's sloganeering. There are threats to kill us. In each of these groups, we see a few locals, but there are more people from the outside.'

The celebration of festivals in Chhapra, a stronghold of the popular former chief minister Lalu Prasad Yadav's RJD, had also changed. Ram Navami and Mahashivratri were being celebrated more publicly than before, with processions that were jingoistic rather than religious. Internet videos showed hundreds of young men wearing saffron headbands, on bikes, scooters and on foot, brandishing swords and shouting 'Jai Shri Ram' to a soundtrack of techno.[2] Not all their chants were religious. 'Ask for milk and we will give you kheer. Ask for Kashmir and we will cut you down,' goes one. These, said Mobin, were shakti pradarshans, demonstrations of strength, during which too, for every twenty locals, there were eighty from outside Chhapra.

No lives had been lost, yet, when I visited. 'People are getting beaten up. But no one has been killed,' said Mobin. Even in the biggest of these incidents in August 2016, when a video of a Muslim boy desecrating Hindu idols went viral, damage was limited to arson and rioting.[3] The boy's house was attacked and sixty-five shops belonging to Muslims were torched.* 'If controlled in one place, they flared up elsewhere. It was mayhem everywhere.'

The scale of violence might have been small, but the communal pot seemed to be on the boil constantly. Little here was unique to Chhapra either. 'It's the same story in Gopalganj, Bettiah, Motihari, Champaran and Narkatiaganj,' Mobin said. All of these, which lie in Bihar's northwest quadrant, were seeing a sudden uptick in communal violence. I had heard similar narratives in other parts of the state too. Communal tensions were also on the rise in Darbhanga, close to the centre of the state in Araria, in Bihar's northeast; and in Bhagalpur, over to the east on the southern bank of the Ganga. Between 2014 and

---

* One of those, selling footwear, belonged to the Mobins. At last, I thought, a leader who belonged to the same economic strata as his people.

early 2017 alone, the state witnessed no less than seventy communal incidents, each qualitatively different from those that had occurred before.

This was the biggest change I found in Bihar.

———

To understand this shift, 1989 is where we should start.

That year, Bhagalpur, the third biggest town in Bihar as of 2020, saw what were described as the worst Hindu-Muslim riots in India since Partition. These riots connoted a break in the history of post-Independence communal violence in Bihar, social activist Arshad Ajmal told me. 'Riots before and after it have generated very different levels of insecurity for Muslims.' He was sitting in his office in a semi-populated residential colony in Patna, where houses had come up on some plots, while others stood barren, with grass, sewage and garbage gathering in them. From here, the fifty-something director of the Patna-based Al-Khair Charitable Trust, which worked for communal amity, had been observing religious violence return to the state.

Before 1989, he told me, encroachment of qabristans used to be a trigger for riots. As villages grew and needed more land, whenever non-Muslim residents claimed any portion of the graveyards, riots ensued. Another trigger was religious processions. In already tense areas, when Hindus tried to enter Muslim-dominated neighbourhoods or vice versa, processions would catalyse violence. 'Otherwise, processions were mostly filled with women, children and young men. They were a time of celebration. If you look at Chhath Puja processions, these don't provoke tensions even now. Their spirituality hasn't been compromised. That is how all processions used to be,' said Ajmal.[4]

It was a gentler time. 'Ram used to be a loving character in the Muslim psyche, not someone frightening. He was an ideal character. What people used to hear [in processions] was "Sitaram, Sitaram", not "Jai Shri Ram", which is much more martial.' Violence lasted a week at the most, and then the curfew would be lifted. They also did not spread far. 'When there were riots in Rourkela or Jamshedpur, they stayed local. They did not have any effect on Patna.' But the most striking quality was the equanimity with which society absorbed them. 'People might have died, but no one ever felt they would have to leave. Something was there in those societies which gave people this strength. They knew mistakes would happen.'

This conversation with Ajmal revealed an older baseline on community relations. 'After 1947, the India that was created, because of [Jawaharlal] Nehru and freedom fighters like Maulana Azad, reassured Muslims about India. Azad did that by asking, "Where will you go after cutting your roots?" They restored people's belongingness. Till 1989, [despite occasional communal violence], people did not leave their bastis.'

And then, L.K. Advani revived hard-line Hindutva as the BJP's core ideology. The Ram Janmabhoomi campaign, seeking to build a temple for the god Ram at his purported birthplace in Ayodhya, got underway.

On the twenty-second of October in 1989, as the Sangh Parivar was collecting bricks in Bhagalpur for the Ram temple, a procession triggered tensions in Fatehpur village. Two days later, while one procession passed peacefully through Tatarpur, a Muslim-dominated area, after agreeing not to raise provocative slogans, a second one was halted by the locals when some members shouted rallying cries like 'India is for Hindus, Muslims go to Pakistan' and 'Children of Babur, either go to Pakistan or the graveyard'. Over the preceding days, criminal elements, as Warisha Farasat writes, had been spreading rumours that 200 Hindu students living in the town had been killed by Muslims and that 32 Hindu boys had been murdered and their bodies dumped in a well. The state government had ignored these warnings.[5]

In Tatarpur, matters escalated rapidly. Crude bombs were thrown at the Hindu group from a Muslim high school. The procession, in turn, turned into a mob and attacked nearby Muslim settlements. As the news reached other processions, they too went on a rampage. That was the start of the 1989 riots in Bhagalpur. In all this, the local police played a partisan role, not protecting Muslims from the rioters. Muslim settlements were attacked over the next three days.[6] According to official figures, 1,070 people, most of whom were Muslims, were killed and 48,000 displaced. No less than 11,500 houses in 195 villages were destroyed. So were 68 mosques and 20 mazaars, or tombs.[7]

In Chanderi village, children were torn apart with trishuls, axes and swords. Rioters chased old men and women around the village before cutting off their hands and feet and killing them.[8] 'It [the riot] was massive, engulfing villages as far as forty-five kilometres from Bhagalpur. It started as a fight between goondas, but the mobilisation was so strong the rioting spread,' said Ajmal. When asked about this mobilisation, he said, 'Cadre-building. Due to the Shilanyas [the foundation ceremony for the Ram temple], the Right had assembled a cadre in Bihar. Communal mobilisation is a prerequisite for a riot.'

After 1989, the long-established feeling of belongingness of the Muslims came under attack. 'A new narrative began. People began to say this is not the place for Muslims.'

This manufactured sentiment did not get far. In 1990, the great subaltern rebellion of dalits, other oppressed castes and Muslims installed RJD's Lalu Prasad Yadav as Bihar's new chief minister. Wary of cleavages within his social justice plank, he was vigilant about communal violence. Famously, when the Vishva Hindu Parishad (VHP)'s Praveen Togadia landed in Patna, he was sent back. Even more famously, Yadav stopped Advani's rath yatra once it entered Bihar. Every time there was a riot, he would visit the place of violence the very next day. 'In Sitamarhi, he travelled to the district and stayed there for seven days. He went from village to village. With that, he created a lasting impression. A peace returned. Muslims took heart that the government would act.'

Ajmal, however, found himself contemplating a troubling question. 'Could only casteism stop communalism?' Both are ways of slicing and dicing the electorate. If religious parties seek to amass votes by dividing voters along religious lines, caste-based parties stress caste schisms. Between them, India toggles between casteism and communalism. Indeed, under Yadav, Bihar did not see more riots like the Bhagalpur one. The ones it did see, like Nawada (1990) and

Sitamarhi (1992), stayed local. As a corollary, however, as dalits and other marginalised groups gained political power, the state saw a rise in caste violence. Dominant-caste militias like the Ranvir Sena and Sunlight Sena (reminiscent of detergent ads) attacked dalits. In turn, dalits joined Naxal groups that attacked dominant-caste people.[9]

Then the pendulum swung again. In 2005, Bihar eschewed Yadav and voted in Nitish Kumar's Janata Dal (United) (JDU) and the BJP. In the ten years that followed, under the renewed umbrella of a supportive state government, the Right's attempt to remake the electorate resumed.[10] This was when the processes that showed up in Bajitpur, Chhapra, Araria, Darbhanga and elsewhere were set in motion.

These took two forms. First, a newer set of festivals, privately observed till then, began to be celebrated more publicly, like in Chhapra, and were spread out over many days, a deliberate act.[11] Unlike Dussehra, which has to be celebrated on a particular day, Ram Navami or the puja of Santoshi Ma come with greater latitude. This allowed organisers to conduct religious processions in different towns on different days, taking as much as thirty to forty-five days to cover the entire district. Weapons were brandished, and more virulent slogans came in. The cadre, found Ajmal, also travelled from one town to another. This enabled them, despite having small numbers, to project strength. Conducting such processions over a month only added to communal tensions and stoked any local resentment.

Even as these processions terrified Muslims and created the perception of a majoritarian groundswell, a second set of processes began. Sister outfits of the Sangh Parivar expanded in the state, each focusing on sharply defined segments. By 2017, when I reached Bihar, the Jhuggi Jhopdi Sangharsh Morcha was working with the urban poor. The Bajrang Dal was reaching out to mostly dalit youth in western Bihar. Vanvasi Kalyan Ashram was active among the especially disadvantaged dalit communities. Shiv Charchas were spreading across the state, reaching out mostly to dalit women and getting them to congregate every day to worship Shiva.[12] These efforts sought dual goals—reconfiguration of caste relations and creation of a local cadre.

Shiv Charchas, for instance, were brought to Bihar around 2012 by one Harendra 'bhai'. According to Ajay Pandey, the priest of a temple outside Chhapra, Harendra bhai was born into the landowning bhumihar caste in the city of Siwan. 'He and his wife Neelam set up Shiv Charchas in Jharkhand before moving back to Bihar.' Arun Kumar Das, a dalit activist from the nearby village Baniyapur, filled in more gaps when I met him at Mobin's house in Chhapra. Shiv Charchas were not excessively ritualistic. The prayers were in Bhojpuri, the local language, and the deity worshipped was Shiva, who attracts a more syncretic following than the other gods in the Hindu pantheon. 'There's no set pattern of praying,' said Das. Pandey said something similar. 'Sometimes there's bhajan-kirtan [singing of prayers]. There's some katha prasang [narration of religious lore]. It can either be held as per the schedule in the temple, or the women can ask for them to be held. Say someone's boy is unwell, his mother might vow to organise a Shiv Charcha if he got better.'

As the Charchas took root, the organisers found some women to be more enthusiastic than others. 'Such women are given the responsibility to go to other villages as facilitators,' said Rupesh, a human rights activist in Patna. In this way, a local leadership structure took form. Charchas were also an attempt to efface jaati [sub-caste]. 'For the first time, all the women are interacting with each other,' Pandey claimed. 'The feeling of jaati is gone. This is a great transformation.'

But the project had an ideological contradiction at its heart. Pandey opposed jaati but defended the varna system. The latter cleaves Indian society into four broad classes according to occupation and is a central reason for the absence of upward mobility for people in the country. Jaati, on the other hand, refers to subsets of these four classes. What I saw in Chhapra added to my doubts about this 'transformation'. At the Shiv Charcha I witnessed, the women praying in the temple were more affluent than the ones in the nearby hamlet of paswans, a dalit sub-caste, and in the huts behind the temple. Only one woman at the prayer meeting was from these settlements. The rest were from dominant castes. Women in both the settlements baulked at the thought of spending four hours in the middle of the day praying. 'It can run really long,' said one young woman in the paswan tola. 'People might have gone if they didn't have work.'

Her brother, a muscular young man in his twenties, who worked as a watchman, was more aggressive in his scorn. 'When we have ceremonies at our house, brahmins don't eat with us. Then, we are from a different community.' Shiv Charchas, he said, sought to embrace people like him only in the name of religion, not humanity.

———

In 2013, Nitish Kumar abruptly tied up with Lalu Prasad Yadav to form the Mahagathbandhan, a grand anti-Congress, anti-BJP coalition, and the Sangh Parivar's march in the state was stalled. In turn, the right wing amped up its polarisation campaign in the run-up to the state polls in 2015. When it lost, it tried even harder. Till the break between Kumar and the Sangh, Bihar had seen communal mobilisation but no rioting. That changed now.

In 2017, Chhapra had about 1.25 lakh voters, 40 per cent of them Muslims and dalits, who traditionally voted for Yadav's RJD. In the 2015 state elections, the party won six assembly seats in Chhapra, the BJP won two, while the Congress and Kumar's JDU got one each. If the BJP took dalits into its Hindu fold, it would gain at Yadav's cost. The rhetoric against Muslims was part of this strategy. 'We are the enemy because we are with Lalu,' Mobin told me. It was working. Fissures between dalits and Muslims were growing. In Bajitpur, as Mobin said, the six boys named in the police FIR for Shamsher's murder were all dalits.

As scholars like Mohammad Sajjad of Aligarh Muslim University in Uttar Pradesh have detailed, similar patterns of polarisation mapped to the demographics of constituencies were playing out elsewhere in Bihar as well. Between 1995 and 2017, Sajjad told me, the mallah community, classified as scheduled tribe in the state, had consolidated its hold over the floodplains near Vaishali and Muzaffarpur. 'This resulted in conflict between them and the local rajputs [a dominant community].' The BJP was trying to 'foment anti-Muslim feelings amongst [the mallahs] in the hope that they and the rajputs would become one voting bloc'.

At one level, this is a tiredly familiar tale. 'Fascist spontaneity is manipulated spontaneity, organised spontaneity,' the academic Jairus Banaji said in a talk titled 'The Political Culture of Fascism'.[13] More surprisingly, however, even as these processes unfolded, Kumar's government, in alliance with Yadav's JDU, was not reining in even violent actors like the Bajrang Dal. 'I called Lalu-ji and told him, "How long will all this continue? It's very surprising all this is happening in your government,"' said Mobin.

A cynical politics was underway. Spying a chance to be prime minister if neither the Congress nor BJP mustered a majority in the 2014 national polls, Kumar had broken off with the BJP.[14] When Modi swept to power in the centre, the Mahagathbandhan ensured Kumar stayed chief minister in Bihar. But as the BJP's polarising campaign in Bihar gained strength, Kumar knew that his position was becoming shaky. So, he did not crack down the way Yadav had. Instead, he aligned with the BJP in 2017 to protect his perch in the state.

This calculation imposed heavy costs on Muslims. Given Kumar's inaction, opportunistic local actors, not just right-wing leaders, were looking to profit. 'Every village has multiple brokers,' said Sajjad. 'They are affiliated to different political parties. They are all playing their own games.' As I heard in Bajitpur, this could even be to force the Muslims out. In the village, a young Muslim man, who wanted to remain anonymous, told me, 'People in our village say, "If we want, we can kill you. Now you people should leave the village."'

'In most of the state,' as Ajmal told me, 'there's tension, and the air's one of terror.' With the state government being unresponsive, Muslims in Bihar were turning to anyone who would listen to them. For months after that trip to Bajitpur, I got calls from the Muslims there, asking for help, as well as updates on fresh troubles and the slow progress on the

case against Shamsher's killers. By then, I was in Gujarat. I forwarded
their messages to Ajmal and others in Bihar. Gradually, the community
realised my incapacity. The calls petered out.

———

The story of Bihar's decline, from an empire in the third century BCE
to a suzerainty under the Mughals, and from a suzerainty to a colony
under the British, is well known. The state was at its peak under the
Mauryan empire when the Ganga was integral to trading. As the
academic Anand A. Yang writes in *Bazaar India*, 'Vessels capable of
accommodating five hundred merchants were known to ply [the
Ganga] in the ancient period; it served as a conduit for overseas trade,
as goods were carried from Pataliputra [later Patna] and Champa [later
Bhagalpur] out to the seas and onto ports in Sri Lanka and South East
Asia.'[15]

After nearly a 'millennium of brilliance', to use Yang's phrase,
Bihar's lustre faded. Under the Mughals, the centre of power in the
subcontinent shifted from Bihar to the west towards Delhi and Agra,
and then, under the British, to the east towards Calcutta. When the
British entered, Bihar was still a centre of trade in cotton, silk goods,
rice and opium. During the colonial rule, the state's decline deepened.
From the 1830s, the volume of foreign cloth dumped in India rose
steeply. By the 1860s, the value of English goods disposed of in Patna
was, writes Yang, 'in one estimation, at least four times the value
of cloth of native manufacture'. By the 1870s, fabrics from textile
mills of Kanpur and Bombay also reached Bihar. Between these two
developments, Bihar saw deindustrialisation.[16]

Farmers were forced into cash crops like indigo. Compounding
matters, revenue collection from cultivators in Bihar (and in Odisha,
present-day Jharkhand and erstwhile undivided Bengal) was especially
coercive. As the British spread across India, they used three systems
of revenue collection from cultivators—ryotwari, mahalwari and
zamindari. In the first, farmers paid tax to the state government. In the
second, villages were grouped into tax-paying units to pay a combined

sum. Bihar ended up with the third, in which zamindars served as intermediaries between the state and the peasant. They became minor satraps. 'Darbhanga, the largest of the great zamindars, possessed an estate ranging more than twenty-four hundred square miles and an annual income of approximately 4 million rupees, a scale on a par with many a princely state. ... Hathwa's property, although small, nevertheless encompassed 1,365 villages, was inhabited by more than 391,000 people, and produced an annual rental of almost a million rupees,' writes Yang.[17]

When M.K. Gandhi came to Champaran, this was the world he saw, said M.N. Karn, the former director of the A.N. Sinha Institute of Social Sciences. 'There were the landless, and those with hundreds and thousands of bighas. That is how the Indigo Satyagraha started. It was built around social inequality, political discrimination and landlessness.'

These scars ran deep. Even after Independence, Bihar struggled to get to its feet. One reason was the zamindari system, said Shaibal Gupta, the director of Patna's Asian Development Research Institute. In the mahalwari and ryotwari systems, tax to be paid was determined by the State each year, so it had a reason to boost production and productivity. A part of the tax revenues, consequently, went into infrastructure like roads and bridges. It also resulted in the creation of a local bureaucracy for tax planning, collection and administration. In the zamindari system, however, satraps collected a predetermined amount as tax every year, employing coercion, irrespective of droughts and other conditions that affected agricultural production. With predetermined cash flows, the colonial State had no incentive to boost local development. Bihar was left with little infrastructure and weak administrative systems.

The zamindari system also established a link, one that continues to this date, between land ownership and political power. It is one reason why, since Independence, land reforms in Bihar remained a non-starter. In the first forty years after Independence, the state unit of the Congress and the bureaucracy were dominated by the landowning elite—bhumihars, rajputs, thakurs and brahmins. Land redistribution did not take off, despite both peaceful movements like Bhoodan and violent uprisings like Naxalism.

Then, Lalu Prasad Yadav became Bihar's chief minister in 1990. This was when the vast majority of the people got a voice in the state, said D.M. Diwakar, a former director at A.N. Sinha Institute. Under Yadav too, however, material improvements in people's lives, including land reforms, eluded Bihar. One reason was financial. He was in power during the Ninth, Tenth and Eleventh Five-Year Plans—a fifteen-year period when Bihar's allocations from the central government were low.

Yadav compounded matters too. Accusing the bureaucracy (rightly) of bias towards the dominant castes, he weakened it. When he could not find candidates from marginalised castes, positions were left vacant. Analysing government recruitment data for 1996–2006, A. Santhosh Mathew, an IAS officer, and Mick Moore, a professor at the Institute of Development Studies at the University of Sussex, wrote in an academic paper, 'Between 1996 and 2006, only 30,000 new primary school teachers were recruited against the 90,000 that were required. The pupil teacher ratio, which was already 90:1 against the national norm of 40:1, worsened to 122:1.'[18]

Over time, deeper fissures emerged. '[Ram Manohar] Lohia had said, "To break the top, build alliances at the base," said Ajmal. Which meant, in Bihar, numerically dominant other backward castes (OBCs, as classified) like the yadavs needed to join forces with the kurmis, a smaller OBC group, and the dalits. 'But the yadavs became feudal instead. There was progress and peace for the Muslims, but the Hindus were chafing at the lack of development,' explained Ajmal. This was because Lalu Prasad Yadav did not create job reservations for the economically backward classes (EBCs). Land reforms did not happen either; his own caste group of yadavs had massive landholdings in districts like Madhepura.

Divisions grew within the social justice coalition. This is when Kumar, who belongs to the kurmi community, left the coalition and joined hands with the BJP in 2005. His move was welcomed across

Bihar. Even social activists felt that although Bihar had progressed on social justice under Yadav, it now needed to focus on development. Kumar seemed to be the right person for the role. Unlike Yadav, he could not count on support from one numerically powerful caste group. Instead, he had to show tangible improvements to build a base. The only leverage he had, said Diwakar, was development.

Kumar's initial decisions inspired confidence. Unlike Yadav, who weakened the bureaucracy and ruled through informal political networks, Kumar sought to revive the bureaucracy by weakening the political class and operating through a 'core team' of senior IAS officers instead. As the academic Jeffrey Witsoe writes in *Democracy against Development*, even when 'Nitish distributed ministerial posts out of political compulsion, corrupt ministers were teamed with secretaries with honest reputations, constraining the influence of the former'.[19] The bureaucracy, fearful Yadav might return, threw its weight behind Kumar.

That there was more money to spend helped. From 2005 onwards, as India's economy accelerated, central allocations to states rose, including to Bihar. In 2005–2006, the state's total revenue stood at Rs 17,837 crore.[20] By 2016–2017, it stood at Rs 124,608 crore, largely on the back of central allocations.[21] During Kumar's first term between 2005 and 2010, law and order improved. So did power supply. Better roads were built.

Since then, however, Bihar lost the plot again.

———

In 2002, while testing groundwater quality at borewells and handpumps across Bihar, Ashok Ghosh and his colleagues in the Department of Environment and Water Management Studies at Patna's Anugrah Narayan (A.N.) College found astonishingly high levels of arsenic in large swathes of the state. Arsenic concentrations between 10 and 40 parts per billion have been linked to heart disease, impaired lung function and skin lesions like melanosis and keratosis, known precursors to skin cancer. Ghosh and his fellow researchers found concentrations as high as 3,880 parts per billion.[22]

Even at 100 parts per billion, the health impacts are dire. In Tilak Rai ka Hatta, a village in Buxar district, no less than 80 per cent of the handpumps had arsenic in groundwater. Of these, arsenic concentrations in every three out of four pumps were above 100 parts per billion. Studying the morbidity in this village, Arun Kumar, a researcher at the Mahavir Cancer Sansthan, a charitable hospital for cancer treatment in Patna, found that 28 per cent of its households had skin-related problems, 86 per cent suffered from gastritis and 57 per cent from liver-related problems, and 64 per cent experienced a loss of appetite. Some families in the village, like that of Ganesh Rai, had very high mortality. 'Seven members of his family died before crossing fifty-five years of age. One at the age of thirty,' Ranjit Kumar, a member of the research team, said. Going by the descriptions, their ailments might have been cancers, he added. Rai too was suffering from cancer.

Over millennia, arsenopyrite, a conjugate of arsenic and iron, washed down from the Himalayas to settle in the riverbeds of the Gangetic plain. In the 1970s, as the use of motorised pumps for agriculture and handpumps for drinking water expanded—because states like Uttar Pradesh and Bihar encouraged people to drink groundwater instead of surface water, which had high bacterial content—groundwater levels fell. Arsenopyrite came in contact with air and split into arsenic and iron, both of which entered water, crops, animals and humans.[23]

Less fathomable was the Bihar government's response. In 2017, fifteen years after high arsenic levels were reported, there was still no agreement on the scale of the problem. Bihar's Public Health Engineering Department, tasked with supplying clean drinking water to people, pegged the number of affected districts at 13, blocks at 50 and habitations at 1,590. These numbers were challenged by researchers at A.N. College, Bihar Agriculture University and Mahavir Cancer Sansthan. According to them, as many as 37 of Bihar's 38 districts had high arsenic levels. Citing the instance of Bhagalpur, they asserted that the state government was undercounting. While government data said that only 4 blocks of the district's 16 had high arsenic levels, a study by the scientists at the Bihar Agriculture University in Bhagalpur found high levels of arsenic in 13 blocks.[24] According to them, arsenic contamination of groundwater was one of the biggest public health crises facing India, and Bihar, in 2016.

Even in the 1,590 habitations where the state government accepted arsenic contamination, its response was grossly inadequate. In Shahpur, a village near Bhagalpur, high arsenic levels were discovered around 2007. Remedial action followed four years later when a company from Gurgaon installed arsenic filters in the village on a government contract. It was in charge of the filtration unit for four years but never returned after installation, said Tripurari Prasad Singh from Shahpur, who was appointed as the caretaker of the filtration unit. A second company then ran the franchise for eighteen months but did not visit the unit either. A third company was running it when I visited in early 2017. In all this period, filters, which should have been changed every eight to nine months, had not been changed even once.

This was a wider pattern. Nupur Bose, a professor at A.N. College, had seen units where the filtered, processed water had higher arsenic levels than the unprocessed water—filters, entirely saturated, were leaching arsenic. A 2013 study by the Netherlands' Delft University of Technology, echoed her statement. Its researchers, who travelled across Bihar, found that filters showed arsenic levels 'above the legal limit' and flagged the lack of replacement as a reason.[25]

On being asked why these companies were not hauled up, an official in the Public Health Engineering Department in Bhagalpur blamed the state government. In 2010, Bihar centralised these tenders, giving progressively larger tenders for installing and running these units. This tied the hands of the local machinery. The official cited two Gurgaon-based companies that won these tenders in 2009–2010, one for 400 units and the other for 300 units. Both failed to meet their targets. 'The first set up just 80 or 90 filters, while the second set up about 50.'

Yet, it was not easy to penalise them. Local companies could be hauled up by the district office or questioned by the locals. But with the contracts awarded from the state capital, all that the local Engineering

Department could do was write letters to the head office in Patna. 'When we try and suspend a company for not doing its work, it goes to the courts,' said the official. The companies often got a stay order. 'Any hope of transferring the task to another company gets delayed.'*

The larger healthcare crisis went unaddressed. At the driveway of the Mahavir Cancer Sansthan, families, each of whom seemed to have travelled a long way, sat huddled, holding their bags close. The lobby was so crowded it resembled the ticket purchase hall of a train station.

When I reached his room, Ghosh—who, seeing no effort from the state to fight arsenic poisoning, had joined the hospital as its head of research to continue working on the crisis—asked me, 'Does Mahavir look like a general hospital or a cancer speciality hospital?' The Tata Memorial Hospital in Mumbai, one of the most famous cancer treatment facilities in India, gets about 25,000 patients every year from all over India, he said. In contrast, Mahavir got 22,000 patients in 2016 from just Bihar, Uttar Pradesh and Nepal, most of whom were suffering from gall bladder or liver cancers, both associated with arsenic toxicity.

A map of Bihar, colour-coded to show the districts from where a majority of the patients came, hung on the wall behind him. Most patients were from districts with high arsenic concentrations, such as Saran (where Chhapra was), Bhagalpur, Darbhanga and West Champaran. 'Surgery has a two-month waiting list even though the disease might become inoperable by then. We have a children's ward. Mostly leukaemia. Cancer is usually traced back to cigarettes and chewing tobacco. That is what we are told. But these kids could not have consumed tobacco,' said Ghosh.

---

* Attempts to understand why bidding was centralised were unsuccessful. S.N. Mishra, executive engineer for monitoring at the Public Health Engineering Department did not respond to my phone calls seeking a meeting. Emails to K.N.P. Verma, the minister in charge of the department, and Anshuli Arya, the department's principal secretary, also went unanswered.

Bihar government's failure to address issues most central to the lives of its people showed up again and again. At a time when states like Kerala were seeing an epidemiological transition, with the number of infectious diseases falling and chronic non-communicable ailments like diabetes and cancer growing, Bihar was replacing one set of infectious diseases with another. Since 2006, the state's disease burden had seen three large changes. Infectious diseases like kala azar, measles, diphtheria, pertussis and polio were less common by 2017. People, instead, were falling to new diseases like drug-resistant tuberculosis, dengue, chikungunya and Japanese encephalitis. Also, some of the old infectious diseases, like hepatitis A and E, malaria, pneumococcal meningitis and typhoid, were claiming more patients than before.[26]

I picked up the incidence of dengue, rapidly rising in the state since 2012, for a closer look.[27] To spread, an infectious disease needs a pathogen, a vector and a biological tipping point. For dengue, the pathogen is the virus. The vector is *Aedes aegypti*, a mosquito with a distinctive striped abdomen. The tipping point refers to the concentration of pathogens in a body needed to overwhelm its defences. *Aedes aegypti* picks up the virus when it bites people who are infected or are reservoirs, that is, those who are asymptomatic or do not contract the illness but carry the pathogen in their bloodstream. The greater the number of reservoirs in a population, the greater the probability the vector will carry that pathogen.

Since 2010, numbers of *Aedes aegypti* had increased in Bihar. Warmer winters spurred by climate change extended the months during which they remained active. The lack of predictable water supply and poor garbage removal created conditions for it to breed. Bihar's focus on sand flies, in its attempt to eradicate the kala azar disease, or black fever, might have also resulted in mosquitoes taking over the ecological niche of the sand flies.

Many workers from Bihar worked in cities badly affected by dengue, like Delhi. Most of them lived in conditions where *Aedes aegypti* flourished—around stagnant water and discarded garbage and scrap. Underpaid and having to send money home, they did not eat well, which left them vulnerable to the disease. They travelled home for Chhath Puja at the height of the dengue season in November. Returning with them, the pathogen found plentiful vectors and a susceptible population. As we saw in Tamil Nadu, poverty leads to malnourishment, which impairs immunity. Poverty also results in people living in marginal conditions—poor access to water, low quality housing, poor sanitation—in which dengue thrives.

To curb the spread of dengue, which has no vaccine, Bihar had to reduce the numbers of *Aedes aegypti*. Better disease surveillance was also needed. The dengue virus has four serotypes. One or the other ravaged the population each year—immunity for only the previous outbreak built in people, leaving them vulnerable to the other three. The state had to move beyond responding to outbreaks to anticipating them, said Ragini Mishra, the lead epidemiologist at the central government's Integrated Disease Surveillance Programme (IDSP) in Bihar. She pointed out the questions that health authorities should ask: 'What is the vector density before the monsoon? What pathogen is it carrying? Which serotype? And then prepare accordingly.'[28]

In Bhagalpur's Sadar Hospital—a ruined complex of old colonial buildings, some standing and others claimed by undergrowth—was the office for vector-borne diseases. The day I walked into their office, its field staff had fortuitously gathered for a review meeting. In response to my question about their readiness for dengue, they mapped out the department's hierarchy. 'The state medical officer has medical in-charges reporting to them. Each medical in-charge has block health workers and block health in-charges reporting to them.' This system was honeycombed with vacancies. 'There should be eight medical in-charges, but seven have retired and only one remains,' said one fieldworker. 'There used to be sixteen block in-charges, now there are zero. There used to be seventy-one block health workers. Now there are three.'

At the neighbouring zonal office for malaria, tasked with controlling the disease in eight districts, a senior official was sitting in a bare room, in a cabin constructed from plywood sheets and containing nothing but a desk and two chairs. 'We have a sanctioned strength of a hundred and forty people. What we have is six.' He spent most of the chat detailing the politics that had landed him in Bhagalpur, with the occasional lapse into pathos, 'If I could get a car and a computer, I could start doing my work.' He looked quite woebegone.*

As for surveillance, there were two ways of confirming a dengue infection. One was the highly accurate enzyme-linked immunosorbent assay (ELISA) test, which took twenty-four hours and could be conducted only at a laboratory. The other option, an instant diagnostic kit, was not as accurate but gave an answer in just five to ten minutes. Bihar was counting only ELISA-positive tests as confirmed cases, even though only six medical college hospitals in the state conducted them. This automatically brought down the number of confirmed dengue cases.

This was a pattern. In the past, the state government had claimed that the IDSP's estimated number of dengue cases was too high, said Mishra. As things stood, however, even the IDSP was undercounting dengue incidence, because only some private hospitals sent in their data, recording just the lower limit of dengue cases in Bihar. This absence of accurate numbers allowed the state to downplay the threat of dengue.

Bihar could least afford this dereliction. Sadar Hospital, the biggest government hospital in Bhagalpur, did not have a blood bank and could not carry out the platelet infusions required for treating severe cases of dengue. Or take Krah, a settlement abutting the tiny town of Silao, about twelve kilometres from Bihar Sharif, the headquarters of Nalanda district. Even as incidence of past scourges like jaundice, diarrhoea and hepatitis B fell, Krah was racked by dengue in 2015. As many as 100 of those living in this densely packed, predominantly Muslim settlement

---

* I emailed questions about dengue outbreaks and their control to R.K. Mahajan, Bihar's principal secretary for health, and to Madan Prashad Sharma, state programme officer for malaria and other vector-borne diseases in the state. They did not respond.

of about 1,000 families contracted the disease. 'We never had such an outbreak earlier,' Mohammad Ilyas, a young tailor, said.

Walking around, I saw impoverishment. In one house, a middle-aged couple was making beedis, a common source of employment here. It took, they said, twelve hours to roll 1,000 beedis. For every 1,000, they made Rs 100. Plastic waste lay everywhere, on the ground and in clogged drains. Some of the houses, mostly single-storeyed structures with unplastered walls, had come up on low-lying land. With houses clustered close together, rainwater had nowhere to drain. Fetid ponds stood sandwiched between them.

In the absence of sanitation facilities, waste water flowed out of homes and pooled up in vacant plots nearby or merged with stagnant rainwater. Cattle, ducks, hens and goats rooted through this slush. 'No vehicle comes to collect garbage,' said Shafiq Alam, a young man in his early twenties. Local sanitation workers came occasionally but only swept the main street and dumped the waste in the lake on the other side of the settlement.

Things were not always this dire. Till 1982, Krah, bounded on one side by a lake and on the other three by fields, must have been pastoral. It mutated after local communal riots that year. As Muslims flocked together for safety, houses came up wherever there was land. The original village, with its old houses and painted walls, became surrounded by the ghetto. As its population grew, civic amenities did not keep pace.

Back in Silao, with its bhumihar majority, a group of men blamed Krah's outbreak on Muslims. 'People, animals, all live together. There is filth everywhere,' they said. What undermined their thesis was the pile of plastic waste and pool of stagnant water just beyond where they themselves sat.

———

Extraordinary neglect of its people was the central leitmotif of Bihar.

With 160 beds and an inflow of 500 to 600 new patients each day, the district hospital of Muzaffarpur, 71 kilometres north of Patna, should have had 48 full-time doctors and 52 nurses. What it had, in 2017, was less than half of that: 12 full-time doctors, 24 part-time doctors and 28 nurses. The intensive care unit (ICU) should have had 4 doctors but had just 1. The unit for newborn babies, which should have had 4 paediatricians, was also managing with just 1.[29]

Of the 38 districts in the state, 17 had no more than 3 government doctors for every 1 lakh people. The district of Siwan, for instance, had just 1 doctor for every 1 lakh people. The highest, Sheikhpura, had 8 doctors per 1 lakh people—or 1 for every 12,500. As we saw in Punjab, the level prescribed by the WHO is 1 for every 1,000.

Education was the same. Nitish Kumar had made headlines for distributing free cycles to girl students. Less had been written, however, about the acute shortage of schools and teachers in the state. While the Right to Education Act, 2009, mandated student-teacher ratios at 30:1 in primary schools and 35:1 in upper primary, the ratios in Bihar's districts hovered between 43:1 and 96:1 in 2017. 'Things are especially dire in high schools', said educationist Manas Bihari Verma, when we met in Darbhanga. 'In high schools here, you will see between 2,200 and 3,000 students enrolled in the ninth and tenth classes each.'

He traced this astounding number to the centre's Sarva Shiksha Abhiyan scheme, which makes education free and compulsory till the eighth grade. Thanks to its funds, Bihar had lots of middle schools but had not built a commensurate number of high schools. So, after finishing their eighth, students had no choice but to enrol in the few high schools that existed. In 2016, a photograph of students at a school in Vaishali, between Chhapra and Muzaffarpur, being helped to cheat in school exams went viral. The *Indian Express* found that the school had 5 classrooms and 1,700 students.[30]

The education this yielded was a travesty. Some students joined private coaching classes. Others made do with these schools where teachers, trying to cope as well, slotted students into batches that came in on alternate days.

Or take land reforms. Landholdings continued to be badly skewed across Bihar. In Ratnauli, a village near Muzaffarpur, no more than 10 to 20 families of the 1,500 families in the panchayat owned land. The rest eked out a living as sharecroppers. Mabina Begum, a sharecropper in her fifties, had to give the landowner half her harvest, adhia in local parlance. Cultivating ten katthas (a local unit of land approximately equivalent to 3.125 decimal, 100 decimals equalling 1 acre) of land, her eventual income from farming was just Rs 5,000.

This is why land redistribution was vital for Bihar's economically poor. And sure enough, after coming to power, Nitish Kumar constituted a land reforms commission under retired revenue and rural development secretary D. Bandopadhyay, but failed to implement the recommendations the commission made in 2008.[31]

Begum explained why MGNREGA was essential for people like her. 'If we get work for a hundred days, that comes up to Rs 17,700.' But this was where the great paradox of Bihar reared up again. She did not get any work in 2014 and just twenty days in 2015, for which she was yet to be paid as of October 2016, when we met. Things had reached such a point of desperation, said Begum, that even people in their fifties were migrating, to seek work in backbreaking brick kilns.[32]

———

For the longest time, the lack of 'development' in Bihar was blamed on the rule of the dominant castes. When Lalu Prasad Yadav came to power, but 'development' continued to lag, the blame was placed on him, poor state finances and a recalcitrant, weakened bureaucracy. After 2005, however, none of these excuses held. The state's financial condition improved. The bureaucracy supported Kumar. His governments drew support from both dominant castes and OBC communities.[33]

Before the 1990s, political contest in Bihar was between dominant caste groups, like brahmins and bhumihars. Between 1990 and 2005, it turned into a tussle between OBCs and so-called forward castes. Then, starting in 2005, EBC communities allied with so-called forward caste groups to oppose the dominant OBC group of the yadavs. And then, in the 2015 election, the EBC communities joined hands with the yadavs against the so-called forward castes. This trend of increasingly unpredictable caste alliances, said Karn, made the state government even more fearful of alienating anyone. He attributed Kumar's failure on land redistribution to this fear: 'His government does not want to try anything that shatters the status quo.'

This rising fluidity of caste alliances engendered a flux in development policies. According to Rupesh, every party in the state tried to court caste groups that did not support them. 'When Nitish came to power with the BJP, he had the support of the middle castes but not the yadavs. To woo them, social security got an emphasis. The performance of the public distribution system and the condition of anganwadis improved.' This focus, however, shrank once Kumar entered into an alliance with Yadav in 2015. The big question before Kumar in 2017 was how he could get the middle class to vote for him. That is why, when the middle class supported demonetisation, Kumar did too, said Rupesh.

Electoral outcomes do not impact welfare policies in Tamil Nadu, since both the dravidian parties in the state stick to them. State priorities in Bihar, on the other hand, seemed to see-saw more widely.

A second reason the state neglected its poor was the misappropriation of development funds. Like the Northeastern states, Bihar too lacked a large formal economy politicians could extract rents from. Compounding matters, in the last two decades, state politicians saw old cash cows wither. The kidnapping mafias lost ground as law and order improved. The creation of Jharkhand in 2000 took away the coal-bearing areas. More recently, after Bihar introduced prohibition in 2016, cash flows from liquor vends dried up as well; an illicit network, like the one in Gujarat, was yet to establish itself while I was there. In such a context, the biggest economic engine in the state was its government.

MLA candidates had to spend as much as 'Rs 3 crore to Rs 4 crore, sometimes Rs 10 crore', for the elections, said Devendra Nath Ray, chief of the *Dainik Bhaskar* bureau in Muzaffarpur. Some of this money came from businesses owned by politicians. In Patna, they ran several hospitals and malls, and ploughed the proceeds into politics. But the biggest source was the government. Leaders at the panchayat level siphoned off development and welfare funds.[34] Politicians at higher levels made money off appointments, government programmes and construction. Both ate into the capacity of the state and the capital available for development work. 'Delivery [of services] is very hard in Bihar,' agreed an IAS official who did not wish to be identified. 'All professions have been decimated. Whether you take engineering or education or health services, they are all broken.'[35]

In response, Kumar created a command-and-control mechanism called Bihar Vikas Manch in which all departments got targets, and their performance was monitored. With the underlying sclerosis unchanged, this went nowhere. As a former officer on special duty to Yadav told me, 'How does it help to monitor key metrics when the delivery mechanism itself has collapsed?'

———

Like remoras to a whale, narratives cling to every state. They persist long after they stop being true. Punjab is the state of cancer, drugs and the Green Revolution. Tamil Nadu has excellent public delivery of healthcare and education. In Bihar, Nitish Kumar is Sushasan, Good Governance, Babu even though the State remains absent.

This void does not stay empty for long. Society steps in, creating imperfect replacements to the State.

In Bihar, one of them was local strongmen. In *When Crime Pays*, the political scientist Milan Vaishnav writes about Anant Kumar Singh, the leader from the bhumihar caste in Mokama near Patna and bahubali, local strongman. Despite the many criminal cases against him, people voted for Singh as he got their work done in a town where the government functioning was weak.[36]

Then, there were market actors, like the Career Plan Coaching Centre. Located in Geetwas, a small village near Araria in northeastern Bihar, it was not much to look at—a tiny room, perhaps four by three metres, tightly packed with benches and desks, housed in an unplastered brick structure whose other half was a garage. It offered tuitions for students between classes eight and twelve. But, as Gautam Kumar, a mathematics graduate in his mid-twenties who set up the centre after failing to qualify for a junior government post, explained, he did not merely provide supplementary education to students lagging in one or two subjects. He taught the entire school curriculum. Bihar's education landscape was packed with entrepreneurs like Gautam Kumar. They operated a wide range of establishments, from teaching institutions located in village shacks to coaching centres in towns and cities to plush air-conditioned schools.

A third set was non-governmental organisations. The WHO and the union government's IDSP kept tabs on the state's disease burden. The Bill and Melinda Gates Foundation was working on fertility, malnourishment, and IMR and MMR reductions. Others like the international NGOs Engender and Jhpiego worked on family planning and population stabilisation.

The resulting outcome, a matrix of State failure and imperfect alternatives, shaped everyday life in Bihar.[37]

Take the strongmen. Not only did they perform some of the functions the state government should have—from resolving small disputes to ensuring that the administration listened to the locals—but also ensured their caste or region got the resources it wanted, to stay locally dominant. As Witsoe writes, a strong territorial undertone runs through the electoral politics of those who claim to be caste leaders. Control over local resources—'agricultural fields, roads, marketplaces, polling booths or any other place with economic, political or social importance'—is key.[38] In their quest to protect caste interests, however, bahubalis also ended up skewing access to government support and control over local resources in favour of a small number of people. The rule they established was often majoritarian, if not entirely lawless.

As for the market, running on profits, it was limited in scope. It found education attractive but not garbage disposal, as the piles of rotting waste in the towns and cities of Bihar showed. It also delivered uneven results. At the lower end of the education sector, the quality of teaching in the coaching centres was uncertain. At the higher end, where schools followed accredited syllabi, parents complained about high fees. Shyam Jaipuriyar, a BJP member I met in Banka, spent half of his monthly income of Rs 20,000 on school and transport fees for his two children. 'We only manage because we live together as a large family.' Market interventions in healthcare were similarly high-priced, cutting off most residents of the state. The poor who could not access charitable institutions simply died, said Ghosh. Private hospitals were beyond their grasp.

Lacking the profit motive, NGOs worked in areas where markets would not enter. One instance was disease surveillance. These organisations, however, came with their own suboptimalities. They had their priorities and organisational constraints, focusing on chosen metrics, like IMR, over wider improvements in community health. Their reach was limited to the regions they served. In those parts of Bihar where the Bill and Melinda Gates Foundation was active, work on population stabilisation was underway. Not elsewhere. Kala azar was being fought, but dengue was going unchecked.

It was a patchwork quilt of coverage that was anything but uniform across the state.

———

'What are the largest changes you have seen in the last five or seven years?'

In every state, this question had yielded sharp answers. But not in Bihar. The only substantial change I found was the rise in communal tensions. Other processes—migration, State functioning, disease burden—seemed to be playing out as ever.

I found large changes only when I looked at the informal economy. With a small formal economy and a poorly functioning government, Bihar's haats, bazaars and their attendant value chains supported most people. It was here that deeper shifts, in livelihoods and mass sentiment, showed up.

———

Sudhanshu ran a small strip of shop on Patna's busy Boring Road. Ten metres long but just two metres wide, it housed two personal computers, both loaded with music and movies downloaded from the internet. This was his livelihood. Boring Road, with a government college and several dozen coaching centres, was a beehive of students. Every day, several of them visited the shop to purchase the latest movies and songs for their phones and pen drives.

Downloaders like Sudhanshu could be seen all over Bihar. Some sat in shops, like him. Others operated from pushcarts, with batteries hooked to laptops. Yet others sat in village bazaars, with laptops perched on fruit crates. All of them were surrounded by a welter of phone cables. The entertainment they provided was affordable. At Geetvas village market near Araria, downloaders charged Rs 10 for one gigabyte of music. Sudhanshu, who did not look a day older than twenty, charged Rs 10 for a film.

One sleepy afternoon in March, I asked him about the current hit films. He opened a folder on his computer and started clicking on files to highlight their names even as he listed them out: 'Akhil: The Power of Jua, Heart Attack, Businessman 2, Shivam, Viraat, The Return of Raju ...' Each of these was from south India, mostly in Telugu, dubbed into Hindi for audiences in the north. 'We have more people coming here for Tamil and Telugu films than for films in other languages.'

South Indian films had been soaring in popularity across Bihar since 2011.[39] The people in this Hindi heartland identified better with these films rather than Hindi or even Bhojpuri cinema. At Sudhanshu's shop, a class eleven student, preparing for the entrance exam to the Indian Institute of Technology (IIT) at a nearby coaching centre, walked in. His parents lived in Patna, but he stayed in a small rented room near the coaching centre. Apart from attending coaching classes, he studied for six hours every day. When there were no classes, he would watch movies, mostly south Indian films. 'I like these stories. There's one with junior NTR, where the son wants to fulfil his father's dreams,' he said, referring to the popular Telugu actor N.T. Rama Rao Jr. In Tamil Nadu, since 2000, new directors had come up who, reported the *Hindu*, went 'back to their roots in the villages and [told] stories of their land, far away from the culture of studios or sets'.[40] Some of these stories pivoted around vigilante justice. Others talked about aspirations. Yet others talked about caste.

Youngsters in Bihar identified with these stories. Bollywood no longer represented their lives. This trend transcended Bihar. According to Debjeet Sarangi, a Bhubaneswar-based activist working on sustainable farming, youngsters in Odisha too were gravitating towards hyper-violent films from the south. 'The local youth have a lot of anger about the lack of opportunities in their life,' he said. Later, on reaching Ahmedabad, I asked the two young men working at my hotel about the movies they watched.

'Madrasi,' they said.

———

Octogenarians Lallan Singh and Ganesh Singh had seen the main bazaar of Udhwantpur, a village eight kilometres south of Ara town in western Bihar, change beyond recognition since 2005. Some of the old-timers—a farm equipment workshop, a grocer, a sweet shop—were still around. But many more new businesses had come up: three chemists, as many beauty parlours, a video-photography store, a cell phone repair shop and another selling recharge vouchers, a banking correspondent, and a store each for footwear and garments.[41] The market's caste composition had changed too. 'On this street, along with baniyas, you now have shops of rajputs, yadavs, brahmins and backward caste people,' the two octogenarians, one retired from the army, the other a farmer, both sitting at the halwai's, told me.

Apart from these, there were two other trends, which I had also been told about in Tamil Nadu. One, there was a striking hyper-specialisation. Some shops only sold phones, others only repaired them, or only sold recharge vouchers or music-and-movie downloads. There were no overlaps. Second, most of these new establishments were barely profitable. Most sold products made elsewhere. All they earned was the 'retailer margin' and made about Rs 5,000–Rs 8,000 a month. The halwai business was more profitable than many of these new businesses, said the octogenarians.

These changes are clues to deeper changes playing out not just in Bihar but across India. The first, obviously, is unemployment, which pushes people towards smaller and smaller economic niches despite the meagre earnings they provide. The second is reverse migration. Salaries of migrant workers fall as they age. Tired of living on small sums away from home, most of them head back by the time they are forty, intending to set up a small shop or start some other business.*

Their return is also facilitated by India's turn towards cash-based welfare programmes. If these work well, they are a source of income closer home. Even if they do not work well, said Sanjay Paswan, a senior leader in the Bihar unit of the BJP and a lecturer on labour relations at Patna University, money still trickles down. Take MGNREGA, he said. Village headmen retained villagers' job cards and fraudulently claimed their wages. But a part of this money still went to the job-card holder, who, assured of getting Rs 1,000 from here would pick up some other work to complement it, said Paswan.

Apart from MGNREGA, Paswan pointed out that Bihar ran about twenty welfare schemes that gave out cash, like pensions, Indira Awaas Yojana and scholarships. Together, he said, these schemes blunted the marginal economics of the livelihoods that awaited them back home. If the average monthly income was Rs 6,000, these schemes together might bring in another 20 per cent or so, he added. Caste and local politics played a determining role here. 'About 10 per cent of the people

---

* When I met Vijay Singh Ballia in Sriperumbudur, he was working as a warden in a garment factory. His monthly income was Rs 8,000. Fatigued by a life that forced him to subsist on Rs 3,000 and his family on the remaining Rs 5,000, he was thinking of returning to Uttar Pradesh and starting some small business there. Even if it netted him just Rs 6,000, it would still mean more cash in hand for his family.

in the village are still deprived of all schemes. They belong to the most marginalised communities,' said Paswan.

———

Overnight, on 8 November 2016, Narendra Modi denotified Rs 500 and Rs 1,000 notes as legal tender. It was an extraordinary moment. India, all of a sudden, lost no less than 86 per cent of all legal tender.

I put aside my work on arsenic contamination and queued before ATMs every day for a week, coaxing out Rs 2,000 at a time, building up a cash reserve I could travel with. And then, I did two transects across the state. The first dropped southwards, from Raxaul, on India's border with Nepal, to Bettiah and Gopalganj, before cutting east towards Darbhanga. I returned from there to Patna, before travelling further south, towards Gaya, Bodh Gaya and Nalanda. A second trip took me east again towards Bhagalpur and the town of Banka, close to the border with Jharkhand. These trips gave me a window seat to what economists confirmed as well—demonetisation dealt a bigger blow to incomes, investments and livelihoods in the informal economy than to black money.

In Bihar, given the overriding centrality of the informal economy in everyday life, the blow fell even harder. By the tenth, the price of cauliflowers in Bettiah, where Gandhi had stayed during the Champaran Satyagraha, crashed from Rs 12 a kilo to Rs 1.* At the Maroofganj mandi, which supplied to shopkeepers across Patna, both supply and demand for cooking oil, spices, rice, wheat and pulses

---

* Families, even those with savings in banks, could not withdraw. To stretch the cash with them, they slashed spending. As prices collapsed in the mandi, both traders and farmers were hit. Mostly sharecroppers, the latter had just finished the kharif harvest and now needed to sow the rabi. With little money coming in, they found themselves borrowing and sowing on less land than usual. See: M. Rajshekhar, 'Cauliflower Sells for Rs One a Kilo in One Bihar Market as Demonetisation Depresses Demand', *Scroll.in* (30 November 2016), scroll.in/article/822860/cauliflower-sells-for-rs-one-a-kilo-in-bihar-as-demonetisation-depresses-demand.

declined sharply a week after the announcement. But oddly, the prices did not budge. The lack of liquidity was to blame. In the absence of cash, nobody could read this market, and it froze at the last price it knew.[42] Neither the traders at the mandi nor I had ever seen anything like this before. Businesspeople fed their families with painfully accumulated working capital. Families ate into their savings, or just ate less. One businessperson told me: 'I now have less than what I had started my business with.'[43]

I met people by day and watched television news by night. Much of this suffering went unreported. Media motormouths and smug economists instead informed us that all great social change comes at some cost. As Eugene Lyons writes about the defenders of Stalinist Russia in *Assignment in Utopia*, their sophistry did not distinguish 'between a natural evolutionary economic process developing inevitably through decades and centuries, and an arbitrary decision by a handful of men, compressed into a few months of terror'.[44]

The media also elided over the simple fact that illicit monies in India were held, not as cash under the mattress, but in land, real estate, gold, equities and offshore accounts—all of which remained untouched. Instead, the rich easily swapped the old notes for new ones. In Tamil Nadu, a CBI raid on sand miner Sekar Reddy revealed Rs 170 crore in new notes.[45] Shortly afterwards, income tax authorities found Rs 30 lakh in new notes and five kilos of gold in the house of Tamil Nadu chief secretary, P. Rama Mohana Rao.[46] The poor, on the other hand, afraid their meagre cash savings would turn worthless, queued up for hours at banks, trying to exchange those notes.

———

Bihar, the fifth state in this hitchhiker's guide to democratic palsy, faced complex challenges. Dengue was one instance. But not all its causes, like the warming of winters which let *Aedes aegypti* live around the year, were in the state government's control.

We saw this earlier. Fish stocks were falling in Tamil Nadu because sea surface temperatures were rising globally. Odisha's ore export boom ended when the US sub-prime crisis hit China. The centre's decision to redirect payments to state treasuries hurt Mizoram's HIV programme. And yet, none of these states took even the adaptive or mitigative steps they could. Tamil Nadu could have stopped the flow of effluents into the sea. Odisha could have boosted its steel sector. Punjab could have strengthened farm extension. Bihar too could have strengthened disease surveillance.

A reason for this inaction lies in the four traits—centralisation, extractiveness, dominance and clientelism—that reduce political parties into weak problem-solving agents. Another lies in fiscal constraints. In the last two decades, the economic independence of states has shrunk. They have slowly yielded their sources of revenue to the centre, the GST being the latest instance. At the same time, not only do payments from the centre, as we saw in Mizoram, increasingly come with fixed uses, but also curbs on state borrowings are rising. This is about fiscal deficit control, said Abhijit Sen. 'Importing more goods than it exports, India is very dependent on foreign inflows. Given this continuing balance of payments crisis and given that neither the Reserve Bank of India nor the centre want destabilisation of the rupee, they keep a tight leash on fiscal deficits, at the centre and at the states, mostly by deciding whether to help a state borrow or not.'

Effectively, every state has a set financial space in which its government has to operate. India sticks to keeping the deficit low even at the cost of hurting the people. State debt, as Laura Bear writes in *Navigating Austerity,* has ethical, political and fiscal dimensions.[47] How did it come to be seen as a purely technical question of monetary debt? One reason is a bureaucrat-led State. As Odisha showed, it privileges fiscal discipline above developmental needs.

One way to escape this bind is to boost union and state revenues. This, however, comes with its own complications. We no longer live in a time where labour and capital are tied to the land, with the State dominating both. Capital is highly mobile now, which has left labour facing a world of uncertain employment and governments bending backwards to attract capital.

An outcome of this is an avalanche of decisions that prioritise investments over people. This is why India continues to weaken her pollution and labour laws and why even cash-strapped states give out tax holidays.

Which brings us to the crisis facing political parties.

———

Till recently, as the sociologist Zygmunt Bauman writes in *Liquid Modernity*, the legitimacy of governments rested on their role in fighting the uncertainty haunting their subjects.[48] But now, as capital slips out of the State's control and pushes workers into uncertain lives, 'the divorce between power (the ability to see things done) and politics (the capacity to decide what things are to be done)', Bauman and the political scientist Leonidas Donskis write in *Moral Blindness*, has resulted in 'a ludicrous, degrading and all too manifest incapacity of nation-state politics to perform its function'.[49]

As they fail to perform their role, nation-states face a crisis of legitimacy. And country after country sees a rise in 'political apathy, loss of political interest and commitment, and a massive retreat of the population from ... institutionalised politics'.[50] In India too, opinion polls show a dipping taste for democracy and rising preference for autocratic or military rule. A 2017 survey by Pew Research Centre, for instance, found that 55 per cent of the people in the country wanted an autocrat.[51]

As this disenchantment deepens, it is not just citizens who run the risk of ending up with something worse, political parties feel threatened too. Electoral democracy is how they and their funding networks access power. As disillusionment grows, they might find themselves voted out by political rivals, or replaced by strongmen, religious leaders or fresh political formations. And so, moving from state to state, I saw five ways in which parties tried to retain legitimacy—denial, diversion, cultism, elections and endorsements.

The first, denial. States manipulate data to hide problems. Bihar did not count dengue cases and underplayed the arsenic crisis. Tamil Nadu fudged exam results and focused on IMR and MMR improvements to suggest that its people were healthier than before. This is a wider pattern. India also fudges its forest cover numbers,[52] GDP numbers[53] and job creation numbers.[54]

The second, diversion, takes two forms. Political leaders blame others for any crisis. As Tamil Nadu's water crisis worsened, instead of reining in sand mining, pollution and rampant groundwater extraction, the state blamed neighbouring Karnataka and Kerala for not giving it enough water from interstate rivers.[55] At other times, politicians distract people with a different crisis, one they can pretend to address. The state 'has to seek other, non-economic varieties of vulnerability and uncertainty on which to rest its legitimacy,' as Bauman and Donskis write. 'That alternative seems to have been located (first and most spectacularly, but by no means exclusively, by the US administration) in the issue of personal safety: whether they arise from pandemics, unhealthy diets, criminal activities, anti-social conduct by the "underclass", or most recently, "global terrorism".'[56]

In Mizoram's autonomous district councils, leaders blamed Mizos for the underfunding. In Tamil Nadu, S. Ramadoss of PMK incited vanniyars against dalits. In Bihar, the BJP was trying to turn specific communities against Muslims. In 2019, Amit Shah, the union home minister, called Bangladeshi migrants 'termites' and used the NRC in Assam—which has the power to determine whether a person is a citizen of India or not—to shore up legitimacy for the BJP. These are dangerous games. As Vasily Grossman writes in *Life And Fate*, 'When people are to be slaughtered en masse, the local population is not immediately gripped by a bloodthirsty hatred of the old men, women and children who are to be destroyed.'[57]

Morality, or wanting to be fair, is a more universal trait than we recognise. As the primatologist Robert Sapolsky writes in *Behave*, other species too show a sense of justice. Human morality certainly runs deeper than our cultural institutions, laws and sermons.[58] Which in turn means that people have to be taught to hate.

This is a scientific process. The human brain has a propensity to cleave people into 'Us/Them' categories and is all too willing to label 'Others' with homogenous, unappealing qualities. It also, as Sapolsky writes, links visceral and moral disgust bi-directionally. Bite into rancid food, and the insula, the part of the brain which processes 'gustatory disgust', lights up.[59] The insula also lights up when we think of something we find morally disgusting—like violations of social norms or individuals stigmatised in a society. 'There are numerous ways to get someone to think an "Other" is so different that they barely count as human. But as propagandists and ideologues have long known, if you want to get someone to *feel* that an Other hardly counts as human, there's only one way to do it—engage the insula. And the surest way to do that is through metaphor.'[60] Metaphors that strip people of their individuality and thus facilitate moral disengagement.*

The third, leadership cults. Political parties idealise their leader and describe them in heroic and worshipful terms. This image, inevitably exaggerated, is projected through a party's communications. This cult of the leader, normally seen in authoritarian regimes, is quite prominent in India. In Odisha, Naveen Patnaik is projected as a reluctant politician and as Mr Clean. J. Jayalalithaa is Puratchi Thailavi, Revolutionary Leader, or simply Amma. Nitish Kumar is Sushasan Babu. Right from his days as a chief minister, Narendra Modi styled himself as a no-nonsense leader out to deliver 'development'. Days after announcing

---

* It is an explanation that closely mirrors Victor Klemperer's reason for the rise of Nazism. A linguistic professor of Jewish descent living in Dresden during the Nazi years, Klemperer writes that speeches by Adolf Hitler and Joseph Goebbels were not the most powerful Hitlerian propaganda tools. The masses either did not understand a lot of these or were bored with the endless repetitions in the speeches. Nazism, instead, permeated German society through words, idioms and sentences, structures repeated a million times and accepted mechanically without conscious thought. 'Words can be like tiny doses of arsenic: they are swallowed unnoticed, appear to have no effect, and then after a little time the toxic reaction sets in.' See: Victor Klemperer, *The Language of the Third Reich* (London: The Athlone Press, 2000), 15–16.

demonetisation, Modi came on television to say he had taken on people who might not let him live and that if he was proved wrong after fifty days, he should be hung. Bauman again comes to mind:

> With the issue of the credibility of people in public view replacing the consideration of what the business of politics is and ought to be; with the vision of a good and just society all but absent from the public discourse ... people become the passive spectators to a political personage who offers them his intentions, his sentiments, rather than his acts, for their consumption.[61]

Centralisation is one reason for the rise of leadership cults. In the absence of strong local leaders, the high command has to win elections by itself. Another factor is the sycophancy that concentration of power spawns. Yet another is the desperation of the masses. Describing the widespread economic distress in the 1960s and 1970s in Tamil Nadu, which pulled people towards M.G.R, the social scientist M.S.S. Pandian quotes Eric Hobsbawm in *The Image Trap*, 'Men can live without justice, and generally must, but they cannot live without hope.'[62] The media plays a role too. Instead of seeing politics as processes and issues, as Jacob Hacker and Paul Pierson write in *Winner-Take-All Politics*, it 'endlessly analyzes the great personalities who dot the political landscape, their psychologies and strategic acumen, their personal appeal and personnae, their eloquence and gaffes'.[63]

The fourth, elections. India's political parties focus on winning elections—not just union or state polls but also municipal, zilla and panchayat polls—and use the favourable outcomes to suggest unswaying voter support for policies. Along the way, we see an outcome where rising State incompetence coexists with evermore sophisticated constituency-level electoral strategies and rising electoral roll manipulation.[64] The news media plays along, depicting even by-polls as referendums on the central leadership. This, again, is a larger slide. For the media, write Hacker and Pierson, 'governing often seems like something that happens in the off-season. Even then, most of the conversation focuses on how [a government decision] sets things up for the next election.'[65]

The fifth, endorsements from religious leaders, media and judiciary. As we saw in Punjab, politicians forge links with religious leaders. Gurmeet Ram Rahim supported the Congress in 2007, and then the BJP in 2014, in both the Haryana and Lok Sabha polls. That year, Kailash Vijayvargiya, in charge of the BJP's election for Haryana, took forty-four candidates of his party to seek Rahim's blessings.[66] In India, religious leaders like Jaggi Vasudev have defended demonetisation and the Citizenship Amendment Act. This pursuit of endorsements extends beyond new-age gurus. Four of the seven trustees of Gujarat's Somnath temple are BJP leaders— Narendra Modi, L.K. Advani, Amit Shah and Keshubhai Patel.

These are symbiotic arrangements. Religious bodies need political support. Religious sects looking to grow across the world, for instance, need foreign policy support. Also, as they grow, sects are likely to have fissures and factions. When a guru dies, competing factions need powerful friends to gain control.[67] Little here is unique to India. In Sri Lanka, some Buddhist monks and the government had a similar symbiotic arrangement. In return for support, these monks defended the State attacks on the Tamil minority.[68]

Similarly, as at the time of demonetisation, the media tries to manufacture support for government policies. Or, as in Odisha, distracts people from more pressing issues. As this book went to press, Bihar's election dates were announced. The media, however, ignored more pressing issues to focus instead on the politics between Nitish Kumar and the BJP, and the suicide of a Bollywood actor from the state.

As for the courts, one instance should suffice: the Supreme Court refuses to schedule habeas corpus hearings for Kashmir.

———

Each of these responses compounds India's problems. Data fudging blinds us to reality. Diversion deepens fissures in the country and pushes us closer to communal, caste and ethnic conflagrations.

Cultism accentuates political centralisation, weakens party democracy and sets the stage for demagogues to come to power. As Ambedkar warned in a speech to the Constituent Assembly: 'Bhakti, in religion, may be a road to salvation of the soul. But in politics, Bhakti or hero-worship, is a sure road to degradation and to eventual dictatorship.'[69]

Seeking legitimacy from elections not only keeps parties in constant campaign mode but also reinforces the short-term bias built into democratic politics in which politicians are always under pressure to show quick results. This, coupled with weakening State capacity, pushes politicians towards populist schemes that do not demand a lot from the State. In Tamil Nadu, for instance, compared to the messy politics involved in reducing caste and gender discrimination, Amma Baby Kits were a cinch.

Growing links between politicians and religious bodies create their own problems. As the illegalities of the self-proclaimed godpersons grew, politicians helped ward off serious crime investigations against these religious leaders.[70] Similarly, when the media starts legitimising the government, not only does its watchdog function take a pounding, but also consensual reality suffers. People, increasingly unsure what to believe in, replace understanding with conspiracy theories and blind trust in the leader.

This leaves one last question, as I move to Gujarat: how do people respond to State failure?

6

The State That Chose Majoritarianism

I was borne along by a flood of memories. Waiting for the rain to stop at Damparengpui. A truck standing outside a garishly painted house in Keonjhar. A former factory owner pushing a bicycle laden with phenyl through an emptying industrial zone in Ludhiana. A sand mining quarry outside Villupuram. A moonlit night at a petrol pump outside Pathankot, trucks laden with stones slowly moving in the distance. A Shiv Charcha in a small temple outside Chhapra.

The train crossed Delhi's borders. Gujarat, the next day. An old fear, of not comprehending what I was seeing, was back. I was on the move constantly, collecting information faster than I could absorb. What was I missing in this blur of movement?

I flipped back to an early passage in J.D. Taylor's *Island Story*, his account of cycling around pre-Brexit Britain, and read it again.

> One of the roots of political idealism is a moral demand to do more, think more, be a better person. Its demands take the form of *this is what we need to do* to get from A (now) to B (a better world), be it through consciousness-raising, grassroots democratic participation, multitudinal insurrection, counter-hegemonic strategic optimism … whatever. A more frank way of posing the problem is to consider what stops people getting from A to B. What features of the terrain block passage, inhibit desire, forbid trespass?[1]

Taylor had pedalled out to understand why despite 'an economic downturn, worsening living standards and welfare and wage cuts, are so many voting conservatively, thinking pessimistically, acquiescing in all this?' I had set out on a quest too. Setting out with an inchoate urge to refamiliarise myself with India, I had found larger questions. None of the states I had travelled in worked for the people. In each, the practice of democracy was faltering. Hardest to understand was our loss of collective purpose. Old worldviews had been discarded without a newer common direction replacing them. What we had, instead, was the buzzword of development, thrown around like confetti by politicians and people alike, but never elaborated into a vision of the people, the society we want to become.

Later that night, my thoughts turned to the state that remained, Gujarat, and how different it was from the other industrialised state in my roster, Tamil Nadu. Both had different equations between business and politics. In Tamil Nadu, politics had always been in the driving seat. Not so in Gujarat. At one time, if its telia rajas, or edible-oil barons, had been powerful enough to choose chief ministers, in more recent times, some of India's biggest business houses have been operating from here. The logic underpinning their politics was different too. The dravidian parties agreed on welfarism, and even when they drifted, did so into populism. In contrast, Gujarat had majoritarianism. Taking the state's landslide mandate for Narendra Modi after the 2002 riots as the moment Gujarat embraced majoritarianism, a conservative milestone, it had been so for fifteen years when I was on my way there. As the rest of India weighed the idea of a Hindu Rashtra, this trip to Gujarat was a chance to see life in a society that had already made its choice.

For the first time in this reporting project, I was travelling with a couple of pre-configured questions. Rhapsodies about the Gujarat Model were a big reason India voted for Modi in the 2014 general elections. In the months before the elections, WhatsApp forwards with photos of the Sabarmati riverfront in Ahmedabad, the state's broad highways and more, juxtaposed with similar projects in Europe, had done the rounds. In these images, Gujarat seemed to have leap-frogged the rest of the country. The mechanics of this transformation, however, were poorly understood. Most accounts were celebratory rather than analytical, drowning out criticisms of the state's unimpressive record in the human development index (HDI). However, Gujarat repeatedly returned Modi to power. Perhaps progress in the state needed a closer look. The state had, for instance, set up a cell for climate change, as opposed to Punjab and Tamil Nadu, which, despite climate change wreaking havoc on everyday life, were blank on adaptation and mitigation.

Local governance, missing from my reportage till now, would be one more area to examine in Gujarat. Recent events in the state had added a couple more questions. Since 2015, patidars, a landowning caste counted amongst the BJP's supporters, had repeatedly taken to the streets complaining about shrinking economic opportunities and demanding reservations. It was a demand that sat poorly with the state's claims of 6 per cent–7 per cent growth in agriculture.[2] There was also rising caste violence, as in Una, a town in western Gujarat, where seven members of a dalit family were beaten up by cow vigilantes in July 2016.

I wondered how these questions themselves would fare. This was a country where politicians 'borrowed' documents to win contracts; MLAs paid stipends to people in their constituencies; candidates rejected in assembly polls ruled as ever; health departments simultaneously delivered three different outcomes; and 1,500 students enrolled in one classroom. I would probably hear about changes and processes wilder than I could imagine.

———

Rajesh Mehra moved to Surat in 2013. A trader in the 'saree-blouse' business, he used to buy thread from Silvassa in Dadra and Nagar Haveli, get blouses stitched back home in Amritsar and ship them out to wholesalers who, in turn, sold them to retailers across India. When this business model slipped into losses as cheaper blouse-making units came up in Surat, Mehra, in his mid-forties, left his family behind and shifted to Surat, but the thread went to Amritsar as before. Mehra

hoped his new perch, a shop in the basement of an old textile market
near Ratan cinema, would help him better market his wares.

Surat, midway between Ahmedabad and Mumbai, was India's
largest producer of synthetic fabrics. As of 2017, no less than 40 per
cent of all man-made fabrics produced in India came from here. It
especially dominated the polyester saree market. Buy one anywhere in
India, in the glitziest metropolitan mall or a rural market, and, even
today, the chances are it would be from Surat.

Four years after the move, Mehra was still struggling to find his
feet—earning Rs 32,000 in a good month, keeping Rs 10,000 for his
expenses in Surat, sending Rs 10,000 to his family in Amritsar and
another Rs 10,000 back to his village—and beside himself with worry.
Till 2017, Indian companies paid a welter of taxes, like VAT, sales tax
and excise duty. When we met in June 2017, less than a month remained
before all these taxes would be replaced by the GST. Levied on every
unit in a value chain, GST intended to curtail tax avoidance.

The whole cluster was panicking. No more than twenty-five firms
here were what business reporters call vertically integrated units.
Surat's Laxmipati Sarees, for instance, bought polyester yarn from
outside but did the weaving, printing and post-production work, like
embroidery, in-house. The rest resembled a weaving firm called VK
Tex. Working out of a long, narrow building in the Pandesara industrial
area outside Surat, it only made grey fabric, rough weave yet to be
coloured and printed. Surat had tens of thousands of such firms. Most
had an annual turnover between Rs 1 crore and Rs 5 crore. Small in
size, they focused on no more than one or two of the stages through
which yarn becomes garment. Running about 7.5 lakh looms, these
clustered around Surat's 65,000 traders. Working out of the 250 or so
textile markets in the city, the traders collected orders from wholesalers
and got garments made, guiding commissions through the city's thicket
of weavers, printers, processors, embroiders and transporters.

Under GST, this disaggregated value chain seemed likely to pay as
much as 20 per cent more tax than its vertically integrated counterparts.
Bigger companies bought raw material and equipment at lower rates,

spreading their administrative and manufacturing costs over a larger volume of production. In contrast, the companies in the disaggregated value chain lacked economies of scale. Also, as service providers, its traders would now have to pay GST. As a result, under this new tax regime, while the larger firms would only pay GST at the time of buying raw materials, the informal economy chain would be taxed every time a consignment changed hands. These factors, along with doubts on whether they could meet the tax's compliance requirements, made small firms fear for their viability.[3]

Industry representatives were feverishly trying to meet the union government. Workers and owners were marching in the streets. Some traders had left the business. Mehra himself was surrounded by unsold stock worth Rs 3 to Rs 4 lakh, a consignment for which he did not have bills. Wholesalers, unwilling to pay the full GST once the new tax regime would kick in, were not buying. He had run out of ideas. 'I can't go back. I have a family to maintain. I will have to look for a job here.' At one point during our conversation, he distractedly asked if it was easy to learn English. A little later, his gallows humour surfaced. 'Or I can go back home, and we can all eat [free meals] at the gurudwara's langar.'

The national media arrived. Surat hit headlines day after day. Some reports projected these businesspeople as victims of a rushed law. Others denounced them as habitual tax evaders criticising a good law. In this turmoil, a deeper shift was missed. Even before the GST, Surat was already in trouble. Competitive advantage had been leaving its micro, small and medium businesses to eddy around larger units.[4]

Through the 1980s, Surat's designs sold well for as long as four years in the market before starting to taper downwards. By the mid-1990s, this life cycle was shrinking. Customers gravitated to new products like polyester sarees that were half a metre longer than the standard five metres. 'The longer the saree, the more the pleats,' explained Sanjay Saraogi, the forty-six-year-old managing director of Laxmipati Sarees. Costlier sarees were selling better. Surat used to price sarees at Rs 80– Rs 400. Then, Saraogi found that sales of his more expensive sarees, priced at Rs 1,000–Rs 2,000, were growing faster than before.

'Till the 1980s,' he said, 'sarees were mostly to cover the body. Women didn't see them as fashion and, in any case, had a limited budget.' By the 1990s, both purchasing power and customer tastes were changing. There was also a long overdue correction in who the purchaser was. 'Before the 1990s, men used to buy sarees for women. It is when women started stepping out to buy, that demand for choices grew.' Technology played a role too. As shuttle-less looms like inkjets and waterjets came in, customers' expectations of quality and design rose beyond what powerlooms could deliver.

Surat was slow to respond. Its traders and wholesalers did not pick up these signals. Between 1990 and 2000, the city also saw businesspeople from Kathiawar in Gujarat's Saurashtra region, whose returns from mainstays like diamond trade and farming were falling, enter its textile trade. Better capitalised, these new entrepreneurs had a hundred looms or more, while most weaving units in Surat had no more than five or six. Running on greater scale, these units produced at lower costs. They, along with rising imports of man-made fabric from China, put pressure on smaller units, which could neither easily scale up and reduce their manufacturing costs nor invest in innovation and new machines to be competitive.

Inkjets and waterjets were expensive. With innovation too, the dice were loaded in favour of big firms. They could spot consumer trends faster. Saraogi had placed 450 salesmen in the stores of his biggest wholesalers. Selling only Laxmipati Sarees to the retailers who came to place orders, they WhatsApped real-time information on market preferences back to the head office. 'We have a thermometer for the whole of India,' he said.

The outcome was a double movement. On the one hand, powered by booming consumer demand, Surat grew immensely between 1990 and 2006. In 1990, the cluster had no more than ten or eleven textile markets. In the next sixteen years, pulling away business from cities like Kolkata, it added another two hundred and forty. Within the city too, it was a time of intense competition. 'Even salesmen working in companies took shops on rent and used them to branch out on their own,' he said.

At the same time, its weakest units, like small powerlooms running out of central Surat, began dying out. Gradually, the minimum scale required for survival rose. A manufacturer told me, 'At one time, twelve powerlooms made for a viable business. Then, a business with five to six waterjets was considered viable. Right now, units with eight to twelve waterjets are viable. The new scale of viability will be minimum twelve to thirty-six looms.'

In 2017, powerlooms still ran in the industrial estates that surrounded Surat but had fallen silent inside the city. Here, they mostly showed up in the shops of scrap dealers. The rooms and sheds housing them had been repurposed—some were taken over by other textile trades like embroidery, while others served as parking spaces for two-wheelers. The communities operating these looms left the trade. Moving around in Surat, I ran into weavers who now drove autorickshaws or lived off the income from renting out their premises.

This was not just market forces at work. In 2015, as imports of Chinese man-made fabric began rising, the local industry association, the Surat Chamber of Commerce, asked the union government to impose anti-dumping duties. Its request was ignored. India, however, did levy these on the import of polyester chips and yarn. As the journalist Paranjoy Guha Thakurta wrote in the *Economic and Political Weekly*,

> In the teeth of opposition from the polyester using industry in India, the central government on 25 July [2014] imposed an anti-dumping duty on imports of purified terephthalic acid (PTA), a critical intermediate that is used in the production of various polyester products. This decision will almost entirely benefit only one corporate entity, that is, RIL [Reliance India Ltd].[5]

A curious asymmetry was at work. In India, only two companies, Reliance and Mitsubishi Chemical Corporation made PTA, Thakurta told me. Less than fifty companies converted these chips into yarn. Beyond yarn, however, the value chain fragmented into thousands of enterprises. In Surat alone, over 100 dealers sold yarn. About 10,000 weavers, ranging from units with a few powerlooms to large businesses with dozens of shuttle-less looms, wove that yarn into grey fabric. This then went to 400–450 mills and processing factories in and around Surat. Beyond them lay another maze of small units—some decorated sarees with embroidery, others with diamonds and borders sewn on them—employing thousands of migrant workers.

Unable to access cheaper polyester chips from China, units in Surat had to buy from Indian manufacturers. However, once their finished fabrics reached the market, they had to compete with cheap, imported Chinese fabric. This was one reason manufacturers were adding scale. Lowering other costs was a way to stay viable.

Surat was just one hub. There were other clusters, like Bhilwara in Rajasthan and Bhiwandi in Maharashtra, that produced synthetic apparel, employing workers from across the country. 'If this industry shuts down, there will be an employment problem not just here but also in Maharashtra, Bihar, Odisha and Uttar Pradesh,' said a member of the city's industry association.

Yet, policy favoured only one end of this value chain. Abhijit Sen called this a national problem. 'India is protecting input suppliers but not anyone else.'* The costs ran deep. Even as Surat's production capacity rose, the town was going to see the shuttering of units, predicted Dhirubhai Shah, the managing director of Shahlon Industries, a real estate and yarn manufacturing company. 'Surat has 7 lakh looms operated by 10,000 companies. In five years, that will come down to 2,000 companies. We have 400 to 500 companies in processing. We will see similar consolidation there as well.'[6]

It was not the only cluster in the state where micro, small and medium enterprises (MSMEs) were in trouble. No less than 60,000 units in Ahmedabad were sick, the scholar Tridip Suhrud told me. As

---

* This applied not just to the textile industry in Surat. When India erected import barriers to protect the country's steel makers from cheaper imported steel, engineering firms exporting finished products lost their global competitiveness. In edible oils too, as we will see, government policies benefitted a handful of oil importers at the cost of the country's oil mills and oilseed cultivators.

Gujarat pushed subsidies towards a few large groups, smaller firms in the state's chemical clusters and the ceramic cluster of Morbi were also falling sick.[7]

It was a complete about-turn. In *The Shaping of Modern Gujarat*, political scientist Achyut Yagnik writes about the post-Independence ambition to transform Gujarat into a mini-Japan. Accordingly, apart from investing in large public sector initiatives in heavy industry, the state promoted MSMEs.[8] But, as they slipped into distress, the state began seeing something new. As in Punjab, where businesspeople had diverted working capital loans to buy land, and Odisha, where earnings from the iron ore boom had flowed into gold, real estate and colleges, Gujarati businesspeople too began investing in stock markets instead of ploughing money into their MSMEs. In all these states, returns from financial speculation seemed to outperform productive investments.[*]

---

[*] By the end of 2017, hit by demonetisation and GST, industries were generating returns of about 11 per cent, and debt instruments, like bonds and debentures, were yielding around 6 per cent–7 per cent. In contrast, investments in stocks, directly and through mutual funds, were yielding annual returns above 20 per cent. Firms like Marwadi Shares were fast accreting customers. Till 2015, this stockbroking firm in Rajkot was adding about 1,000 new customers every month. By 2017, this grew to 6,000 new customers a month.

At one level, this shift resembled what India saw in 1993–1997. At the time, when their businesses went into a slump, a generation of businesspeople moved their savings into the stock market. What was new this time was where this money was going. Till 2016, Gujaratis had a range of investment vehicles to choose from—land, stock market, bank savings, gold, day trading, moneylending, informal exchanges for commodities and stocks (known as dabba trading) and more. By 2017, that range shrank. Land rates had plateaued. Demonetisation had made people wary of investing in gold. After crackdowns by the Securities and Exchange Board of India, money flows into dabba trading slowed as well. The only informal instrument still in use was moneylending. Most money seemed to be going into stocks and mutual funds.

This could get risky. In the old days, Gujaratis used to invest in formal and informal instruments to hedge risk. Now, as more and more money flowed into the bourses—creating the paradox of soaring stock markets amidst a slowing economy—shares could get overvalued all too easily. See: M. Rajshekhar, 'Why

This is one reason why, today, even as India's economy slows, the stock market climbs and climbs.[9]

————

Dhirubhai had a mischievous sense of humour. A burly, mustachioed farmer in his late forties, he grew groundnuts on three acres along the highway connecting the old, princely capital of Junagadh to the fishing harbour of Verawal. He was talking about his crop when the conversation veered to Kisan Call Centres (KCC). These were set up across the country in 2004 to provide information on crops, government schemes and more to farmers via a toll-free number.

At the best of times, remote call centres are an inferior replacement to gram sevaks—fieldworkers employed by agriculture departments—whose understanding of both farming and local politics make them more effective at introducing modern farming knowledge to farmers. In addition, the bureaucratic impulse to staff positions at these centres at the least cost possible, fills them with young agricultural science graduates who lack the experience of farmers.

Dhirubhai and his friends would call 1551, the toll-free number for KCCs, say that their groundnut trees had a problem, describing the symptoms in extravagant detail—yellowing leaves, drooping branches, the works—and once the 'tele-advisor' would start to advise them, they would yell, 'Groundnuts don't grow on a tree,' and hang up.

'I will show you,' Dhirubhai said and dialled the number. He stood with the phone pressed against his right ear, while two other farmers and I looked on, wondering what fresh botanical sickness he would invent. No one answered, and he eventually hung up. We went back to talking about his groundnut crop.

In a good year, he harvested 100 kilos of groundnuts for every Rs 4,000 he invested. The minimum support price, at which the

---

Small Businessmen in Gujarat Are Quitting Industry and Turning to Financial Speculation', *Scroll.in* (26 September 2016), https://scroll.in/article/851343/why-small-businessmen-in-gujarat-are-leaving-industry-for-financial-speculation.

government is supposed to buy, was Rs 4,400 in 2017. The state government, however, did not buy from the farmers, and Dhirubhai got only Rs 3,500 for 100 kilos from the traders.[10] Despite oil being the most valuable by-product of groundnut, the price oil millers paid for groundnuts had fallen steeply since 2002.

Oil millers were in trouble too. At its peak, this part of western Gujarat had as many as 1,400 oil mills. In the 1980s and 1990s, these telia rajas were so powerful they chose the chief ministers of Gujarat. Things were different in 2017. As many as 500 of them had shut down. The ones still around survived by mixing groundnut oil and palm oil, or passing off palm oil as groundnut oil.

The share of groundnut oil in India's edible oil market fell from 15 per cent in 2000 to 1 per cent by 2017 because of rising imports of palm oil, the cheapest edible oil in global markets.

Since 2005, the centre had been slashing import duties on crude and refined palm oil, produced largely in Malaysia and Indonesia. In 2005, India's import duty on crude palm oil was close to 80 per cent. By 2008, it was down to nil. It rose to 15 per cent by 2017, but even at this rate, imported palm oil was much cheaper than local oils. And so, India's dependence on imported edible oil climbed from 3 per cent in 1992–1993 to 75 per cent by 2017.

This decimated India's oilseed economy. Dhar, a city in Madhya Pradesh's Malwa region, saw farmer protests in 2017 as soybean, which yields soybean oil, sold at Rs 70 per kilo, far below the MSP of Rs 105 per kilo. The same year, in Punjab and Haryana, mustard fetched Rs 3,100 per quintal, well below the MSP of Rs 3,700. Rapeseed too sold below the MSP of Rs 67 per kilo at Rs 55 per kilo in various states.

None of the commonly advanced explanations for import duty slashes—inflation targeting and World Trade Organization caps on import duties—survived scrutiny. Edible oil had too small a weight in India's wholesale price index for its prices to matter. In the mid-2000s, the US successfully did challenge India's imposition of a 300 per cent import duty on soybean oil, but it was not binding on other oils. A third hypothesis, that import duties might have been kept low due to high global prices, did not hold either. Even when international prices fell, the duty was not revised.

This slash in import duties also paradoxically occurred at a time India was trying to become self-sufficient in oilseeds. Back in the mid-1980s, when the country's foreign exchange problem was worsening, edible oil was the second biggest commodity it imported. To counter this, in 1986, India launched a technology mission for oilseeds to boost domestic production. The National Dairy Development Board was asked to replicate its milk cooperative model for the oilseeds sector.

In 1989, as M.V. Kamath writes in *Milkman from Anand*, edible oil brand Dhara was launched.[11] Initial results were good. Groundnut production rose from an average of 6.59 million tonnes a year between 1984 and 1989 to 8.1 million tonnes between 1994 and 1999.*

Then came the first setback. In 2001, after a trip to Malaysia, the then prime minister Atal Bihari Vajpayee reduced the import duty on crude palm oil from 75 per cent to 65 per cent.[12] A change in the industry's value chain was to blame. As I reported:

> Till the 1980s, the groundnut oil value chain in India had been an uncomplicated two-step affair—farmers grew the crop and oil mills crushed it. [Since then] this chain has lengthened. Oil refining companies came up. They processed crude oil, not oilseeds, to produce refined oil. The sector also saw the entry of palm oil exporting countries like Malaysia and Indonesia and importing companies like Adani Wilmar, Cargill and Bunge. Players in this value chain had conflicting interests. In the old days, farmers wanted high prices while the Telia Rajas wanted to buy groundnut at low rates. Now, eager to reduce their dependence on local production, refined oil makers wanted India to import crude edible oil.[13]

---

* In the same period, production of other oilseeds rose from 12 million tonnes to 25 million tonnes.

As imports of crude palm oil rose, the price of oilseeds fell. Farmers began switching to cotton. Average annual groundnut production between 1999 and 2004 came down to 6.1 million tonnes.

Bigger slashes followed once the Congress-led UPA government came to power in 2004. Import duties on crude palm oil gradually came down from 80 per cent in 2005 to zero, and stayed there till 2013, before rising to 2.5 per cent, 7.5 per cent and then 15 per cent. With duties on refined palm oil getting axed as well, imports of these too rose from 3.6 per cent of total palm oil imports in 2006 to 31 per cent in 2016–2017.[14] Rising imports of refined palm oil helped importers and the refining industry in Malaysia and Indonesia. But it hurt Indian refiners, who wanted a higher duty differential between imported crude oils and refined oils. As I reported:

> Take a clinical look at India's edible oil policy and you will see how government policy has … hewed to the needs of whoever is the biggest player in the value chain. At one time, policy was influenced by the Telia Rajas. As their star dimmed and the refiners stepped in, the government obliged them by enabling crude oil imports. Under the UPA, government policy further tilted in favour of select large companies that were importing refined oil as well as exporting countries like Malaysia and Indonesia. [These companies] were 'always trying to shape policy,' said [Abhijit] Sen. In contrast, 'the farm lobbies were not very effective.'[15]

Instead of being self-reliant in oilseeds as it had set out to become, India became the world's largest consumer of imported edible oil. In 2017, it was the third largest item India imported, worth Rs 70,000 crore.* This shift hurt the second pillar of Gujarat's rural economy

---

* Sharad Pawar headed both the Ministry of Agriculture and the Ministry of Food Supplies under the UPA. He did not reply to my emails. K.V. Thomas, the minister of state in these ministries during the second term of the UPA government between 2009 and 2014, claimed not to know why the import duties had been slashed. 'Our policy is always to help the farmers. We were trying to take a balanced view [between] farmers and refineries,' he said. It was lowly

and contributed to an agitation by the patidar community, for who groundnut was a principal crop.

The community, however, demanded restitution, not in the form of higher import duties, but reservations in government jobs.

———

If MSMEs and groundnut production were two pillars of Gujarat's economy, Amul was a third. In 2016–2017, the federation reported Rs 27,043 crore as sales turnover. With farmers getting Rs 36.6 per litre on average, the cooperative handed Rs 65.8 crore to 36 lakh large and small dairy farmers across the state every day. They were also paid annual dividends. The cooperative, a retired Gujarat Cooperative Milk Marketing Federation official told me, was why farmer suicides were rare in Gujarat. Beneath these numbers, however, Amul was weakening.

By the 1980s, as the era of the Gandhians came to an end, in a development that paralleled the autonomous district councils of Mizoram, the dairy unions had grown into the biggest economic engines of their districts. Given their capacity to extend loans, employment, contracts and more, local politics pivoted increasingly around control of these cooperatives. Slowly, even as union membership became more broad-based, with the government distributing cattle among adivasis and women, control of the management concentrated with the dominant castes. In north Gujarat, chaudharys dominated the milk unions, while the southern and central regions were the strongholds of patels.

This new generation of milk union leaders, the regional satraps, comprised people like Banas Dairy's Parthi Bhatol, who belonged to the chaudhary community. This was when Amul began to weaken. In 1975, the cooperative had begun using elections to democratically choose leaders. Dairy farmers chose village society heads, who chose directors, who chose district milk union chairpersons, who chose the GCMMF chairperson. It was a system meant to ensure accountability to the farmers.

———

rhetoric again. For most of his tenure, import duty on crude palm oil stood at nil, which was against farmers' interests.

To maintain their hold, district chairpersons began creating 'panels' of loyalists who would contest elections to become directors. The candidate for district chairperson with the more successful 'panel' would have the numbers to win the elections. Money spent on campaigning rose. By 2017, as Rasulbhai, a dairy farmer in Banaskantha, told me, 'Before polling, for three weeks to a month, candidates for directorships take village milk society heads [who vote in director elections] away for a tour. They are brought back only on the day of voting.' Most farmers could no longer afford to contest elections at the village level. With the rise of panels, dairy farmers also lost their say on whom to appoint and could only choose between candidates with loyalties not to the farmers but to those vying to be the chairperson.

According to a National Dairy Development Board official I met in Rajkot, those who won elections 'made that money back through inflated labour contracts, purchase contracts and employment contracts'. Bhatol said that this had become commonplace in the other dairies since 2005, but denied that it happened at Banas. 'In transport contracts, directors and others take bribes of twenty paise per litre of milk.'

To understand the financial implications of this capture, I took a closer look at Banas Dairy. Located in north Gujarat's Banaskantha district, it was the largest, and so, presumably, the best-run milk cooperative in the Amul family. Of the 1.8 crore litres of milk Amul bought every day in 2017, 0.41 crore litres were procured by Banas Dairy. In aggregate terms, the dairy was doing well. Milk procurement was up. Total revenue and net profit had risen too.[16] These numbers, however, are misleading. Total revenue and net profit include other income, like dividends from the federation. When only operating numbers (revenues and costs) are considered, the dairy shows a loss for five of the ten years for the period between 2006–2007 and 2016–2017. Adding depreciation to operating costs shows worse numbers: Banas Dairy posted an operating loss in nine out of ten years.[17]

This was new. In a doctoral thesis submitted in 2004, Arvind Patel had compared the financials of nine Amul milk unions between 1993 and 2003. At that time, Banas had posted operating profits all ten years. Even factoring in depreciation, it had posted profits six of these ten years.[18]

What changed? The share of milk purchase and transport in operating costs, for one, went up steeply between 2006–2007 and 2014–2015.[19] In an email, Bipin Patel, the managing director of Banas Dairy, told me that milk procurement costs had risen because the dairy paid 'record milk prices to our milk producers.'. What he did not reveal was that this rise in milk prices in Banaskantha was not steady but sporadic. They rose in 2012, 2013 and 2015. In two of those years, elections were held at the dairy. According to a retired senior official of GCMMF, Bhatol hiked milk prices before the elections 'to retain power, resulting in surplus milk entering Banaskantha from Rajasthan and an accumulation of stocks'. Bhatol again denied this accusation, while claiming that it was the other chairpersons who practised this.[†]

These patterns—rising operating costs and boosting prices before polls—echoed in other dairies too. An accounts manager of Dudhsagar Dairy confirmed facing pressure to increase milk procurement prices before elections. In 2007, a news report flagged over-employment at Baroda Dairy, pointing to employment being doled out to those close to the board members. The dairy, procuring

---

* I emailed questions to Banas Dairy's chairperson Shankar Chaudhary and managing director Bipin Patel, asking about the operational losses and the falling profit margins. Chaudhary did not respond to the email. In his reply, Patel cited figures for the rise in the dairy's annual turnover. 'The annual turnover of our union for the year 2016–2017 was Rs 7,552 crores which was Rs 993 crores in the year 2006–2007,' he said. 'The average milk procurement for the year 2016–2017 was 42.94 lakh kg per day which was 11.97 lakh kg per day in the year 2006–2007.' But he did not respond to specific questions on the dairy's operating losses.

† I met Patel and R.S. Sodhi, the managing director of GCMMF, while working on this report. I followed up on those conversations with emailed queries about the drift in Amul, spanning weakening fidelity to cooperative principles to weakening financials. In their responses, both insisted everything was fine at Amul.

'hardly three lakh' litres per day, had a staff strength of 1,550.[20] That year, Kaira Union procured three times as much milk with just 1,150 people in its rolls.*

Even while these processes were underway, Amul began facing turmoil on another front. Politicians were moving in. As the retired GCMMF official told me, 'Anyone who wants long-term power has to control people institutions [like cooperatives]. And dairy is the biggest in Gujarat. Of the 17,000 villages in Gujarat, 16,500 are covered by dairies.' At Banaskantha, in 2015, Bhatol was voted out.

An annexation set in motion in 1998 was finally complete. That year, the BJP had tried to influence the chairperson selection by changing the composition of the Banas board. The dairy, at the time, had twelve members representing talukas in the district, two nominees of the state government, one nominee each of the GCMMF, the National Dairy Development Board and the Registrar of Cooperatives, with seventeen members in all. However, on the day the chairperson was to be elected, the Keshubhai Patel-led BJP government nominated two fresh people to the board. The state government was overstepping. 'It had no

---

* In April 2018, more accusations of corruption emerged. Between January 2015 and December 2018, Kaira Union had bought 8,700 tonnes of cheddar from a private dairy in Erode, Tamil Nadu, called Milky Mist, even though Kaira itself had a cheese-making plant, as did its sister dairies at Banaskantha and Sabarkantha.

It showed cooperation between dairies was weakening. What's more, despite being prohibited by the federation, these 'outside-federation' transactions had continued for three years. No one—not Kaira's internal auditor, not its board of directors (which included Sodhi himself), not GCMMF's monthly planning and coordination meetings, where, as the former GCMMF official said, 'all MDs come together and decide production, dispatch, sales and inventory', not the state government auditor, flagged them. It was more proof that Amul was in trouble. Four milk unions—Banaskantha, Sabarkantha, Kaira and Mehsana—accounted for most of Amul's milk procurement and controlled as much as two-thirds of the voting power on the GCMMF board. Between 2013 and 2017, three of these faced accusations of financial mismanagement. See: M. Rajshekhar, 'Amul Federation Could Be Soured by Corruption Charges Against Its Oldest Cooperative in Gujarat', *Scroll.in* (16 April 2018), scroll.in/article/875332/amul-could-be-soured-by-corruption-charges-against-its-oldest-cooperative-in-gujarat.

shareholding in Amul. It did not stand guarantee for our loans. It had no right to interfere,' the retired GCMMF official told me. The matter went to court, where Amul's stance was upheld. Even under subsequent chief ministers, the trend continued. 'Amul kept going to the courts and getting stays,' he said.[21]

These efforts redoubled after Narendra Modi became chief minister in 2001, said the former elected official at Banas Dairy. Under Modi, pressure on dairy chairpersons to join the BJP went past blandishments into coercion, claimed the official. Bhatol had to face audit objections. At the same time, the BJP began putting up its members for chairpersonship.[22] In this period, the party also stepped up its attempts to gain control over credit cooperatives. As C.N. Tarapara, the managing director of the Rajkot District Cooperative Bank told me, 'The bank had a rough time when it was under Congress leadership. The BJP government filed forty-three cases against it. It's only when the management changed that all the cases were taken back.'

The BJP's control over cooperatives was one way to weaken both the Congress and local power structures. At the same time, party leaders also saw a chance to consolidate their own position in the district, even if, between credit and milk cooperatives, the former was 'not as big financially as milk cooperatives', said Arjun Modhwadia, a Gujarat Congress leader.*

At Banas Dairy, after losing the previous election for chairperson, the BJP put up Shankar Chaudhary, the state's health minister at the time and the party's MLA from the district, in the 2015 elections. Bhatol, said the former elected official at Banas, was called to Gandhinagar, where the government sat, and was told to create a panel where half the people would be loyal to Chaudhary. Bhatol refused. 'He said:

---

* Much of *Ear to the Ground*, as you see by now, was a sampling exercise. In Odisha, to study the speculation that followed the iron ore boom, I had chosen engineering colleges. In Punjab, to study rising religiosity, I had picked up deras for a closer look. In Gujarat, lacking time to study political party takeovers of both credit and milk cooperatives, I picked up dairy for a closer look. In dairy, I zoomed in on the biggest milk union.

"[Shankar Chaudhary] has the [cooperative] bank. He's the MLA. He's the minister. Why does he want the dairy too?'" the official said. Chaudhary won. The Bhatol camp alleged electoral malpractice.

It was the start of a new chapter. In Banaskantha, Anand and Ahmedabad, most people described Bhatol as someone primarily interested in remaining powerful locally for which he was willing to shift political allegiances. From supporting the Congress, he gravitated to the BJP after Modi became the chief minister. The satraps usually had little political ambition. The new flock of chairpersons, however, had political careers. All were members of the BJP. Five were current or former MLAs.

What did this mean for Amul? When asked, both R.S. Sodhi, the managing director of GCMMF, and Bipin Patel struck sanguine notes. The first, in his email, said there was nothing wrong with politicians leading milk cooperatives. 'Responsible and selfless political leaders founded Amul 70 years ago and therefore politics remain inherent in the organisation.' Earlier, when I met him, Patel had echoed this. 'You can't separate politics from society. Once the board sits down, it takes off the cap of the political party and thinks about the farmers. There is no adverse impact.'

These statements, however, don't sit well with Amul founder Tribhuvandas Patel's views. He, as Kamath writes, was categorical that the cooperatives would fail if politicians entered them, viewing them as opportunities for patronage. Verghese Kurien, who stayed at the helm of GCMMF till 2006, had also resisted the entry of politicians till the end.[23] Accountability falls when power gets concentrated. Few were likely to challenge Shankar Chaudhary's decision, for instance. As an MLA and a state cabinet minister, he had an unassailable position in Banaskantha. As we saw in the Introduction, Chaudhary was accused of 'misusing his position' in the government to get permissions for a 150-seat medical college set up in May 2018, the first to be run by a milk cooperative.

Another factor likely to diminish opposition was the criminal records of several of these chairpersons. Amul chairperson Jetha Patel was arrested in a rioting case in the aftermath of the 2002 communal violence in the state. He was a district BJP leader at the time.[24] The charges were later dropped, with the police citing insufficient evidence.[25] The vice chairperson Jetha Bharwad, who won the assembly election from Shehra constituency in 2017, faced charges of rape and kidnapping, according to his affidavit for the 2012 assembly election. The same year, Shankar Chaudhary's affidavit listed three charges related to murder, four for rioting while armed with a deadly weapon and three for attempted murder.[26]

————

As dairy, MSMEs and farming declined, the state's capacity to create wealth was falling. Protests like those of the patidars and Surat's businesspeople were one manifestation of anger. But the BJP was not too worried. It had complete control over Gujarat. Credit and milk cooperatives were only one lever of control. But the party's capture of the state ran deeper, employing religion and fear.

From the late 1970s, writes Achyut Yagnik, 'a large number of Savarnas began to join new Hindu Sects such as the Bochasan sub-sect of the Swaminarayan sect, Swadhyay Parivar and Asharam Ashram'. This was partly to 'gain entry into new networks of social security and patronage'.[27] There is an important distinction here. While caste organisations, like the Patidar Samaj, belong to a single community, sect networks are more ecumenical, open to a wider array of caste and class groups. 'Swadhyay has a strong following amongst the dominant community—businessmen, architects, brahmins, bureaucrats, judges,' said Lancy Lobo, director of Vadodara's Centre for Culture and Development. 'The Swaminarayan sect has a base of peasantry and the patel community. Others like Morari Bapu have a following among businessperson. Several OBC communities follow Asaram Bapu. Sub-sects within the Swaminarayan Sampradaya sect, like Bochasanwasi Akshar Purushottam Swaminarayan Sanstha, have NRIs [non-resident Indians] and people in central Gujarat as their followers.'[28]

According to Suhrud, if control over cooperatives helped the BJP influence voters through patronage, sects performed the same function, but by controlling minds. The Sangh Parivar's courtship of these sects was amped up under Modi. As chief minister, he would 'chair meetings and special functions of the Swaminarayan sect', said Bhadrayu Vachharajani, a sociologist based in Rajkot. 'So much so that when the sect's leader died, people remembered how close Modi was to him, and said Modi should become its new head.'

So is the case with temples. As we saw in the previous chapter, four of the seven trustees of Gujarat's Somnath temple are BJP leaders— Modi, L.K. Advani, Amit Shah, Keshubhai Patel.[29] 'This is an effective way of moving politics in India,' Suhrud said. 'People may not take what the BJP and the RSS say seriously. But this is the temple's head saying it. So, what we see once campaigning stops is that the sadhus come out.' The patidar community might be angry because of thinning economic prospects, but the message from religious leaders, that religion has to be protected, was a powerful mode of diversion.

What accompanied this was the party's use of fear. On the one hand, it positioned Muslims as a threat, one that only the BJP could control. On the other, it had its own access to violence. In a piece she wrote after the BJP scraped back to power in the state in 2017 with ninety-nine seats, the journalist Revati Laul nailed both.

> Ever since the demolition of the Babri Masjid 25 years ago, the well-oiled machinery of the Hindu Right has instilled the fear of the 'other' in the minds of every aspirational, gold-earring wearing Gujarati. The auto-driver summed it up. 'Madam, Modi is a *daku*. But he is doing one thing that is making us vote for him again and again. He is keeping the Muslims in their place.'[30]

The seeds of this fear were sown a long time ago. Till the 1970s, most civil society in the state wanted a plural society, the political scientist Ghanshyam Shah told me. By the 1980s, that changed. 'In the late 1970s, children's books came, cartoon books, which ridiculed Muslims. These were brought out by some Vaishnavite sect.' According to him, the riots in 1969 were a major reason this polarisation started. Communal riots had till then been local and spurred by local issues.

But the 1969 riots were qualitatively different. Leading up to these, between 1962 and 1969, a series of events unfolded in the state. The number of communal incidents rose steadily. Gujarat also saw agitations over 'gau raksha', cow protection, with big processions of sadhus. In 1963–1964, when the demand for a ban on cow slaughter was raised, the state government gave in. 'Those in power were not anti-Muslim,' said Shah. 'But they did not understand. At that time, all this [unrest] was blamed as a creation of China. This created a different narrative. Muslims are Pakistanis. They do not have a loyalty to India.' In a report on these riots, Poorna Swami wrote in the *Caravan* magazine:

> According to the Reddy commission, relations between Hindus and Muslims began to especially wither after the Chinese invasion of India in 1962. The axis that China formed with Pakistan soon after, as well as Chinese support of Pakistan during the India-Pakistan war of 1965, had stirred suspicion among some sections of Hindus. They allegedly began to question the loyalties of Indian Muslims, recalling the split allegiances of Muslims during Partition.[31]

These processes, riding on local unemployment as textile jobs moved to Surat and away from Ahmedabad, eventually resulted in large-scale communal violence, starting in the city and spreading to nearby towns like Nadiad, Vadodara and Anand, and unfolded over September and October. Unofficial numbers pegged the number of dead as high as 2,000, most of them Muslims. These were the most severe Hindu-Muslim post-Partition riots in the country, until the Bhagalpur riots in Bihar twenty years later.

'There was,' added Shah, 'a certain exaggerated confidence in the inevitability of the democratic project as well. At that time, the intellectuals never questioned. [They] thought these threats would be taken care of automatically by education and urbanisation.' So, they did not create organisations or mobilise to fight the disinformation campaign. 'Maybe they did not have the patience. Or they thought ideas themselves would change society.' On the other hand, those who wanted a society that hewed to their notion of traditional culture, and was anti-Muslim and anti-Christian, worked at building an alternative narrative. 'It slowly culminated in an anti-Muslim and, now, completely polarised society. It is now very difficult to talk about secularism. Those aberrations have been institutionalised and legitimised.'

On this edifice stands the BJP's project of frightening the Hindus. I got a glimpse of this one morning I took an auto to the bus stand in old Ahmedabad. Later that evening, a rath yatra was to be taken out. All of the old city was lined with police. And yet, every time the auto turned into a bylane, I saw local Muslims going about their lives. Women were drying clothes, shops were open, halwais were frying sweets. There was little to suggest tensions were high. When I told Jyotsna Yagnik, the former trial court judge who had pronounced Babu Bajrangi and Maya Kodnani guilty in the 2002 riots that followed the burning of the train coach at Godhra, about the paradox a few days later, she laughed. 'The police bandobast? That is not to frighten the Muslims. It is to tell Hindus, "See how much we do to keep you safe."'

Gujarat's fear project also extended beyond demonising Muslims. Laul wrote in the *Wire* about an adivasi farmer who sacrificed two days of daily wages and spent on bus fare and food to get to his village and vote.

> 'Why have you spent about 2,000 bucks just to vote when you have no money for food and live in a tarpaulin tent on the road?' I asked him. Fear was the reluctant but honest reply. 'Fear of what,' I persisted. 'The fear of having your name struck off the ration card and BPL card and the *panchayat* coming to your home and threatening you if you don't comply.' As he finished speaking, the other men—all tribals—standing with him nodded in agreement. Twenty-two years of the BJP has driven that point home. It is a well-oiled machine, which does not mean that it delivers on any of its election promises. It means one thing only. It delivers fear with regularity and precision.[33]

Clientelism goes hand in hand with coerciveness. Under Modi, this project of fear intensified further. 'Anyone who speaks against Modi from inside the BJP gets finished either physically or politically,' Gordhan Zadaphia, a BJP leader in the state, told the *Caravan*.[33] Girish Patel, a human rights lawyer, further described this quilt of fear. 'Section 144 is everywhere. Meetings are not permitted. This is a police state.'[34]

The Gujarat Model slowly emerged from the shadows.

If tight control over the state and the centrality of fear were two features, a third was the state's bias towards large companies. Under Modi, as the economist Indira Hirway wrote for the *Wire*, Gujarat saw a huge rise in 'incentives and subsidies on investments to the corporate sector to attract investments [and] infrastructure development focused on roads, airports and power.'[35]

The most well-known of firms is Ahmedabad-based Adani Enterprises. The backstory goes thus:

With elections scheduled in Gujarat in 2002, Advani replaced the former chief minister Keshubhai Patel with Modi, a political novice at the time, choosing him over senior state leaders like Suresh Mehta and Kashiram Rana. 'Advani was planning to make a run for prime minister, and Gujarat was a key state for the BJP,' Zadaphia told me in 2013. 'To make sure he controlled Gujarat, he wanted an outsider in charge in the state who would be dependent on the party high command for his legitimacy.'

Modi took charge in 2001, knowing he would have to win the state elections. At the same time, he did not want to depend on Pramod Mahajan, who was managing the BJP's finances, for funds. 'This is his personality. He doesn't want to depend on anyone for anything,' Achyut Yagnik told me in 2013. As I reported:

> According to Yagnik, Modi wanted his own source of funds, but this was not easy. Industry was suspicious of this RSS man who had taken charge of Gujarat. Modi was suspicious of

industry. 'In his first year, Modi kept all businessmen at an arm's length. He suspected they were taking undue advantage of the state economy,' says a senior bureaucrat in the state energy & petrochemicals department. 'Modi distrusted Adani due to his rapid rise and thought he was too close to Keshubhai.' According to him, it took Adani a year, from October 2001 to September 2002 to find his way into Modi's inner circle. This was partly due to the 2002 elections. Two other factors contributed. After the Gujarat riots, when some CII leaders criticised Modi, a group of local businessmen—including Adani, Indravadan Modi of Cadila, Karsanbhai Patel of Nirma and Anil Bakeri of Bakeri Engineers—established a rival organisation called the Resurgent Group of Gujarat (RGG) and threatened to leave CII.

And then came the Vibrant Gujarat Summit and the [Rs] 15,000 crore commitment from Adani, who wanted to grow big in a state that had Reliance. 'He too wanted a break at that time,' says the Gujarat CII official. 'And this is how he angled for it. Just like Modi needed a break.'[36]

After this, multiple instances of the Gujarat government favouring Adani Enterprises were flagged. To take one instance, between 2006 and 2009, the Gujarat State Petroleum Corporation bought natural gas from the open market and sold it to Adani Energy at a price lower than the purchase price. The Comptroller and Auditor General (CAG) said the company received an undue benefit of Rs 70.5 crore.[37]

A fourth feature of the Gujarat Model was an extraordinary centralisation of power. As Girish Patel said about Modi's rule in Gujarat: 'The chief minister controls everything. Like the US presidential system, this is a chief ministerial system. The difference is that in the first, the president is strong but the Congress is independent and it controls the president. What you have here is more extreme. One man's word is final. Some decisions don't even go to the cabinet. You saw that in the case of Tata and land. Legislative functioning is dysfunctional. The assembly is called only when constitutionally required. The questions asked are ones prepared by the government.'

In his profile of Modi for the *Caravan*, the magazine's editor-in-chief Vinod Jose described how the BJP leader got rid of his rivals in the party.[38] Parallelly, Modi also concentrated decision-making at the Chief Minister's Office. With that, administrative autonomy weakened. As Patel told me, 'Even IAS officials have personal loyalty to him. The police too is under his complete control. We saw that in 2002 and in its aftermath. Things continue like that even after 2014. Even now, the chief ministers are replaceable characters. The Congress too used to appoint state chief ministers. But that was by competition. People [are now] chosen on the metrics of ideology and rigidity. You see this elsewhere too. The government now considers the ideological bent of the leaders, even the judges, before appointing them.'

With that, the nature of the State changed. 'People close to the leaders have a better chance of getting promoted,' retired police official R.B. Sreekumar explained. This resulted in an 'anticipatory sycophancy for career advancement'. Slowly, the administration, police and even the judiciary hewed closer to Modi's majoritarian worldview.

This showed up repeatedly. The state administration worked better in non-Muslim areas. As a report in the *Wire* showed, in the Muslim ghetto of Juhapura in Ahmedabad, there was no street lighting, gardens or parks, and no asphalt roads beyond the four-lane axis crossing the ghetto.[39]

Majoritarianism cast a yet longer shadow over Gujarat than just active discrimination against Muslims. It was the reason why all minorities in the state—not just Muslims, but also dalits and adivasis—fared poorly on health and education indices. As an explanation for why the state's expenditure on health and education were low, a senior official in the current BJP chief minister Vijay Rupani's office said, 'The state believes it should work on roads and create conditions for enterprise, that people will take care of schooling and health.' This line of thinking ignored the simple fact that Gujarat's upper- and middle-caste Hindus were more affluent than its minorities. While patidars could have their own medical colleges and hospitals, Muslims, dalits and adivasis were left out in the cold.[40]

As books like *Kafkaland* and *Splintered Justice* detail, the state's criminal justice system too worked better for Hindus than Muslims.[41] Jyotsna Yagnik corroborated their conclusions. Around 2009, she began observing that 'investigations of police officers were getting erratic, varying according to the religion of victims and attackers.' Even judges were not immune to religious bias. Before Yagnik delivered her Naroda Patiya order on the 2002 riots, a fellow judge told her: 'We all hope you will protect the faith.'[42] Ghanshyam Shah explained the underlying thinking to me: 'To protect the religion, others have to be attacked. As a Hindu, you have a duty to protect those who have carried out this dharma.'

If majoritarianism was a fifth feature of Modi's Gujarat Model, a desire to highlight the state's capability under him was the sixth. As chief minister, he created showcases, like the Sabarmati riverfront, Gift City and Vibrant Gujarat conventions, each of which was promoted widely to suggest that Gujarat was in the throes of radical, modernising change. The riverfront, for instance, mimics similar structures in the West. 'Politics is the use of symbols to unite people,' said Suhrud.

All this, however, brings us to a fresh question. As expected, minorities were not doing well in Gujarat. The odd thing was, as the patidars' protest, the travails of MSMEs and the decline in Amul showed, the majority community was not doing well either. Who was gaining from Gujarat's majoritarian project? Ghanshyam Shah had an answer to that question. It served the interests of a few.

———

India's track record on climate adaptive/mitigative urban planning has been dismal. Most buildings and houses use construction material that absorb heat and drive up cooling costs. Cities have low and decreasing tree cover, and rising hard spaces. As Bangalore found in 2017, even after heavy rains, there is little groundwater recharge.[43] In city after city, lakes, which can recharge groundwater, are being killed through real estate development. Little thought is given to water supply. Instead, as water scarcities loom, cities source water from farther and farther away. Peri-urban areas are a different kind of a nightmare. In state after state, panchayat presidents have allowed even five-to-seven-storeyed buildings outside municipal boundaries. 'When the municipal corporation expands its limits, it finds these strange places where buildings are standing, but there are no roads, water supply or sewage,' said G.K. Bhat, the founder of Taru, an environmental consultancy based in Ahmedabad. 'The whole place works only on groundwater.'

Against this wider landscape of climate catastrophe, Gujarat claimed to be a leader. Its cities had plans that sought to manage the worst fallouts of climatic stress. Ahmedabad had a roadmap for heat waves.[44] Surat had a blueprint to tackle floods.[45]

Climate change was adversely affecting Gujarat too. On the one hand, the frequency of extreme events, like heavy rains and floods, was rising.[46] On the other, the state was also seeing subtler changes like gradual increases in temperature. Think of the first as a shock. The second as a stress.

Shocks and stresses pose different challenges for a city. Shocks come with cascading fallouts. Heavy rains first cause traffic jams, then flooding, and then, if conditions do not improve, the city starts shutting down. 'Cities depend on networks—a flow of milk, a flow of food, cash for ATMs,' said Bhat. 'As one urban system fails, it incapacitates the others. And cities see a progressive network failure.' He was in his office in a high-rise near the Ring Road. As Ahmedabad rushed towards work far below, he drew an analogy with living systems. 'These [urban failures] are not independent failures, but multi-organ failures. Every failing organ incapacitates the rest, reaching social unrest and epidemics in its higher reaches.'[47]

Stresses, on the other hand, trigger a spiral. Days were getting hotter in Ahmedabad, for instance. In May 2016, the mercury touched 50°C.[48] The previous high had been 47.8°C in 1916.[49] The difference between day and night-time temperatures was falling as well. 'At one time, even if the mercury went up to 45°C, nights were pleasant and temperatures came down to [between] 25°C and 26°C,' said Saswat Bandopadhyay, a lecturer in the Department of Planning at Ahmedabad's CEPT

University. 'But now,' he added, 'they [difference between day and night-time temperature] come down just half as much, to [between] 32°C and 34°C.' In response, those who could afford it installed air-conditioners, which warmed up the city further.

Zoning is one way to respond to such challenges. A city vulnerable to floods needs spaces where the water can pool, and one facing high temperatures needs more cooling green cover. Urban planning is a good place to see how adaptation and mitigation were being mainstreamed in Gujarat, one of the most urbanised states in the country.

Rajkot, the fourth-biggest city in Gujarat—after Ahmedabad, Vadodara and Surat—located in the centre of the Saurashtra region, was urbanising fast. People, pushed by the state's weakening rural economy and pulled by Rajkot's industrial and service economy, were flocking here. The city, like the rest of the Saurashtra region, was low on water. Its development plan for 2031 says: '[Rajkot Municipal Corporation] is able to supply only 20 minutes of water daily as against the benchmark of 24 hours.'[50] Here is what I found during *Ear to the Ground* on how the city was doing on adaptation and mitigation:

> On some fronts, Rajkot is doing well. To make the city more energy-efficient, Rajkot's Municipal Corporation has made solar heaters mandatory. Rainwater harvesting is mandatory too. These efforts, however, are undercut by other decisions. As it expands, Rajkot is leaving very little room for environmental sinks like green zones. As a city grows, it should leave about 30% of its surface area for green zones and environmental sinks, said Mahesh Rajasekar, a former environmental consultant with Taru. 'What holds true for a nation also holds true at a smaller, ward level.'
>
> But Rajkot's old city has a green cover of about 2%, and its periphery does not fare any better.[51]

Try to understand why the city took some measures but not others, and you will arrive at a curious division of labour. In 1973, when Rajkot became a municipality, its municipal corporation was responsible for urban planning. That changed in 1976, when Gujarat passed the Gujarat Town Planning and Urban Development Act. Following this, urban development authorities were set up in Gujarat's biggest towns, and planning responsibilities were divided between these new bodies and the municipalities.

While municipalities would handle town plans, the urban development authorities would draw up development plans. The difference is one of scale. Development plans work on larger areas— required for planning the city's expansion—and look twenty to thirty years into the future. They map the broad contours of a city such as residential, industrial and green zones and road networks. Town plans, on the other hand, flesh out development plans in more detail, and work on shorter timeframes.

At Dholera, pitched as India's first smart city, Gujarat used eminent domain—the power of the State to appropriate private property for public use—to acquire land. Not so in Rajkot. Here, land ownership stayed with individuals. The only restriction on how landowners used their land was zoning. This resulted in authorities coming under pressure to allot land for profitable uses. There was, said an official, a lot of pressure to not zone land as green. It is not surprising that land owners lobbied. Urbanisation unlocks land values and can make people wildly rich. But such zoning makes the city vulnerable to climate change.

'India's democratic architecture for a town means it should be run by the urban municipal corporation, which reports to locally elected councillors,' said Bandopadhyay. However, what Gujarat created, through the urban development authorities, was a system run by bureaucrats who reported to the Urban Planning Department and the Chief Minister's Office, leading to a political capture of municipal functions.

Eight of the ten members in the Rajkot Urban Development Authority (RUDA) board were bureaucrats. Their decisions, complained RUDA planners, were overruled by Gandhinagar. This was corroborated by Nilesh Virani, president of the Rajkot Zilla Parishad and a board member of RUDA: 'If a politician is the chairman, the interference will be visible. So, they only make bureaucrats the chairman.'

The deeper game plan is clear enough. Politicians can monetise urbanisation in two ways. One way is to enter the real estate business, and the other is to extract rents from favourable zoning decisions. Compounding matters, lines between the party and landowners blurred as well. 'Rajkot has ten to fifteen major groups who are very active in politics, the builder space and education,' said Kaushik Mehta, the editor of *Phulchhab*, a Gujarati language newspaper headquartered in Rajkot.

This engendered, yet again, an outcome where gains were privatised but costs were public.* The cities that emerged from this planning process, said Bandopadhyay, had basic infrastructure like roads, water and drainage but showed little attention to related questions like public health. The hydrology of these spaces was completely distorted as well. Local water bodies were hemmed in. If a region came under the 'no go' area, influential people got it changed. 'If there's a water body, then no more than ten metres is left on either side,' said Bandopadhyay. This increased the risk of flooding. At the same time, given the lack of attention given to water supply while expanding, these cities began depending on water imported from elsewhere. Each ward, said Mahesh Rajasekar, should have had a green space no more than a kilometre away. In Rajkot, however, green spaces lay in the periphery, even though the city was already heating up. A town planner with the Rajkot Municipal Corporation said: 'Our summer temperatures are now around 46°C to 47°C. They are up by one degree.'

In all, Rajkot took small steps towards sustainability while drilling away at its ecological foundations. This is a wider critique. The state's Climate Change Department rolled out programmes for LED lighting and made rainwater harvesting compulsory but stayed mum on wider deficiencies like inadequate green zones. 'What you have in Gujarat is an outcome where the resilience and development plans do not talk to each other,' said Bandopadhyay.

---

* I sent questions to Vijay Rupani, the chief minister, and Vikrant Pandey, the chairperson of RUDA. They did not respond.

Such slips showed up repeatedly. Ahmedabad created a Heat Action Plan but continued to chop trees. By 2030, vegetation would cover just 3 per cent of the city's area.[52] Surat created plans on how to mitigate floods, but stayed silent when the Essar Group built an embankment that cut the delta of the Tapi, which flowed through Surat, by half. Or take Gujarat itself. It pushed projects like the Sardar Sarovar Dam, claiming water needs, but did nothing to curb water pollution in the state.

———

I stood at the beach in Dandi and tried to imagine the day Gandhi marched here. I was back at the sea some weeks later, this time at the fishing harbour of Verawal. Looking at juvenile sharks and rays, only a little bigger than my hand, pulled in by fisherpeople, I recalled a similar trophic collapse in Tamil Nadu. Gingerly stepping into the dirty sea, I recalled a small, clean stream running over rounded stones just beyond the village of Zochachhuah in Lawngtlai, Mizoram, where the Kaladan Highway left India and entered Burma. I stood before a burnt train coach outside Godhra railway station, ground zero of this inflammable new India.

What happens to a society after it embraces majoritarianism? In Gujarat, the majority community was fissuring too. It was getting harder for kadva patels to get a house in a leuva patel colony and vice-versa. This was new, said Vachharajani. 'Before the Gujarat quake, we did not know which of our neighbours were leuva patels and which were kadva patels.' Religious display had become more overt as well. 'Earlier, we never saw a juloos [procession] at Janmashtami. Now, all of Rajkot is taken over by processions.'

In Gujarat, said Ghanshyam Shah, 94 per cent of the labour was in the unorganised sector. 'They start working at twenty-two years of age and work till sixty. If they have to save for old age, they have to hold multiple jobs. In this context, there is very little outside [their] caste [or community] to support people. In [such] conditions of insecurity, people bank on each other. Primordial loyalties get strengthened. Each caste had a traditional support system. That is now strengthened as a caste-only support system.' He gave the instance of student hostels to explain this. 'The first patidar chhatralaya came up around 1916 or 1917 in Surat. Then, similar structures came up for anavil brahmins in south Gujarat. These were meant to support people who wanted to study but could not. But now, some patidar chhatralayas allow only mehsana patidars.'

What he said next nailed what I had been seeing all along. 'To get support from one's caste group, you need to indicate that you are a reliable member of the community.'[53] This was why displays of religious faith were rising not just in Gujarat but across India. Every community has its codes, identity and symbols. In this age of insecurity, people have to show their fealty to these symbols. One has to be, Shah said, an ideal member of one's community. This was why leuva patels had grown newly loath to rent out houses to kadva patels. Even in Mizoram, the 'spirituality' of people was gauged by whether they kept their day of rest.

The outcome is a fatal misstep Ambedkar foresaw. 'If the individuals in a society are separated into classes, and the classes are isolated from one another and each individual feels that his loyalty to his class must come before his loyalty to everything else, and living in class compartments he becomes class conscious, (he is) bound to place the interests of his class above the interests of others. (He) uses his authority to pervert law and justice to promote the interests of his class and for this purpose systematically practises discrimination against persons who do not belong to his caste (class?) in every sphere of life.'

In such a society, he writes, where classes clash and are charged with anti-social tendencies, governments cannot govern with justice and fair play. 'They might be of the people and by the people, but they would not be for the people. It will be a government by a class for a class. A government for the people can be had only where the attitude of each individual is democratic, which means each individual is prepared to treat every other individual as his equal and is prepared to give him the same liberty which he claims for himself.' Democratic society, he writes, is a prerequisite for a democratic government.[54]

But when was India ever an equal society?

———

Despite these fissures, Indian democracy—embedded with the ideology of socialism, self-reliance, modernisation, liberal democracy, secularism and anti-imperialism—still had a certain capacity for achievement. The country built a heavy industrial base and cleared the ground for the Green Revolution, writes Balagopal.[55] Notwithstanding elite capture, it attacked poverty and curbed the worst of caste, gender and religious discrimination. The citizens, feeling things would improve further, stayed invested.

But now, this structure is succumbing to entropy. In every state, democratic institutions, ripped free of the founding values of a young idealistic democracy and hijacked by power structures, are declining into disorder and unaccountability.[*] Nowhere is this corrosion more acute than in the country's political parties. Across the country, the use of money in elections has been rising. Political party finances remain opaque; all parties, staunch enemies most of the time, jointly oppose any application of the Right to Information Act to their finances. The number of politicians with criminal cases has been rising. A swelling proportion of elected representatives have become far wealthier than the people they purport to represent. In tandem, state after state has become repressive and intolerant towards dissent and opposition.

Right through this decay, we, the people of India, have held an idealised notion of Indian democracy in our heads and have dismissed features like the ones above as aberrations. Yet, if the same deformities show up repeatedly, are they mere aberrations or deeper truths about our democracy?

I had started with the naive notion that democratic protest was thriving in India. I no longer think so. In state after state, I saw people take to the streets only when expropriation became too blatant.

---

[*] One sign of this unaccountability was the frequency at which my questions to politicians and bureaucrats went unanswered.

More insidious forms of dispossession—like nobbled education and healthcare delivery—went unchallenged.

It was not that people did not care. They were, instead, normalising these dispossessions. As Paul Oliver writes in *Blues Fell This Morning*, on the role of blues music in the lives of African-Americans under Jim Crow Laws in the United States, 'In rural areas where education levels were low and the people knew no better environment, there was little with which to compare their mode of life.'[56] They knew they could not change the world but had to live in it. In the USA, blues music slowly built that public awareness about a shared injustice. 'The maturity of the blues came with the dawning realization that an equal place on earth was a basic right and perhaps within the bounds of possibility.'[57]

In India, what facilitates that normalisation is the collapse of institutions that should reveal these dispossessing processes—like the media and trade unions—and folklore. Bereft of these, people understand some expropriations, but not all. Many fall for diversionary conspiracy theories peddled by parties and their disinformation architectures. Others resort to more atomised responses.

Some, like the fisherpeople of Vedaranyam and the forest guards of Dampa, responded by mining their local environments more intensively. Those who could not, turned to debt or migrated. Young women from Lawngtlai in Mizoram worked in Chennai; young men from Uttar Pradeṣh and Bihar worked in Aizawl and elsewhere; I found people from Manipur in Thanjavur, Tirupur and Hosur; and a young woman from Konta, deep in Naxal Chhattisgarh, at a textile factory in Sriperumbudur. These were individual responses to systemic failures. Apart from these, people fell back on kinship structures, like sects in Gujarat, caste in Tamil Nadu, and religion in Punjab and Mizoram. I finally understood why the Mizos watched Korean soaps, yearning for a wider kinship.

Instead of challenging the rot in political parties, such responses strengthen them. No wonder that processes of dispossession and marginalisation, like the ones described in this book, continue to intensify in this country.

Conclusion

I found State failure in all the six states I reported from. Governments failed to deliver health, education and justice. Self-interested political parties, entirely unable to deal with the challenges before their state, hid their failure through denial, diversion, leadership cults and endorsements from others. Watchdog institutions rarely held power accountable. Citizens fell back, not on democratic remedies, but on caste and religious structures to keep insecurity at bay. In all, Indian democracy seemed more performative than real.

In *How Democracy Ends*, the academic David Runciman writes, 'The question for the twenty-first century is how long we can persist with institutional arrangements we have grown so used to trusting, that we no longer notice when they have ceased to work.'[1] In India's states, these arrangements include political parties, legislatures and democratic watchdogs like the police and the press. All of them continue to function but do not deliver what they should. Democracy, as Runciman writes, seems to be failing 'while remaining intact'.

We now know democratic projects are fragile. The United States voted in Donald Trump. Russia, after the fall of the Soviet Union, became what Hungarian sociologist Bálint Magyar calls a 'post-communist mafia state' instead of choosing Western democracy.[2] Cambodia, despite a nation-building push after the fall of the Khmer Rouge, slipped into neo-authoritarianism under its current prime minister Hun Sen.[3] Turkey, a postcolonial beacon under its first president Mustafa Kemal Atatürk, now languishes under Recep Tayyip Erdoğan's authoritarian rule.

If democracy was malfunctioning in all the six states I surveyed, how was the union of states faring? India has been described as a patronage democracy, an electoral democracy, a feudal democracy, a flailing democracy. None of these definitions, however, captures the full messiness I saw— like the slide into oligarchy and the rise of intreccio.

I was still mulling over that question when the dysmorphia of the Gujarat Model took root in Delhi.

———

Democratic decay and State failure were the running themes of *Ear to the Ground*. Fears about both gradually hit national headlines.

First came the belated realisation that coups are not the only threat to a democracy. The world also has, as the political scientist Nancy Bermeo says in Runciman's book, 'executive coups', when those in power suspend democratic institutions; 'election-day vote fraud', when the electoral process is fixed to produce a particular result; 'promissory coups', when democracy is taken over by people who then hold elections to legitimise their rule; 'executive aggrandisement', when those already in power chip away at democratic institutions without overturning them; and 'strategic election manipulation', when elections fall short of being free and fair, but also stay shy of being stolen outright.[4] As Runciman writes:

> People manipulate elections because the appearance of victory at the ballot box is what gives them the authority to rule. Promissory coups and executive aggrandisement require the appearance of democracy be maintained, because the success of the coup depends on people believing that democracy continues to exist … as democracy gets more established, it gets harder and harder to overturn it by force or outright fraud. … [At the same time] the more democracy is taken for granted, the more chance there is to subvert it without having to overthrow it.[5]

What India has experienced under Modi is executive aggrandisement. The difference between the BJP and other political parties in the country is not one of moral character, as the party claims. The success of India's political parties hinges on a few building blocks: winning elections through not just political promises but also ground-level constituency manipulation; social media (disinformation) architectures; access to formal and informal finance; curbing challenges, be it from elections, India's federal structure, watchdog institutions or civil society; and the cult of the leader. These apply to the BJP as well. What sets the BJP apart from its rivals is its greater proficiency in the use of these building blocks.

As these blocks fell into place for the BJP, two things followed. First, the party launched the ideological reconstructions to remake India into a Hindu Rashtra. But that is not the only outcome. Means are more real than the professed end, as Eugene Lyons warns in *Assignment in Utopia*. 'They harden into a system of power and privilege which must postpone the end in order to maintain itself.'[6] This is what happened in Gujarat. The ideological project was overtaken by the BJP's drive to stay in power. Even the majority community did not do well in the state under its government. Instead, the party set in motion a project of fear to keep the Hindus insecure about Muslims, even as economic gains flowed to a few.

In its first five years, as the academic Tarunabh Khaitan describes in the paper 'Killing a Constitution with a Thousand Cuts', Modi's National Democratic Alliance (NDA) government attacked accountability mechanisms—elections, institutions and democratic commons.[7] Campaign finance was made more opaque with the introduction of electoral bonds,[8] and pliant officers were elevated to the Election Commission and anyone less than entirely pliant was hounded out.[9] When the BJP lost a state election, the party cobbled together post-poll alliances and got governors to swear the BJP into power while it tried to get rival MLAs to defect.

Institutions meant to check the centre took a hit as well. The BJP refused to allow the single largest party in the opposition to appoint a leader when it fell three seats short of the required number;[10] bypassed the Rajya Sabha, where it did not have a majority, by tabling critical legislation, such as the Aadhaar and Other Laws (Amendment) Bill, 2019, as money bills, which do not require the upper house's approval;[11] gifted two Supreme Court judges plum post-retirement perches—P. Sathasivam was made the Kerala governor[12] and Ranjan Gogoi was sent to the Rajya Sabha;[13] politicised the CBI further;[14] gave itself additional powers over the Central Information Commission;[15] sent a pliant mandarin, famous for his press conferences during demonetisation, over to the Reserve Bank as governor;[16] and left vacancies unfilled in institutions of scrutiny like the National Green Tribunals.[17]

Democratic spaces got bludgeoned. Leaders like Chandrashekhar Azad of the Bhim Army were repeatedly arrested. Foreign contribution licenses of NGOs were cancelled. Universities like JNU were attacked. Students and activists, like Sudha Bharadwaj, protesting the government's excesses were slapped with sedition charges and imprisoned. People, especially those whose voices were inconvenient to the ideological project, like rationalist Narendra Dabholkar, scholar M.M. Kalburgi and journalist Gauri Lankesh, were killed by right-wing sympathisers.

Running alongside executive aggrandisement, which is nothing but 'dominance', were the other three traits of extractiveness, centralisation and clientelism. The BJP outspent its rivals in polls. It saw extraordinary centralisation, with even state polls being fought in Modi's name. Clientelism took a new form with a rising number of state programmes being launched in the name of the prime minister.

The government also began a process of remaking the population. 'The shaping of the New Man is [every totalitarian] regime's explicit project, but its product is not so much a vessel for the regime's ideology as it is a person best equipped to survive in a given society,' writes the journalist Masha Gessen in *The Future Is History*. The regime, in turn, Gessen writes, comes to depend on this newly shaped person for its continued survival.[18] So, the BJP's disinformation architecture, spanning social media and mass media, tried to remake the people in the country into supporters. It told people what to think. It pushed conspiracies about inimical threats to the country. It denounced those opposing the government as traitors and sought to widen the chasms between Hindus and minority communities.

I slowly came to appreciate what Arshad Ajmal had told me in Bihar: 'The battle with the Congress is to deepen democracy. The battle with the BJP is to protect democracy.'

———

Then came the pandemic. For long, as this book shows, India's central and state governments ignored crumbling State capacities in healthcare, taking refuge in denial and data manipulation. COVID-19, radiating outwards from Wuhan to Europe and the Middle-East and then hitting India, ripped that facade off.

Despite warnings, India was slow to respond. Ignoring the WHO's guidelines, the government did not stockpile protective gear.[19] The centre's first aggressive reaction on 24 March 2020 (a previous one involved the prime minister asking middle-class India to clap their hands and bang plates from their balconies) was one of panic. That night on television, Modi announced a twenty-one day complete lockdown starting at midnight, during which people were not to step out except to buy essentials. The decision was born of the knowledge that India's health infrastructure could not deal with the pandemic. Curbing the virus's spread was the best option before the government.

But, as with demonetisation, inattention to detail was evident. The government had not factored in migrant workers. Unable to work, their cash reserves ran low. Worried about their health and that of their families, millions wanted to head home, but buses, trains and planes were not plying. In scenes that called to mind Steinbeck's *The Grapes of Wrath*, epic journeys, spanning hundreds and thousands of kilometres, started all over India by trucks, bikes, rickshaws, cycles and on foot.

The visuals that emerged were chilling: migrant workers being hosed down with disinfectants by the police; a woman pulling a suitcase with one hand while carrying her tired child; another exhausted child asleep on a suitcase being dragged by his mother; an old woman walking home with a pup perched on her shoulders—'It's too young. It will die if left behind,' she told a reporter. This morality of hers was missing in how the migrants themselves were treated by the State. Their decision to walk home was rooted, not just in financial distress, but in a newfound awareness that neither the government nor society would help. As a friend put it, 'That was the government's success. It made people believe in Modi while killing any expectation that the State owes them anything.'

To prepare for the pandemic, some government hospitals were reserved exclusively for COVID-19 cases. Others, in anticipation of a rush, shut down their out-patient departments. Patients suffering from other ailments were denied treatment.[20] Immunisation services took a hit as well. The number of bacille Calmette-Guérin inoculations in April 2020 was half the number in January.[21] States like Bihar, Rajasthan and Kerala even discontinued immunisation.[22]

Old habits, like fudging data, kicked in. As cases grew even in the hinterland, India's Health Ministry continued to deny community transmission.[23] States screened for the disease in areas that did not see a spike in cases, allowing for the reporting of low infection rates. For their part, unwilling to waste a good crisis, the disinformation architectures used COVID-19 to fan further hatred against Muslims, coining terms like 'corona terrorism' and 'corona jihad'.[24]

The government asked people and companies to donate to a new fund, PM-CARES, instead of the existing Prime Minister's National Relief Fund. Unlike the latter, the new fund was not open to audit. Even as questions were raised about what its collections would be used for, the Supreme Court refused to intervene.[25] Crony capitalism kicked in. In one instance, firms close to the BJP got contracts from the Gujarat government for manufacturing ventilators.[26]

The lockdown was extended repeatedly, without consulting the scientific panel set up to advise the government on COVID-19, but it failed to halt the pandemic.[27] Although the economy came to a standstill between March and June, the government did not provide income or food support to the poor. After about two months of lockdown, a rising chunk of Indians became food insecure. In one study by New Delhi's Centre for Studying Developing Societies, 78 per cent of the 25,000 respondents said they found it 'quite difficult' or 'very difficult' to feed their families during the lockdown.[28]

The costs ran deeper yet. The lockdown battered an economy that was yet to recover from demonetisation and GST. In the first quarter of 2020, as the pandemic hit and the lockdown kicked in, India's GDP shrank by 23.9 per cent.[29] GST collections fell. States slipped into a financial crisis. Families, selling hard-won assets to stay alive, found themselves sliding back by ten or fifteen years. Informal credit dried up, even in Tamil Nadu. 'People have not lost trust in others, but in the future,' concluded a team of researchers led by Isabelle Guerin in a paper describing the collapse of the state's informal debt markets.[30]

Like totalitarian projects seen in the past, this government too promised utopia but did not care about individual lives. Through this mayhem, its symbolic projects—like the redevelopment of Rajpath (the ceremonial road that runs from the president's house) and the building of a temple at Ayodhya (at the site where once stood the Babri Masjid that was razed by a mobilised right-wing mob in 1992)—continued. Its response to the unfolding, accelerating economic carnage, instead, was to lift the lockdown even as cases kept rising. India is now expected to have the largest number of COVID-19 cases by the dawn of 2021.[31]

———

The project to lead India into Hindu right-wing authoritarianism has made headway on some fronts and struggled elsewhere.

The BJP has progressed on institutional capture but has fared less well with the states. It has created a robust communication machinery but has lost popularity due to misgovernance. The rent-sharing model has come with its own costs: The companies overlooked by the BJP in preference for those closer to it have soured on the party.[32] Between demonetisation, GST, the government favouring a few firms, and COVID-19, India's economy tanked.[33]

Complicating matters, the BJP's majoritarian project comes with its own contradictions. It wants dalits to boost its vote bank but also defends casteism. It espouses majoritarianism but works only for a few. In the Gujarat elections of 2017, despite its chokehold, the party barely scraped through, winning no more than 99 of the state's 182 seats; it had targeted 150. This is where the historian Stephen Kotkin's explanation in *Uncivil Society* on why even brutal, authoritarian regimes fall comes in. Talking about the fall of communist Europe, he argues that it was not civil society that brought it down. Instead, it was the establishment that dismantled its own house by misruling and making itself susceptible to loss of legitimacy.[34]

Romania is one of the countries Kotkin cites. To repay soaring foreign debt, dictator Nicolae Ceauşescu imported as little as possible and exported as much as possible. State expenditure on housing, education and healthcare dropped precipitously. Not only villages but also cities went dark at night. In the winter of 1984–1985, the regime banned all automobile traffic to conserve fuel. Rationing, even for bread, returned to Romania's cities. People stayed quiet till the December of 1985, when an unrelated spark, triggered by a Calvinist pastor— who summoned his parishioners to protest his upcoming eviction from church land by State authorities—in Timisoara, a town of about 3.5 lakh people, whipped up protests across the country.[35] It was, writes Kotkin, the beginning of a political bank run. Power works if people believe it works. Once the enormous crowds formed, the Romanian communist police State disintegrated.

India saw something similar with the protests against the Citizenship Amendment Act. Unlike what was claimed by many mainstream news channels, Muslims were not the only ones protesting. Students, dalits, adivasis and others marched too. Their uprising fell like rain on India's parched democracy. Till then, India's opposition parties— demotivated by the BJP's rise and lacking value-based reasons for being in politics—had failed to defend constitutional values. Then, from the streets and neighbourhoods across India came a full-throated defence of the Constitution. Protesters read out its Preamble, sang the national anthem and peacefully courted arrest. While the BJP tries to remake the people, its claim of having the national mood behind it is built on instrumentalities like social media dominance, carefully planned electoral wins and a subservient media. For the first time in five years, cracks showed in that edifice.

In February 2020, as Delhi went to polls, the BJP smeared the protestors as traitors. Its leaders led chants demanding the protesters be shot, but the party was trounced in the elections. Later that month, a three-day assault on Muslims in northeast Delhi, with rioters brought in from outside and locals joining in, followed. The police made no efforts to quell the mobs.[36] As of November 2020, fifty-three people were confirmed dead. Most of them were Muslims.[37] In the months since, the State has slapped charges of sedition and incitement on many of the protestors. But not even first information reports (FIRs) have been filed on the BJP leaders who made incendiary speeches. Instead, a Delhi High Court judge who took the police to task was summarily transferred.[38]

Nonetheless, the party's track record of losing elections in the states continued. It has, between 2018 and 2020, lost Rajasthan, Chhattisgarh, Madhya Pradesh, Jharkhand, Maharashtra and Delhi. Yet, it is important not to get carried away. Even if there is a mass outpouring and the party is forced out of power, India might just revert to the previous suboptimality or, given that economic insecurity keeps rising, might fall to the charms of a new demagogue.

———

Seventy-three years after Independence, India is marooned, like Russia,[39] in an ideological project that purports to take the country back to a past of mythic greatness but, in reality, serves a narrow elite. Even as this battle wages, more pressing challenges bear down on the country. While reporting, I saw joblessness, precarity, impaired financials of states, corruption, air and water pollution,* resurfacing caste and communal divides, eroding national competitiveness, a loss of common purpose, intreccio, weakening institutions, fraying ecological foundations and more. At the same time, a set of other processes— for instance, the rise of monopolies and foreign ownership in sectors like infrastructure and energy—continue unhindered, with their own long-term costs.

There are yet others. As GST strips financial autonomy from the states, they are increasingly unable to raise funds for their functioning. This leaves them struggling even more to perform their basic functions, heightens their dependence on the centre, and introduces fresh tensions into state-centre relations. Climate change might upturn global geopolitics as countries look for others to blame. As a climate-change-induced scarcity of resources builds, the world might see a return of Hitlerian politics around *lebensraum*, living space, with countries fighting for a greater share of the planet's resources, warns historian Timothy Snyder in an article for the *Guardian*: 'A problem that is truly planetary in scale, such as climate change, obviously demands global

---

* One winter evening in 2015, after visiting Dera Sacha Sauda at Sirsa in Punjab, I boarded a bus to Delhi, about 280 kilometres away. By nine o'clock, fog settled over the road. By ten o'clock, it was thick enough to make movement almost impossible. The bus cautiously moved along. And then, a thud, a lurch, and the bus slammed to a halt. I saw splatters of blood on the windscreen. 'It was a cow,' said the conductor. We continued to crawl along, reaching Hisar by midnight, and the driver cut the trip short. With Delhi just 180 kilometres away, a fellow passenger and I shared a cab. Seven hours of sleepless vigil followed as the driver, a young man barely out of his teens, working to get his siblings an education, drove ahead with nothing but the dim tail lights of the vehicle in the front to guide him.

Drivers and locals said the fog was man-made. Not only did this part of India have several industrial units and power plants, but also, in October and November, farmers burnt fields to clear the crop stubble left after their kharif harvest. A sudden nip in the air trapped these emissions close to the earth. At that time, most discussions on India's worsening air quality were limited to handwringing about Delhi's worsening pollution levels. But, as the trip showed, the smog covered a far larger swathe of land and probably at higher concentrations than in Delhi. It was a reminder of how rapidly real challenges facing India were growing.

solutions—and one apparent solution is to define a global enemy.'[40] For the COVID-19 pandemic too, China got flagged as a global enemy. If India continues to burn coal because of a weak economy that cannot afford costlier alternative fuels, the country could come to be seen as a global enemy in the fight against climate change. Soaring inequality is another threat we face. India's top 1 per cent have more than four times the wealth held by the bottom 70 per cent of the country, about 953 million people.[41] As the historian Walter Scheidel cautions in *The Great Leveler*, only war and pandemics have successfully reduced inequality in the past.[42] These are all issues we barely acknowledge, let alone resolve. It might be tempting to entrust these issues to an authoritarian figure, but democracy yields better answers.

———

Democracy is indeed frustrating. It allies itself with change, as the writer Lewis H. Lapham writes in *Age of Folly*, 'which engenders movement, which induces friction, which implies unhappiness, which assumes conflict not only as the normal but also as the necessary condition of its existence'.[43] Yet, it creates a more just society than any other arrangement.

It is a lesson the religious majority needs to learn. Complaining about the GST, a factory owner I met in Hosur told me: 'Why is Modi doing this? We voted for him because he would keep the Muslims under control.' Seeing minority communities as a purely religious construct had blinded him to another reality. When it came to religion, the government sided with the powerful, the Hindus, and against the minority, the Muslims. In its economic policies, it sided with big companies, against small and medium ones like his.

As Lapham writes, if democracy means anything at all, 'it means the freedom of thought and the perpetual expansion of the discovery that the world is not oneself'.[44] We are all minorities here. If not by religion, then by where we live, our levels of education, occupation, sexuality, eating habits, the clothes we wear, our hairdo, by whichever markers that set us apart.

It is this democratic project, imperfectly realised as it is, that we are now in the danger of losing. We know how we got here. It first misfired in the states, and attempts to take corrective action fell short. Slowly, the people in the country began doubting, to use Zygmunt Bauman's words from *Liquid Modernity*, 'the benefits which the freedoms on offer are likely to bring them'[45] and voted for a leader who promised strong, decisive leadership and achche din, good days. The question is: where we do go next?

Ours is a time when, as Vasily Grossman writes in *Life and Fate*, history seems to have left the pages of books and come to life. Where it goes next depends on us. 'Though the struggle with the forces of "dogma" has been long and hard, the open society has so far prevailed,' the historian Robert Conquest muses in *Reflections on a Ravaged Century*. 'There is no reason, in principle, why it should not do so in the future if the lessons have been truly learned, and when learned, not forgotten.'[46]

To reclaim our institutions and insist on scrupulous adherence to the practice of democracy, as Angela Davis says in *Freedom Is a Constant Struggle*, we need greater vigilance and solidarity.[47] We have to keep an eye on how the government and other institutions work, not only for us but also our fellow citizens. In some ways, the battle for India was lost when we stopped caring about rural schooling. That created the untrained manpower and the employment crisis—the substrate on which the right-wing has grown, as we saw in Hosur.

Vigilance works. In Mizoram, Lalthanzara had to step down (he won the bypoll, but the Congress lost the next state election). In Odisha, the Kondhs continue to resist Vedanta. In Punjab, despite their chokehold over the state, the Badals were voted out. In the past, in the remote hinterlands of Chhattisgarh, village women trained as health activists have forced the state government's primary health centres to work better.[48]

And then, there is solidarity.

As I moved around, India seemed to be splintering. One afternoon in Bangalore, while writing the second draft of this book, I talked to a polite young man from Assam who worked as a security guard in a gated colony. I asked him about the National Register of Citizens and its impact on the people in his home state.

He responded, 'If they don't have papers, they have to go.'

'Where will they go?'

'I don't know, but they have to leave.'

This is what Bauman and Donskis call an 'adiaphora' in *Moral Blindness*—the decision by a population to withdraw the cloak of conventional morality from a subset of the population such as migrants, minorities and whoever is being classified as the Other at a given moment, leaving them vulnerable to the State and others, without any feeling of sympathy or empathy.[49] This is why India's voting in 2014 pointed at something darker in our psyche, not just the hope for achche din. In those polls, craving faster development, a third of the country showed it was willing to throw a minority community to the wolves. Now, as people struggling to save themselves fall back on exclusionary communities and the disinformation architectures continue their barrage of hate, those fissures are deepening further.

Vigilance and solidarity are not easy. The first comes with the risk of repression. The second does not come naturally to us. Not only is bigotry easier than tolerance, but also hierarchies, as Robert Sapolsky writes, help Us/Them binaries to flourish.[50] And India is nothing if not a hierarchical society. Us/Them feelings also grow more easily in an environment of separation; and our cities and villages are increasingly ghettoised by religion and class.

————

But it helps to think of all this another way. To last, civilisations have to rise to the challenges facing them. The costs of not doing so are extinction—think of the Incas, Indus Valley Civilisation and Easter Island—or a long slide into decay.

In *Paths in the Rainforests*, the historian Jan Vansina describes how equatorial African communities, running their societies per traditions that evolved as their world changed, flourished from 3000 BCE till colonialism. And then, due to the slave trade and missionaries, their traditions faltered and that region lost its adaptive capacity. 'The transition to independence occurred ... without the guidance of a basic new common tradition. ... Today that is still the situation, and the people of equatorial Africa are still bereft of a common mind and purpose.'[51]

As my reporting project progressed, I found myself wondering what India's future would be if it failed to respond to the challenges before it. Would the country end up with self-inflicted austerity as in Mizoram, ruled by a few as in Odisha, by one family as in Punjab, in thrall to one supreme leader as in Tamil Nadu, an absent State as in Bihar or a majoritarian republic that works for a few as in Gujarat?

Or can we reclaim this republic?

Annexure

The State Riddled with Conflict

Manipur is enchantingly beautiful. A tenth of its landscape is a valley, thirty-two kilometres at its widest, only a little bigger than the city of New Delhi. The rest of the state consists of hill ranges close to three thousand metres high and of the same Assam-Burma tertiary range as Mizoram. As my flight flew in, the central valley, carpeted with green fields and dotted with lakes—the largest being the famous Loktak—presented an arresting tableau.

The lives of Manipuris, however, are a stark contrast to these pastoral surroundings. The state—with the Naga community dominating the hills to the east, north and west of the valley; the Meitei community in the valley; and the Zo people, known as Kukis here, in the hills to the south—is one of the most violent parts of the country.

Unrest began before Independence, when Manipur was merged into India. Shortly after this, separationist insurgency reared its head in four Naga-dominated hill districts. In the 1960s, the valley, home to the Meiteis—Hindus, Muslims and Buddhists—who account for two-thirds of the state's 25 lakh people, saw the rise of insurgent groups as well. They were a response to the capture of government contracts in the Northeast and the misappropriation of funds by cronies close to the local chapter of the Indian National Congress, according to E.N. Rammohan, a former director general of the Border Security Force and advisor to the Manipur government.[1] Once the Nagas staked claim over the wider area of Nagalim and issued notices to other ethnic groups like the Kukis, asking them to leave, insurgency spread to non-Naga tribal districts like Churachandpur in the south. Subsequently, insurgent groups demanding autonomous regions for the Hmar people and others also came up.

The result has been a military occupation that has lasted almost as long as India has been independent. The British deployed the Armed Forces Special Powers Ordinance in 1942. It became the Armed Forces (Assam and Manipur) Special Powers Act (AFSPA) in 1958 and has stayed in force, unbroken, ever since. By the early 2000s, however, most insurgent groups in the state had mutated into extortion gangs and grown links with local politicians. Rammohan writes, 'In the elections of year 2000, the different groups were hired by politicians of all hues, both state and national. The groups freely used their guns to intimidate voters and the elections were completely rigged.'[2]

India's armed forces drifted too.* Extrajudicial killings stacked up. In 2004, troops of 17 Assam Rifles tortured and killed thirty-two-year-old Thangjam Manorama.[3] In protest, the activist Irom Sharmila began a fast that would run on for sixteen years, and twelve middle-aged women stripped naked in front of the 17 Assam Rifles headquarters holding banners saying 'Indian Army Rape Us'.

This potted history, with its emphasis on AFSPA, the Indian armed forces, insurgents and a certain non-violent protest, is the media's stock narrative for Manipur.

In 2015, meeting people in Imphal and its surrounding villages, and then in the district of Ukhrul, ninety kilometres to the northeast of Imphal and home to the Tangkhul Nagas, and then in Churachandpur to the south, I found both stasis and change within that larger matrix. Insurgents continued to have links with political parties. In autonomous council elections held shortly before I reached Manipur, insurgent groups in the five hill districts had issued diktats, some prohibiting the Congress from contesting and others banning the BJP from the polls.

---

* See: Kishalay Bhattacharjee, *Blood on My Hands: Confessions of Staged Encounters* (India: Harper Collins, 2015).

Other things were changing as well. The quantum of extortion, while still high, had reduced. A state Congress leader, speaking on the condition of anonymity, said, 'At one time, people were scared to build houses or buy new cars.' A good-looking house, cemented on all sides, used to draw the insurgents' attention. Since 2010, that had been changing. When I visited, Imphal had new car dealerships and hotels. The insurgents had found a new revenue stream of contracts from the state's PWD. 'Every underground group,' said the Congress leader, 'has an overground person it bids through.' If two groups wanted the same contract, negotiations, conducted by the newly formed Coordination Committee (CorCom), an umbrella organisation of seven insurgent groups, would follow.[4]

Even the functioning of the armed forces had been changing. Speaking about an incident in Imphal where a group had demanded money from a hospital, an Imphal-based human rights activist told me, '[The hospital] refused. The amount was too high. Angered, the militant who had come to collect the money threw a bomb inside and was running out when he was caught by some Bihari labourers. And then, he took out an ID card and showed it to them. It said, Indian Reserve Battalion.'*

This was a marked change. Till the 1990s, there were just two sides, said Babloo Loitongbam, the director of Human Rights Alert, an NGO. 'There was the State. And there were militant groups that opposed the State.' By 2015, as the conflict continued, Manipur had a spectrum of armed actors: the army, paramilitary, Indian Reserve Battalion (controlled by the state but paid for by the centre), Manipur Rifles, Manipur Police Commandos, Manipur Police, village defence forces, militant groups managed by the military, militant groups with links to politicians, and then, the groups listed as terrorist organisations under the Unlawful Activities (Prevention) Act—like People's Liberation

---

* I emailed to questions the then chief minister Okram Ibobi Singh, the then principal secretary, Home, Suresh Babu, and the then chief of the army staff General Dalbir Singh Suhag. They did not respond.

Army of Manipur, United National Liberation Front, Kanglei Yawol Kunna Lup, Kangleipak Communist Party, People's Revolutionary Party of Kangleipak and Manipur People's Liberation Front. 'When a conflict goes on for over twenty-five years, local people, militants, even the armed forces start creating their own survival strategies within the violence,' said Loitongbam.

However, even as the nature of the insurgents and the armed forces changed, AFSPA continued as ever. If its continuation is one puzzle, the zones of its imposition is another. The act, which confers judicial insulation upon the Indian army, is not in force in Imphal, which sees the most violence, but in all the hill districts where the ethnic groups, and not the Meiteis, are numerically dominant.

This pattern of selective imposition transcends Manipur. In Tripura too, AFSPA is imposed only in the areas populated by the ethnic groups. 'The indigenous people believe it is a tool of ethnic domination by the ruling [immigrant Bengali community]. Tribals, doomed to eternal neglect, are kept suppressed and at bay by this Act,' writes R.N. Ravi, a former special director at the Intelligence Bureau who led peace talks with the Nagas.[5] Loitongbam agreed, 'I am convinced the imposition of AFSPA in Manipur has nothing to do with insurgency.' Other parts of the country, like central India, he said, see far more violence than Manipur. 'And yet, AFSPA is in force here. Not there.'

The protective umbrella extended by AFSPA to the security forces has changed other aspects of the state as well. While AFSPA gives absolute powers to the military—even allowing it to kill civilians without being hauled by the courts—the state police too behaves as if it is covered under the act. Between January 1979 and May 2012, Manipur saw 1,528 fake encounters by all security forces. Of these, the state's police and commandos killed 377 people. Assam Rifles was responsible for the death of 419 people in such encounters, while joint teams of state police and central paramilitary forces were responsible for 481.

This disregard for the rule of law extends beyond the police to the state administration. In April 2015, a senior police official, Amitabh

Arambam, driving home one night with his wife and two young children, was beaten up by the security guards travelling with the speaker of the state assembly, Thokchom Lokeshwar Singh, allegedly because Arambam had not allowed the speaker's cavalcade to overtake.[6] Arambam had been the second officer in command in a special investigations team set up on 13 January 2011. This unit nailed an army colonel ferrying pseudoephedrine, a drug used for converting poppy into heroin, in three fully loaded SUVs. A few days later, it also picked up the son of T.N. Haokip, Congress leader and former speaker of the state assembly. Shortly after these raids, the team was disbanded.[7] Given this context, it is hard to establish whether the attack on Arambam was coincidence or payback.

Loitongbam traced this culture of impunity to AFSPA, which has also seeped into other institutions. 'As long as you pledge allegiance to national interest, you can do what you like.' National interest had come to be equated with the ruling Congress government in the state, he added. In such an environment, it becomes easy for the government to brand people as anti-national. 'People can be killed on just suspicion.'

In the 1980s, work on the Mapithel Dam in Ukhrul district started. 'Anyone who opposed the project was treated as a militant or anti-government. Protesters were arrested, some were tortured,' said K.S. Thanmi, a candidate for the Naga People's Front. By 2015, whenever villagers tried to oppose the project, the government declared Section 144 of the Criminal Procedure Code, which bans assembly of more than five people.

Those opposing private projects are beaten up as well. In November 2012, public hearings for Jubilant Energy's oil exploration project were conducted in Tamenglong district under the heavy presence of Assam Rifles and Indian Reserve Battalion. In Churachandpur district, two land owners from a village called Lungthulien near Parbung town, who refused to give land for the project, were 'brought to Churachandpur thana and beaten through the night', said F. Doliensung, the joint secretary of Hmar Inpui, the apex association of Hmar people in India.

The collapse of institutions responsible for ensuring accountability enable this impunity.

The state police, deeply implicated in the violence, is unresponsive to complaints. Ravi corroborates this breakdown: 'Against the all India average of police filing charge-sheet in 88% of reported heinous crimes after investigation, Manipur's record is 4%!'[8]

If a police complaint does get filed, the judiciary drags its feet. In a 2012 memorandum, Manipur's civil society organisations report that in Manipur's lower courts, judges refuse 'to cooperate with the victims' families to register an FIR ... and actively discourage any effort to criminally prosecute perpetrators of custodial violence by not taking cognizance of torture and ill-treatment leading to death'. At the Guwahati High Court, their memorandum adds, judges 'award monetary compensation to the families of the victims but remain silent on the prayer for prosecution of the perpetrators of the crime'.[9]

The state Human Rights Commission, at the time of my visit, was defunct as the state government had not nominated new members since 2010.* As for the local press, it depends largely on the government for advertising. Besides, it is dangerous for local reporters and editors to speak out too loudly against local power structures.

During my reportage, Manipur was the only state in which, even in chance conversations with people, I found that they (a man sitting next to me in a van returning from Churachandpur to Imphal) or someone close to them (a colleague of one of the people I interviewed) had experienced violence. There was a widespread anti-India sentiment. In part because AFSPA, as Loitongbam explained, also runs entirely counter to Manipur's ancient conflict resolution codes. These principles, called Chainarol, sought to resolve conflicts by minimising suffering and encouraging amicable ties. It was applied in ceremonial duels,

---

* It got a chairperson in June 2018 but continued to suffer from lack of staff and funds. See: Iboyaima Laithangbam, 'Cash-strapped Manipur Human Rights Commission Observes 22nd Anniversary', *Hindu* (28 June 2018), thehindu.com/news/national/other-states/cash-strapped-manipur-human-rights-commission-observes-22nd-anniversary/article31937682.ece.

in which whoever struck the first wound was declared the winner. Surprise attacks were prohibited. While modern-day humanitarian law prohibits attacks on those who are not active participants in an armed conflict, be it civilians or prisoners of war, Chainarol set rules for the conduct of warriors too. It showed that, as Loitongbam told me, if you maintained humanity in the midst of hostility, peace could be made.[10]

AFSPA and the state police, he said, violated these ideals. 'When an underground [militant] is killed in conflict, no one raises any question. But if you pull out a woman from her house, rape her and then use your power to say it never happened, then that creates anger.'

Villagers at a political rally in Chadong village in Ukhrul district said mob justice was becoming popular: 'There's a total absence of justice. If a thief gets caught in a village, he could be killed by the villagers.' Pradip Phanjoubam, the widely respected editor of *Imphal Free Press*, said, 'A disillusionment has been setting in among the people.' 'They no longer have faith in the insurgents, in religion, in the state. There is no faith in any stream of thought. This is a crisis. It is these unwritten rules [that govern how societies function] that make people behave better.'

Afterword

V. GEETHA

Despite the State is part of and extends the grammar of a genre of writing that has emerged this past decade: reportage which combines fieldwork, research and argument, and transforms into an extended essay. Each individual story in this book—say, on sand mining in Tamil Nadu or arsenic poisoning in Bihar or, what appears to be a bit of whimsy, the popularity of Korean soaps in Mizoram—constitutes an individual narrative moment. This moment opens back in time as well as tips into the present, connecting to other social, political and economic events and developments as these have unfolded within a particular geography and history. Meanwhile, Rajshekhar offers his gloss on the moment, citing ideas and concepts drawn from studies in political economy, finance, sociology, environment and literature. The result: a generous and thoughtful reading experience. Rich detail sits easily with provocative ideas, and description is stirred into argument.

In another sense too, this is new writing. The focus is not 'India', either as an idea or material entity, but an India as it is lived by millions of its citizens: within bounded linguistic and cultural limits, shaped by political traditions that are specific to the region in question and an economic life that is experienced in terms of concrete outcomes and which cannot be easily assimilated to broad theories of 'development'. This is not to say that the 'region', as it is often disparagingly referred to (in contrast to the nation), might be studied as such, detached from the Union of India; only that the region is not to be viewed purely as 'subnational', as it often is, but as integral to our understanding of the nation.

The story of India is thus as much a story of its many constituents and how these constellate together. Rajshekhar does not draw easy comparisons, but he aligns his narratives along a set of coordinates. He argues that extractive practices, clientelism, dominance and centralisation characterise political and economic life in all states, whichever the political party in power, and that these traits define how parties comport and conduct themselves. Each of these practices could be interpreted in broad historical terms, so that we see their unfolding in terms of the longue durée of both development and democracy.

———

Take extractive practices, as these have come to exist in the twenty-first century. Control exercised over the commons, whether these are natural resources or social goods that governments are meant to make available to all citizens; fiscal policies that determine government spending; and rent collected by government functionaries for almost any task they are expected to perform—in a sense, these were built into the planned economy as envisaged by independent India's first generation of rulers.

True enough, India's planners did not view the large-scale public projects they undertook as taking over the commons. In fact, they imagined such takeover, of land, forests, riverine valleys for dam building or power stations, as remaking the commons. But on the ground, this takeover resulted in deepening inequalities. Primary producers were expropriated; a dam did not mean jobs for all those who lost access to land and such commons as there was; and, worse, those dispossessed were forced to migrate and await compensation that refused to arrive, and when it did, did not prove adequate. Ranjana Padhi and Nigamananda Sadangi have written the history of this mode of development as it unfolded in Odisha, through tales of resistance to public projects that were put in place almost every decade since Independence, starting with the signature Hirakud Dam.[1]

This history is demonstrative. It shows how development, in essence, has always meant dispossession. And that a 'public' project did not necessarily mean that it was so in its granular details. To be sure, as mines and hydel stations, factories and dams got made, some of the dispossessed did find their lives upgraded, but such changes were offset by class and caste hierarchies inscribed into the very heart of public sector growth. Townships, for instance, attached to large public projects, were enclosures of privilege, while the labour hinterland, from which casual and contract labour was drawn, was degraded, in every sense of the word, as Jonathan Parry and T.G. Ajay's work on the Bhilai Steel Plant demonstrates.[2]

Further, the secondary aspect of growth, the expectation that such public projects would spur private industrial expansion, remained captive to the license raj, as it was called, and soon enough, graft came to be secured as quasi-legitimate rent. Fiscal outlays for the citizenry worked to an extent when invested in education and health sectors, but such investments were not uniform. Not only were there differences between the states but also within too, as cities fared better than villages, and amongst populations, the most marginal benefitted the least.

Extractive processes in the present are not identical to what we started out with in the heyday of planning. For one, the collusion with capital and a host of private interests, including of the party in power, was not as brazen as it has come to be since the opening of the economy in the 1990s. For another, a new mode of accumulation has emerged, presided over by what might be called the political class as such, through client networks that rake in unaccounted money for the party in power. Government has been denuded of what is owed to it by way of legitimate revenue, and this has either meant that it give up on welfare-related governance or garner rent from private players to finance populist welfarism. Meanwhile, these players are allowed a free run of the environment, whether they speculate or start an industry.

However, the shift from a regulated economy associated with building strong public assets, as it was with a bloated licensing system, to a deregulated one, where private players could forge ahead with greater freedom, has not diminished the power of the Union of India, with respect to its grip over economic life. It has persisted, but in other ways. On the one hand, the State has sought to rework its earlier fiscal arrangements, doing away with subsidies for farmers and micro industries, and not expanding health and education budgets in rational ways. On the other hand, it has brought in an array of schemes that keep the working sections at a suboptimal level of existence, staving off hunger but not ill health or malnutrition. This balancing act, meant as much to secure electoral outcomes as to allay dissent, has not proved easy. Neither the union government that initiated market reforms nor the states that carried these through have been able to fix on a magic formula. Ironically enough, these schemes have since become the focus of citizens' demands, while the more substantial losses incurred on account of economic deregulation have been harder to address.

Meanwhile, the period of market reforms, that is, from the late 1980s onwards, saw the states gradually come into their own, particularly in the economic sphere. They entered into agreements with multilateral agencies and capital, and prepared the ground—literally, through the creation of special economic zones—for market-driven growth. This made for what has been described as a sort of market-driven federalism, in contrast to the unitary federal polity that we had always been.[3] But this did not prove consequential in a democratic sense, as we shall see. Rather, it signified a remaking of class-caste relationships within states, which had its genesis in other developments prior to and in congruence with the moment of liberalisation. I shall return to this in my discussions of 'clientelism'.

The differences that mark current extractive practices, as Rajshekhar describes them, and earlier forms of extraction do not take away from this fact: that the logic of working with natural resources, closely tied to the lives of primary producers, and wreaking havoc on the environment has a long and hoary history, whose details we are yet to fully grasp. Likewise, the fate of the dispossessed, relegated to the sidelines of the development story, is part of a history whose unfolding cannot be tidily separated into the making of the good public sector and the venal private sector. There are crisscrossing lines as well as lines that mark differences; to view matters in this manner could prove sobering and render our demands for transparent governance and democracy realistic.

———

Rajshekhar deploys the term 'clientelism' to describe a mode of organisation of political parties that does not depend on affiliations built bottom up but instead on networks that extend downward from the party through trusted emissaries, especially those who are most likely to deliver votes. Such an emissary could be a political fixer, manager of party assets or conduit for circulating money prior to elections.

Clientelism is not new and, in fact, might be viewed as fairly old and endemic to political life in modern India. Writing on provincial political life in early twentieth century India, David Washbrook calls attention to how patron-client relationships, which secured mutual benefits for both groups, were worked by municipal politicians to retain their leadership positions in local society and, later, at the level of the province or presidency. Local governance thus rested on the power of those who held office to dispense favours and to endorse specific claims put forth by the citizenry. This nexus between those in office and those that addressed them was further fortified by caste and religious loyalties.[4]

However, as democratic life proliferated—with the expansion of the national movement and, in the immediate post-Independence decades, with the growth of local or regional parties, such as the DMK, and the assertive political presence of the Left—old certainties came to be unsettled. Clan and caste were subsumed within broader categories of belonging and fellow feeling, whether of the nation or specific cultural and linguistic identities or socialist comradeship. In any event, this led to the making of political constituencies that were held together by ideology: their relationship to government was contrarian, if not confrontational, and also did not rest only on clan and caste loyalties.

In independent India, democratic claims could not be easily scuttled, and the government had to necessarily answer to popular needs, not just those defended by locally dominant interests. An older style of governance, which had elitist bureaucrats settling matters with locally powerful groups, gave into, or at least learnt to coexist with, an emergent form of rule, which required bureaucrats to heed what political parties and their representatives demanded. And when such parties took office, as S. Narayan points out with respect to the DMK, the local party person, rather than the bureaucrat, came to mediate popular demands and in turn channelise government's responses in ways she thought fit.[5]

Meanwhile, the changing nature of democracy, most visible in the ways in which regional political life developed, meant that the party holding power in the union government also had to heed diverse realities, and the national good, which appeared incontrovertible in the decade of Independence, had to accommodate regional aspirations and needs. The linguistic reorganisation of states aided this process, with economic concerns being defined and fought over in the name of bounded linguistic and cultural constituencies—the Samyukta Maharashtra movement is a case in point. Thus, unitary federalism assumed a cooperative countenance, with states insisting on their stakes in all matters, from the planned economy to issues of governance. This did not take away from the insuperable powers vested in the union government by the Constitution, but it did suggest the need for a politics of pragmatic accommodation.

This is evident in how planning was actualised. The Green Revolution and the setting up of large public sector units spurred major economic changes in the states, at least in pockets. As important such changes were to the advantage of particular classes and communities, eventually, these latter emerged into a new political self-consciousness that came to view state interests as paramount, if not separable from the so-called national interest. K. Balagopal, writing of Andhra Pradesh in

the early 1980s, terms the rise of these interests as representing the
will to power of 'the provincial propertied classes', of those who had
benefitted from the Green Revolution on account of their drawing on
social and real capital and, more importantly, utilising government
subsidies to their advantage.[6]

Reaping advantages from their position in rural society, these classes
in Andhra Pradesh, comprising reddy and kamma landlords, came to
straddle rural and urban worlds. In addition to furthering their agrarian
interests, they went on to invest in non-agrarian activities as well,
acquiring government contracts for public works and licenses for petrol
stations, and investing in cinema, trade and usury. Set in their social
dominance, which essentially was caste dominance, these classes were
ready to rule. The rise of N.T. Rama Rao and the Telugu Desam Party
(TDP), argues Balagopal, with its avowed support of 'local' interests,
has to be placed in this context. While the national Congress had
sought to rule in the name of the national good and through an adroit
manipulation of caste arithmetic, the TDP relied on cultural sentiment
to do with being 'Telugu', and class-caste power in the countryside,
successfully ousting the Congress in the state elections.

Meanwhile, the party became a sort of advance guard of local action
undertaken to keep intact class and caste authority: whether protesting
dalits or armed leftist militants, it sought to keep them in check through
the arbitrary use of State power as well as coercion exerted by local
hirelings. Often, these latter were drawn from the ranks of the poor
amongst the castes that were part of the provincial propertied classes,
and they proved able foot soldiers in protracted class-caste wars. The
TDP thus came to preside over a brutal and bloody playing out of caste
clientelism. At the same time, Rao took to dispensing a slew of welfare
provisions, attempting to reach out to his voters and the party faithful
through a nexus that tied the chief minister to the beneficiaries directly.
But, popular charisma and time-honoured patron-client networks did
not always work well together, until the time Chandrababu Naidu
became chief minister.

Balagopal points out that Naidu proved the man of the hour as far as India's eager capitalists were concerned: his government was pro-business, and he lost no time in rolling back subsidies granted to various social segments and in constraining populist distribution of State largesse. To compensate for the dissatisfaction that arose in response to these moves, Naidu built himself up as an efficient and able manager of issues, and one who would not demur from being amongst the people and heeding their woes. Even as governance came to be highly centralised, whatever benefits that accrued to the people came to be distributed not through local elected bodies, as they ought to have been, but through a well-oiled client network, presided over by party bosses. Clientelism thus came to sit snugly with neoliberal policymaking.

Following Balagopal, we ought to be able to map shifts in modes of extraction, governance and the emergence of clientelist politics in all states. Once we do this, the developments described in this book are likely to appear less exceptionable and more as heightened expressions of political cultures that are both similar and different across states, and which have sought to shape, even as they have been shaped, by electoral democracy.

The similarities include: the race for dominance that has infected political parties and the consequent vitiation of even the limited democracy guaranteed by elections, which in turn are increasingly subject to nepotism and persuasion through illegal cash transfers; the centralisation of political authority in the office of the chief minister, undercutting the power of local leaders; and the retreat from ideology towards rule that relies on what it views as developmental outcomes. The differences have to do with welfare: why is it that some states have not reneged on welfarism? Rajshekhar's account of Tamil Nadu is interesting in this regard, for what it tells us about the relationship between dominance and welfarism. In this context, the historical backstory is worth narrating.

The story has to begin with K. Kamaraj, the Congress chief minister of Tamil Nadu (1957–1963), remembered with affection and respect across the political spectrum. Sensitive to social justice and determined to keep his state's interests in the forefront, Kamaraj ensured that Tamil Nadu benefitted from the era of planning: not only were parts of the state earmarked as Green Revolution zones, but also the state received generous public sector projects. Even as he remained the Congressman he was, he did not renege on social justice concerns, which were central to the politics of the dravidian movement: reservation remained in place, violence against dalits was firmly attended to, and meaningful welfare provisions were made available to the disenfranchised. For example, Kamaraj's government extended the mid-day meal scheme, available until then only in limited schools; children in elementary schools were given free uniforms; special scholarships were made available for children from dalit families; and a massive campaign and budget were pressed into service to build a good public library system.

The DMK (1967–1976) carried on the numerous policies put in place by Kamaraj. It continued to support agrarian growth fuelled by the Green Revolution and encouraged the expansion of private industry and capital. Likewise, it added to the welfare basket: it nationalised transport, used subsidies to give the public cheap rice and built housing for the urban poor. It also sustained reservations in education and government recruitment for dalits and the backward classes. At the same time, it was short on dissent, quelling student and worker protests with an iron hand.

Importantly, the party's tough populism was inscribed within a larger politics of federalism. It thus demanded increased fiscal outlays for the states and greater autonomy in governance, and resisted the imposition of Hindi as the national language. However, its populist federalism notwithstanding, it could not forego electoral alliances with the Congress, then in power in the union government. In a sense, the unitary federalism of the Congress as well as the DMK's politics of state autonomy came up against their limits. The Congress needed to be present in the regions, but it could not do this on its own. A regional party such as the DMK had no choice but to reckon with the overweening authority of the union government. In any event, this made for a pragmatism that has since been the hallmark of dravidian politics, which remains high on rhetoric and accommodative in practice.[7]

This pragmatism acquired a thoroughly instrumental edge when the AIADMK came to power in 1976. The party relied on the charisma of its leader, the actor M.G. Ramachandran, and his on-screen persona—heroic, compassionate and always on the side of the downtrodden—became the face of the dravidian movement. His acts came to define dravidian ideology, rather than the other way around. Anxious to retain power and remain politically relevant, he was less vocal about the federal model that the DMK had foregrounded. He also reset the relationship that the DMK had forged between economic growth, welfare and ideological assertion. Welfarism replaced economic policymaking, and state resources came to be treated as if they were part of M.G.R.'s personal fiefdom.

Economic growth slowed and fell below the national average. Meanwhile, the party cultivated particular caste constituencies; tried to rejig the reservation policy, before returning to what was; and cultivated a client network that included political leaders as well as favoured industrialists. These latter benefitted immensely when M.G.R.'s government embarked on a substantial privatisation of higher education. Given this mix of developments, the state witnessed protests, especially by workers, and also saw a rise in leftist militancy. Unable to engage these discontents politically, M.G.R.'s government turned ferocious. Militants were killed in staged encounters with the police; civil rights groups that protested such killings faced coercion; and, in 1981, M.G.R.'s government passed a bill that made 'scurrilous' or 'indecent' writing a cognisable offence, inviting up to five years' imprisonment. A politics of dominance at any cost, orchestrated by the individual leader presiding over a clientelist network, thus came to stay in Tamil Nadu.

This reached its apogee when J. Jayalalithaa took over as chief minister, and her time in office, across the decades of the 1990s and thereafter, coincided with the neoliberal moment. The DMK too worked economic reforms with efficiency, when it came to rule, initially in 1996 and thereafter in 2006. But it was Jayalalithaa who brought home the dubious harvest: rent extraction, personal asset accumulation, centralisation of authority in the Chief Minister's Office as never before, and the rule of arbitrary power. On the other hand, she did not let go of the state's distinctive mode of governance—keeping social justice concerns in place, growing the welfare basket and insisting on state autonomy.

Welfarism, it might be said, became a substitute for substantive policymaking, be it investing in health or education, creating employment or rendering agriculture viable. Citizens came to be viewed as recipients of State goodwill rather than bearers of rights, as permanently needy, yet deserving only the bare minimum. This, in turn, created an electorate that played the welfare card to its own purpose and, in the bargain, settled for an attenuated democracy, in a political context where parties strived for dominance through measures that were at once conciliatory and coercive.

Economists have lauded Tamil Nadu's growth model, pointing to favourable indices of education and health as well as praising the state's pro-poor policies. Social scientists have argued that the state's reservation policies have brought hitherto marginalised communities to the forefront of politics and governance. These assessments are valid, but they do not tell the whole story. Other balance sheets must also be drawn up to help us critically comprehend the emergence of a politics of dominance and control.[8]

———

Tamil Nadu's tryst with regional autonomy, its determined welfarism and the authoritarian turn that successive governments in the state have sustained—all these indicate that in the neoliberal era, unitary federalism notwithstanding, states can and do transform themselves into more independent entities. The politics of dominance that parties have pursued through the neoliberal era has helped push the agendas and fortunes of regional elites, those provincial propertied classes, as well as their patrons.

It simply will not do to point fingers only at the large democratic deficit that marks the performance of the union government. True enough that the original sin must be laid at its door, at the authority vested in it, and the manner in which it has wielded that authority and continues to do so. On the other hand, there is nothing that the union government has done that has not been carried through in the states: the ways in which the Punjab government has used UAPA against those opposed to its narrow clientelism; the free run given to capital in Odisha; the slow but sure allowance that is being given to the Hindu Right in a state like Bihar, where, once, it was kept out; the contraction of democratic life in Tamil Nadu; the venality of the political class in Mizoram; and the coming together of all these tendencies in Gujarat.

Clearly, the union and state governments mirror each other in complex ways, and their relationship has neither been consistently confrontational nor entirely on terms set by the former. Reading the story of the states together is thus a useful exercise in comprehending how that entity called the 'Indian State' works. On the one hand, there is the union government that possesses overweening and countervailing authority, and state governments are held in check by fiscal and legal constraints. On the other hand, governments in the states seek to work their limited options to advantage, stopping at nothing, whether this has to do with the use of the police to curb dissent, fudge data or put in place market reforms that benefit their cronies.

Meanwhile, the union government watches, waits, collusive or not, and plays its role as guarantor of national sovereignty and security to advance its claims. In the neoliberal era, the former has been identified with, not the people and their right to constitutional remedies, but plutocrats. National security meanwhile has come to mean increased forms of surveillance of and violence against citizens insisting on their rights. These ways of governance have not been unwelcome in the states, unless they interfere with a different political mandate, as in Kashmir or Manipur, or come up against other models of kleptocratic governance.

———

Despite the State posits a complex relationship between development and democracy. One has been pursued in defiance of the other, and as a consequence, both have failed to deliver what they promised to. But meanwhile, the demos, the people of India, have not remained passive, and, in a variety of ways, have navigated the twists and turns of the path that connects economics and politics, growth and justice. They counter extraction by: filing Right to Information petitions, going to the courts, keeping watch on criminal acts of extraction, organising themselves to protest the takeover of their lands and the commons ... And for what it is worth, they work with political parties and their local leaders, seeing in them valuable conduits that help to transfer welfare, market information and political wisdom. At times, they are silently assisted by earnest officers in government, who are often strapped for resources themselves and have to reckon with indifferent colleagues and opportunist politicians.

Sections of the citizenry also seek to work within extractive processes. Enterprising individuals take advantage of whatever opportunities the market offers or governments make available, and set up small and large businesses, take risks and stake their all to win those lucrative contracts, playing clientelism to their advantage. Those who have neither social nor material capital work with bazaar cultures, trust their migratory instincts and travel far and wide to find work, and even when things appear abysmal, look to start all over again.

Hemmed in as all of them are by structures of inequity, practices of graft and violence, and the ever-present menace of an authoritarian and increasingly dissembling political system, they yet refuse to play victim. An enduring image of this resilience was the migrant worker in the time of the 2020 pandemic, who dared to walk home, for thousands of miles, because neither the neoliberal economy that needed her time and labour nor her government who insisted that the effects of growth would in time trickle down to her household, bothered to house her and care for her when she found herself thrown on to the streets and into uncertainty.

Despite the State, the people are.

V. Geetha is a Chennai-based feminist historian, writer and translator.

Notes

INTRODUCTION

1. Ajay Modi, 'Milking Votes', *Business Today* (24 November 2013), businesstoday.in/magazine/focus/chairman-vipul-chaudhary-union-against-gcmmf/story/200274.html.
2. TNN, 'Probe Corruption Allegations at Mehsana Dairy: High Court', *Times of India* (30 November 2013), timesofindia.indiatimes.com/city/vadodara/Probe-corruption-allegations-at-Mehsana-Dairy-High-court/articleshow/26615576.cms.
3. PTI, 'Amul Chairman Vipul Chaudhary Removed', *Mint* (13 January 2014), livemint.com/Companies/9F06SgQnSMvLpPouuC4z6N/Amul-chairman-Vipul-Chaudhary-removed.html.
4. M.V. Kamath, *Milkman from Anand: The Story of Verghese Kurien* (Delhi: Konark Publishers, 1996).
5. Kamath, *Milkman from Anand*, 111.
6. PTI, 'Two Former Gujarat Congress MLAs Join BJP', *Hindustan Times* (27 August 2017), hindustantimes.com/india-news/two-former-gujarat-congress-mlas-join-bjp/story-HnkVLffEkJDhWIkz7BJhCL.html.
7. M. Rajshekhar, 'The Amul Story: How Politics Is Hurting the Economics of Gujarat's Milk Cooperatives', *Scroll.in* (30 November 2017), scroll.in/article/858576/the-amul-story-how-politics-is-hurting-the-economics-of-gujarats-milk-cooperatives.
8. Rajshekhar, '"Amul Is Now a Congress-mukt Federation": How BJP Took Control of India's Largest Milk Cooperative', *Scroll.in* (1 December 2017), scroll.in/article/858585/amul-is-now-a-congress-mukt-federation-how-bjp-took-control-of-indias-largest-milk-cooperative; R.K. Mishra,

'Not Quite Milk and Honey', *Outlook* (16 October 2014), outlookindia.
com/website/story/not-quite-milk-and-honey/292291.

9.   Rajshekhar, 'Amul Is Now a Congress-mukt Federation', *Scroll.in.*

10. Rajshekhar, 'We Need to Get into Mission Mode on Promoting Cooperatives in Right Spirit: Shashi Rajagopalan, Board Member RBI and
Nabard', *Economic Times* (25 July 2011), economictimes.indiatimes.com/
opinion/interviews/we-need-to-get-into-mission-mode-on-promoting-
co-operatives-in-right-spirit-shashi-rajagopalan-board-member-rbi-
and-nabard/articleshow/9355597.cms.

11. Express News Service, 'Gujarat: Centre Nod to 150-Seat Banas Medical
College', *Indian Express* (19 May 2018), indianexpress.com/article/
cities/ahmedabad/gujarat-centre-nod-to-150-seat-banas-medical-
college-5182564/.

12. Peter Pomerantsev, *This Is Not Propaganda: Adventures in the War
Against Reality* (London: Faber & Faber, 2019), 5.

13. Vladimir Netto, *The Mechanism* (UK: Penguin Random House, 2019).

14. Dinesh Narayanan, *The RSS: And the Making of the Deep Nation* (India:
Penguin Random House, 2019), 237–238.

15. Steve Wick, *The Long Night: William L Shirer and the Rise and Fall of the
Third Reich* (US: Palgrave Macmillan, 2011), 238.

16. Laurel Leff, *Buried by the Times: The Holocaust and America's Most
Important Newspaper* (USA: Cambridge University Press, 2005).

17. 'States and Union Territories', Know India, knowindia.gov.in/states-uts/;
'Districts', Know India, knowindia.gov.in/districts/; 'Number of Cities
Towns by City Size Class', Ministry of Housing and Urban Affairs, mohua.
gov.in/cms/number-of-cities--towns-by-city-size-class.php; Richa
Verma, 'India Unclear How Many Villages It Has, and Why That Matters',
IndiaSpend (3 August 2017), archive.indiaspend.com/cover-story/india-
unclear-how-many-villages-it-has-and-why-that-matters-56076.

18. Donella Meadows, *Thinking in Systems: A Primer* (USA: Chelsea Green
Publishing, 2008), 88–89.

19. Rajshekhar, 'Quest for Fast Growth Lands India's Microfinance
Institutions in Soup', *Economic Times*, 8 March 2010, economictimes.
indiatimes.com/news/economy/finance/quest-for-fast-growth-lands-
indias-microfinance-institutions-in-soup/articleshow/5656037.cms.

20. Rajshekhar, 'Crony Capitalism on Modi's Watch Means Invisible Hands
Ensure You Never Go Bankrupt', *Wire* (29 July 2020), thewire.in/

political-economy/crony-capitalism-on-modis-watch-means-invisible-hands-ensure-you-never-go-bankrupt.

21. The Wire Analysis, 'How Sharad Pawar Took on the BJP and Emerged Victorious', *Wire* (27 November 2019), thewire.in/politics/sharad-pawar-maharashtra-ncp.

22. PTI, 'Minorities in India Faced Violent Attacks under Narendra Modi Government: US Panel', *Financial Express* (1 May 2015), financialexpress.com/india-news/minorities-in-india-faced-violent-attacks-under-narendra-modi-government-us-panel/68405/.

23. John Dayal and Shabnam Hashmi, *Democracy and Secularism under the Modi Regime* (India: Anhad, 2015), 365.

24. Bedanti Saran, 'Jayant Sinha Garlands Ramgarh Lynching Convicts, Says "Honouring Law"', *Hindustan Times* (7 July 2018), hindustantimes.com/india-news/hc-has-suspended-sentence-was-honouring-the-law-jayant-sinha-on-garlanding-ramgarh-lynching-convicts/story-oawPKViVZHsVcPAK84zN6N.html.

25. Mohammad Iqbal, 'Pehlu Khan Lynching Case: Rajasthan Court Acquits Six Accused', *Hindu* (14 August 2019), indiatoday.in/india/story/alwar-lynching-pehlu-khan-gau-rakshak-accused-acquitted-1580874-2019-08-14.

26. Praveen Donthi, 'Occupation Hazards', *Caravan* (1 August 2010), caravanmagazine.in/conflict/the-heavy-cost-of-revoking-article-370-in-kashmir.

27. The Wire Staff, 'Cobrapost Sting: Big Media Houses Say Yes to Hindutva, Black Money, Paid News', *Wire* (26 May 2018), thewire.in/media/cobrapost-sting-big-media-houses-say-yes-to-hindutva-black-money-paid-news.

1: THE STATE THAT COULD NOT PAY SALARIES

1. Daman Singh, *The Last Frontier: People and Forests in Mizoram* (New Delhi: Tata Energy Research Institute, 1996), 6.

2. Benjamin Saitlunga, 'Towards a Sustainable Smart City: The Case of Aizawl', Observer Research Foundation (August 2018), orfonline.org/research/43403-towards-a-sustainable-smart-city-the-case-of-aizawl/.

3. M. Rajshekhar, 'Seoul-Stirring Soaps in Aizawl: How South Korean Soft Power Is Changing Mizoram', *Scroll.in* (19 May 2015), scroll.in/

article/728533/seoul-stirring-soaps-in-aizawl-how-south-koreas-soft-power-is-changing-mizoram.

4. Euny Hong, *The Birth of Korean Cool: How One Nation Is Conquering the World through Pop Culture* (New York: Picador, 2014).

5. Singh, *The Last Frontier*, 21.

6. Singh, *The Last Frontier*, 22–27.

7. Singh, *The Last Frontier*, 29–31.

8. Singh, *The Last Frontier*, 57–60.

9. Laldenga, *Mizoram Marches towards Freedom* (India: Lalbiakdiki and Gilzom Offset, 2011).

10. Singh, *The Last Frontier*, 60.

11. Singh, *The Last Frontier*, 60–62.

12. Maitreyee Handique, 'In Mizoram, the Line Between Ancient Code of Selfless Service and Vigilante Justice Wears Thin', *Scroll.in* (8 April 2015), scroll.in/article/716835/in-mizoram-the-line-between-ancient-code-of-selfless-service-and-vigilante-justice-wears-thin.

13. Rajshekhar, 'In a Tiger Reserve in Mizoram, Camera Traps Are Taking Pictures of Gunmen', *Scroll.in* (10 March 2015), scroll.in/article/713794/in-a-tiger-reserve-in-mizoram-camera-traps-are-taking-pictures-of-gunmen.

14. 'Dampa Tiger Reserve', Department of Environment, Forests and Climate Change, Government of Mizoram, forest.mizoram.gov.in/page/dampa-tiger-reserve.

15. Rajshekhar, 'AIDS Is About to Explode in Mizoram and the Modi Government Is Partly to Blame', *Scroll.in* (1 May 2015), scroll.in/article/723915/aids-is-about-to-explode-in-mizoram-and-the-modi-government-is-partly-to-blame.

16. Rajshekhar, 'How the Congress Derailed a Plan to Stop Mizoram's Farmers Burning the Forests', *Scroll.in* (6 April 2015), scroll.in/article/717758/how-the-congress-derailed-a-plan-to-stop-mizorams-farmers-burning-the-forests.

17. T.R. Shankar Raman, *The Wild Heart of India: Nature and Conservation in the City, the Country, and the Wild* (New Delhi: Oxford University Press, 2019), 221–237.

18. Forest Survey of India, *India State of Forest Report, 2013* (India: Ministry of Environment, Forests and Climate Change), 22.

19. Rajshekhar, 'Why Medical Workers Are Taking Personal Loans to Keep Mizoram's Healthcare System Running', *Scroll.in* (5 May 2015), scroll. in/article/724629/why-medical-workers-are-taking-personal-loans-to-keep-mizorams-healthcare-system-running.

20. Mandakini Gahlot, 'High-risk Behaviour', *Caravan* (1 April 2015), caravanmagazine.in/government-policy/government-apathy-india-aids-programme.

21. Henry L. Khojol, '14,000 AIDS Patients in Mizoram', *Telegraph* (1 February 2018), telegraphindia.com/states/north-east/14000-aids-patients-in-mizoram/cid/1440694.

22. 'Amid National Decline, Spike in HIV Cases in Three Northeast States', *Wire* (7 August 2018), https://thewire.in/health/amid-national-decline-spike-in-hiv-cases-in-three-northeast-states.

23. Rahul Karmakar, 'With Nine Cases a Day, Mizoram Becomes State with Highest HIV Prevalence Rate', *Hindu* (13 October 2019), thehindu.com/sci-tech/health/with-nine-cases-a-day-mizoram-becomes-state-with-highest-hiv-prevalence-rate/article29674665.ece.

24. Rajshekhar, 'A New Gateway to the North-East Runs into and Jumps over a Corruption Roadblock', *Scroll.in* (26 May 2015), scroll.in/article/729210/a-new-gateway-to-the-north-east-runs-into-and-jumps-over-a-corruption-roadblock.

25. Rajshekhar, 'Scroll Investigation: Mizoram CM Gave Road Contracts to Firm in Which His Brother Held Shares', *Scroll.in* (29 June 2015), scroll.in/article/736549/scroll-investigation-mizoram-cm-gave-road-contracts-to-firm-in-which-his-brother-held-shares.

26. Budget Speech of Pu Lalsawta, 2014–2015, mizoram.nic.in/budget/budget%20speech%202014-15%20english.pdf.

27. Rajshekhar, 'Scroll Investigation: Mizoram CM Gave Road Contracts to Firm in Which His Brother Held Shares', *Scroll.in*.

28. 'Work on NH-44A: Mizoram CM Targets Party MP Who Is Owner of Contract Firm', *Indian Express* (15 October 2015), indianexpress.com/article/india/india-news-india/work-on-nh-44a-mizoram-cm-targets-party-mp-who-is-owner-of-contract-firm/.

29. Partha S. Ghosh and Deepak K. Mishra, 'Party Dynamics in a Border Region: Meeting the Political Challenges of India's North-Eastern Hill States' (July 2013), researchgate.net/publication/305767890_Party_

Dynamics_in_a_Border_Region_Meeting_the_Political_Challenges_
of_India%27s_North-Eastern_Hill_States.

30. Rajshekhar, 'Scroll Investigation: Mizoram CM Gave Road Contracts to
    Firm in Which His Brother Held Shares', *Scroll.in*.

31. Rajshekhar, 'Scroll Investigation: Mizoram CM Gave Road Contracts to
    Firm in Which His Brother Held Shares', *Scroll.in*.

32. 'Analysis of Criminal Background, Financial, Education, Gender and
    Other Details of Ministers in the Mizoram Assembly 2018', Association
    of Democratic Reforms (2018), adrindia.org/content/analysis-criminal-
    background-financial-education-gender-and-other-details-ministers-
    mizoram.

33. Rajshekhar, 'As Centre Changes Fund-sharing Formula, North East
    Faces an Unprecedented Financial Crisis', *Scroll.in* (23 May 2015), scroll.
    in/article/728152/as-centre-changes-fund-sharing-formula-north-east-
    faces-an-unprecedented-financial-crisis.

34. Rajshekhar, 'A New Gateway to the North-East Runs into and Jumps over
    a Corruption Roadblock', *Scroll.in*.

35. Mridula Chari, 'Mizoram Announces an Oil Palm District, but This Might
    Be a Bad Idea', *Scroll.in* (27 May 2014), https://scroll.in/article/665022/
    mizoram-announces-an-oil-palm-district-but-this-might-be-a-bad-
    idea.

2: THE STATE THAT WASTED ITS IRON ORE BOOM

1. M. Rajshekhar, 'Odisha's Mining Boom Is Over—And Everyone Is
   Scrambling to Cut Their Losses', *Scroll.in* (31 July 2015), scroll.in/article/
   743164/odishas-mining-boom-is-over-and-everyone-is-scrambling-to-
   cut-their-losses.

2. Adam Tooze, *Crashed: How a Decade of Financial Crises Changed the
   World* (UK: Allen Lane, 2018), 242.

3. S.T. Beuria, 'Chit Fund Scam Consumes Odisha', *Deccan Herald* (18 June
   2013), deccanherald.com/content/339585/chit-fund-scam-consumes-
   odisha.html.

4. Rajshekhar, 'Odisha's Mining Boom Is Over', *Scroll.in*.

5. Personal Communication with B. Prabhakaran.

6. Rajshekhar, 'How a Contractor from Tamil Nadu Carved Out an
   Enormous Mining Empire in Odisha', *Scroll.in* (5 November 2015),

scroll.in/article/760562/how-a-contractor-from-tamil-nadu-carved-out-an-enormous-mining-empire-in-odisha.

7. Rajshekhar, 'How a Contractor from Tamil Nadu Carved Out an Enormous Mining Empire in Odisha', *Scroll.in*.

8. Rajshekhar, 'Meet the Odisha MLA Whose Assets Grew by 1,700% in Five Years', *Scroll.in* (6 November 2015), scroll.in/article/761823/meet-the-odisha-mla-whose-assets-grew-by-1700-in-five-years.

9. Ashok Pradhan, 'Independent Candidates Give Parties a Run for Their Money', *Times of India* (13 April 2014), timesofindia.indiatimes.com/news/Independent-candidates-give-parties-a-run-for-their-money/articleshow/33688351.cms.

10. Satyasundar Barik, 'Assets of Candidate Swell by 1,700 Per Cent', *Hindu* (28 March 2014), thehindu.com/todays-paper/tp-national/tp-otherstates/assets-of-candidate-swell-by-1700-per-cent/article5842567.ece.

11. Rajshekhar, 'Odisha's Mining Boom Is Over', *Scroll.in*.

12. 'The Interview That Shook Odisha', *Sambad* (21 September 2014), sambadenglish.com/interview-shook-odisha/.

13. PTI, 'BJD Expels Senior Leader Prafulla Ghadai from Party', *Economic Times* (20 September 2014), economictimes.indiatimes.com/news/politics-and-nation/bjd-expels-senior-leader-prafulla-ghadai-from-party/articleshow/42992177.cms.

14. 'Mining Mafia Causes Rs 200-cr Loss to Exchequer Annually', *Business Standard* (21 January 2013), business-standard.com/article/economy-policy/mining-mafia-causes-rs-200-cr-loss-to-exchequer-annually-111090100070_1.html.

15. 'Much above the Industry Bench Mark', *Second Report on Illegal Mining of Iron and Manganese Ores in the State of Odisha: Volume 2* (Justice M.B. Shah Commission of Enquiry for Illegal Mining of Iron and Manganese Ores, October 2013), 169.

16. Rajshekhar, 'How a Contractor from Tamil Nadu Carved Out an Enormous Mining Empire in Odisha', *Scroll.in*.

17. 'Rs 781 for Every Tonne of Ore It Mined', *Second Report on Illegal Mining of Iron and Manganese Ores in the State of Odisha: Volume 2*, 168.

18. 'Should Have Been At Least Rs 180 Crore', *Second Report on Illegal Mining of Iron and Manganese Ores in the State of Odisha: Volume 1* (Justice M.B. Shah Commission of Enquiry for Illegal Mining of Iron and Manganese Ores, October 2013), 100–101.

19. 'Reaches As High As 75 Per Cent', *Second Report on Illegal Mining of Iron and Manganese Ores in the State of Odisha: Volume 1*, 101.

20. *Second Report on Illegal Mining of Iron and Manganese Ores in the State of Odisha: Volume 1*, 108–109.

21. Ashok Pradhan, 'Independent Candidates Give Parties a Run for Their Money', *Times Of India* (13 April 2014), timesofindia.indiatimes.com/news/Independent-candidates-give-parties-a-run-for-their-money/articleshow/33688351.cms.

22. Rajshekhar, 'How Odisha Squandered Valuable Mineral Resources without Any Gains for Its People', *Scroll.in* (7 November 2015), scroll.in/article/761825/how-odisha-squandered-valuable-mineral-resources-without-any-gains-for-its-people.

23. Biswajit Mohanty, *Chasing His Father's Dreams* (New Delhi: Authors UpFront, 2017), ebook.

24. *First Report on Illegal Mining of Iron and Manganese Ores in the State of Odisha: Volume 1*, 102.

25. Rajshekhar, 'Why Odisha's Empty Engineering Colleges Hurt Students and Not Their Owners', *Scroll.in* (20 October 2015), scroll.in/article/757735/why-odishas-empty-engineering-colleges-hurt-students-and-not-their-owners.

26. Personal Communication with Bijay Mohanty.

27. Ashok Pradhan, 'Not Even 10 Takers for Seats in 20 Odisha Engineering Colleges', *Times of India* (15 August 2015), timesofindia.indiatimes.com/home/education/news/Not-even-10-takers-for-seats-in-20-Odisha-engineering-colleges/articleshow/48490326.cms.

28. Sibdas Kundu, '12-Hour Shutdown Hits Bhadrak Life', *Telegraph* (15 July 2015), telegraphindia.com/states/odisha/12-hour-shutdown-hits-bhadrak-life/cid/1470359.

29. 'JEE: 50 Per Cent Criterion Gone', *The New Indian Express* (24 March 2011), newindianexpress.com/states/odisha/2011/mar/24/jee-50-per-cent-criterion-gone-238354.html.

30. Priya Abraham, 'OJEE Hope for Tech Colleges', *Telegraph* (18 June 2015), telegraphindia.com/states/odisha/ojee-hope-for-tech-colleges/cid/1467844#.VgOQprOY48o.

31. 'Ex Odisha Minister, Son Make Engineering College a Family Fiefdom', *Sambad* (15 August 2015), sambadenglish.com/ex-odisha-minister-son-make-engineering-college-a-family-fiefdom/.

32. 'Board of Directors', KMBB College of Engineering and Technology, kmbb.in/page.php?page=board-of-governors.
33. *First Report on Illegal Mining of Iron and Manganese Ores in the State of Odisha: Volume 1*, 102–105.
34. '47,040 Lakh Tonnes', *First Report on Illegal Mining of Iron and Manganese Ores in the State of Odisha: Volume 4* (Justice M.B. Shah Commission of Enquiry for Illegal Mining of Iron and Manganese Ores, June 2013), 160.
35. Rajshekhar, 'What a Primary School in Keonjhar Tells Us about Odisha's Misplaced Government Spending', *Scroll.in* (24 October 2015), scroll.in/article/758158/what-a-primary-school-in-keonjhar-tells-us-about-odishas-misplaced-government-spending.
36. TNN, 'Odisha Govt to Appoint 5364 Contractual Teachers', *Times of India* (23 October 2014), timesofindia.indiatimes.com/city/bhubaneswar/Odisha-govt-to-appoint-5364-contractual-teachers/articleshow/44915359.cms.
37. 'Odisha Govt Closes 735 Schools after Student Enrolment Declines', *Sambad* (3 July 2017), sambadenglish.com/odisha-govt-closes-735-schools-after-student-enrolment-declines/.
38. Priya Ramani, '"They Don't Feel Sorry": Revisiting Kandhamal 10 Years after the Violence against Christians', *Scroll.in* (26 August 2018), scroll.in/article/891587/they-dont-feel-sorry-revisiting-kandhamal-10-years-after-the-violence-against-christians.
39. PTI, '154 Infants Die in Four Months in Kandhamal Hospitals', *Economic Times* (3 September 2015), economictimes.indiatimes.com/news/politics-and-nation/154-infants-die-in-four-months-in-kandhamal-hospitals/articleshow/48785968.cms.
40. Rajshekhar, 'What a Primary School in Keonjhar Tells Us about Odisha's Misplaced Government Spending', *Scroll.in*.
41. Rajshekhar, 'The Dongria Kondhs of Odisha Now Face a More Formidable Enemy than Vedanta', *Scroll.in* (17 July 2015), scroll.in/article/738955/the-dongria-kondhs-of-odisha-now-face-a-more-formidable-enemy-than-vedanta.
42. Rajshekhar, 'Why Odisha Sees Little Protest Despite the State's Poor Public Services', *Scroll.in* (21 November 2015), scroll.in/article/765719/why-odisha-sees-little-protest-despite-the-states-poor-public-services.
43. Rajshekhar, 'The Dongria Kondhs of Odisha Now Face a More Formidable Enemy than Vedanta', *Scroll.in*.

3: THE STATE CONTROLLED BY ONE FAMILY

1. Amandeep Sandhu, '"We Have Stormed the Citadels of Badal": The Rail Roko Agitation Disrupting Punjab', *Caravan* (13 October 2015), caravanmagazine.in/vantage/stormed-citadels-badal-rail-roko-punjab.

2. Harpeet Bajwa, 'Why Has the Sikh Holy Book Been Desecrated over a 100 Times in Punjab: All You Need to Know', *The New Indian Express* (18 April 2017), newindianexpress.com/nation/2017/apr/18/why-has-the-sikh-holy-book-been-desecrated-over-a-100-times-in-punjab-all-you-need-to-know-1594993.html.

3. Navjeevan Gopal, 'Punjab Clashes: Badals Battle Crisis as Police Firing Kills Two over Holy Book Desecration', *Indian Express* (15 October 2015), indianexpress.com/article/india/india-news-india/holy-book-desecration-badals-battle-crisis-as-police-firing-kills-two/.

4. Abhimanyu Kumar, 'The Lynching That Changed India', *Al Jazeera* (5 October 2017), aljazeera.com/indepth/features/2017/09/lynching-changed-india-170927084018325.html.

5. M. Rajshekhar, 'Ground Report: How Rumours about Cow Slaughter Triggered Riots in Mainpuri', *Scroll.in* (14 October 2015), scroll.in/article/762036/ground-report-how-rumours-about-cow-slaughter-triggered-riots-in-mainpuri.

6. Scroll staff, 'Samajwadi Party Leader Shot, Injured in Mainpuri', *Scroll.in* (28 October 2015), scroll.in/latest/1160/samajwadi-party-leader-shot-injured-in-mainpuri.

7. Sukhwinder Singh, 'Rural Health in Punjab—Needs Reforms and Investments', sikhinstitute.org/july_2010/7-sukhwindersingh.pdf.

8. Ashok Gulati, Ranjana Roy and Siraj Hussain, 'Getting Punjab Agriculture Back on High Growth Path: Sources, Drivers and Policy Lessons', ICRIER (July 2017), icrier.org/pdf/Punjab%20Agriculture%20Report.pdf.

9. Amandeep Sandhu, *Panjab: Journeys through Fault Lines* (India: Westland Publications, 2020), 7–8.

10. Rajshekhar, 'How Climate Change Has Sparked Political and Social Unrest in Punjab This Year', *Scroll.in* (30 November 2015), scroll.in/article/772198/how-climate-change-has-sparked-political-and-social-unrest-in-punjab-this-year.

11. Anupam Chakravartty, 'Hybrid Infestation: The Politics of GM Crops in India', Ritimo (14 May 2018), ritimo.org/Hybrid-Infestation-The-Politics-of-GM-Crops-in-India.

12. Zia Haq, 'Bad Risks, Fake Pesticides Stoke Punjab's Worst Farm Crisis in Years', *Hindustan Times* (7 October 2015), hindustantimes.com/punjab/bad-risks-fake-pesticides-stoke-punjab-s-worst-farm-crisis-in-years/story 8avxcqflwOjANddjhl3cfO.html.

13. Shruti Bhogal and Sukhpal Singh, 'Commission Agent System: Significance in Contemporary Agricultural Economy of Punjab', *Economic and Political Weekly* (7 November 2015), epw.in/journal/2015/45/special-articles/commission-agent-system.html.

14. Akhil Gupta, *Postcolonial Developments: Agriculture in the Making of Modern India* (USA: Duke University Press, 1998), 3–4.

15. Rajshekhar, 'Why Is Industry Fleeing Punjab?', *Scroll.in* (11 December 2015), scroll.in/article/772899/why-is-industry-fleeing-punjab.

16. Personal Communication with Mohammad Yousuf of Cycle Makers Association of Ludhiana.

17. Sudip Chaudhuri, 'Import Liberalisation and Premature Deindustrialisation in India', *Economic and Political Weekly* (24 October 2015), epw.in/journal/2015/43/special-articles/import-liberalisation-and-premature-deindustrialisation-india.html.

18. Rajshekhar, 'Why Punjab's Power Bills Include a Cow Cess and Water Charges', *Scroll.in* (23 January 2016), scroll.in/article/802014/why-punjabs-power-bills-include-a-cow-cess-and-water-charges.

19. Rajshekhar, 'Why Is Industry Fleeing Punjab?', *Scroll.in*.

20. Rajshekhar, 'Every Business in Punjab Leads Back to an Akali Dal Leader (Well Almost)', *Scroll.in* (25 March 2016), scroll.in/article/804998/every-business-in-punjab-leads-back-to-an-akali-dal-leader-well-almost.

21. Rajshekhar, 'Every Business in Punjab Leads Back to an Akali Dal Leader', *Scroll.in*.

22. Rajshekhar, 'Every Business in Punjab Leads Back to an Akali Dal Leader', *Scroll.in*.

23. Rajshekhar, 'Every Business in Punjab Leads Back to an Akali Dal Leader', *Scroll.in*.

24. Prabhjit Singh, 'Goonda Tax Extortionists Now Invade Crusher Sites', *Hindustan Times* (11 April 2014), hindustantimes.com/chandigarh/goonda-tax-extortionists-now-invade-crusher-sites/story-y456rAgdvoGHdkqG8OzZAL.html; Jasdeep Singh Malhotra, 'Rs 20 Lakh a Day Goonda Tax on Sand, Gravel in Pathankot', *Hindustan Times* (21 September 2013), hindustantimes.com/punjab/

rs-20-lakh-a-day-goonda-tax-on-sand-gravel-in-pathankot/story-wv3JaiQvNBG8M9V7YGjEsN.html.

25. Devinder Pal, 'Badal-Kairon-Majithia Clan's Growing Biz Empire', *Tribune* (26 April 2014), tribuneindia.com/2014/20140426/main5.htm.

26. Sukhdeep Kaur, 'How Punjab's Cable Czar Built Rs 321-cr Empire, the "Fastway"', *Hindustan Times* (4 April 2015), hindustantimes.com/chandigarh/how-punjab-s-cable-czar-built-rs-321-cr-empire-the-fastway/story-sDCFgMTkWvbotzNUK75RBI.html.

27. 'Order, Case no. 36/2011', Competition Commission of India (3 July 2012). cci.gov.in/sites/default/files/362011_0.pdf.

28. Rajshekhar, 'Every Business in Punjab Leads Back to an Akali Dal Leader', *Scroll.in.*

29. Nicolas Martin, 'Politics, Capital and Land Grabs in Punjab, India', in *The Wild East: Criminal Political Economies in South Asia*, ed. Barbara Harriss-White and Lucia Michelutti (UK: University College London Press, 2019), 243.

30. Harriss-White and Michelutti, 'Introduction', in *The Wild East*, 1.

31. Harriss-White and Michelutti, 'Conclusion', in *The Wild East*, 322.

32. Rajshekhar, 'Every Business in Punjab Leads Back to an Akali Dal Leader', *Scroll.in.*

33. Devinder Pal, 'Badal Luxury Bus Fleet's Phenomenal Growth Continues', *Tribune* (28 April 2014), tribuneindia.com/2014/20140429/main7.htm.

34. Rajshekhar, 'Every Business in Punjab Leads Back to an Akali Dal Leader', *Scroll.in.*

35. Raman Kirpal, 'Not on TRP Radar, Yet Govt Ad Windfall for Badal Family Channel', *Firstpost* (20 January 2012), firstpost.com/politics/not-on-trp-radar-yet-govt-ad-windfall-for-badal-family-channel-188878.html.

36. Ruchika M. Khanna, 'Empty Coffers, State again Knocks at Centre's Door', *Tribune* (10 January 2016), tribuneindia.com/news/punjab/empty-coffers-state-again-knocks-at-centre-s-door/181678.html.

37. Rajesh Dikshit et al., 'Cancer Mortality in India: A Nationally Representative Survey', *Lancet* (28 March 2012), thelancet.com/journals/lancet/article/PIIS0140-6736(12)60358-4/fulltext.

38. 'National Health Profile 2015', Central Bureau of Health Intelligence, India, indiaenvironmentportal.org.in/content/419189/national-health-profile-nhp-of-india-2015/.

39. Rajshekhar, 'Has Punjab's Obsession with Cancer Robbed Its Poor of Healthcare?', *Scroll.in* (18 March 2016), scroll.in/article/804008/has-punjabs-obsession-with-cancer-robbed-its-poor-of-healthcare.

40. Sandhu, *Panjab*, 431.

41. Prabhjit Singh, 'Testing Times: The Case of Missing Teachers in Punjab Govt Schools', *Hindustan Times* (25 April 2015), hindustantimes.com/punjab/testing-times-the-case-of-missing-teachers-in-punjab-govt-schools/story-uG7xaOsWRSjpkzrBwtKJAP.html.

42. Rajshekhar, 'How the Badals Spread Their Control over Punjab (and Why It Is Eroding)', *Scroll.in* (26 March 2016), scroll.in/article/804076/how-the-badals-spread-their-control-over-punjab-and-why-it-is-eroding.

43. IANS, 'Meet Punjab's Ministerial Family—The Badals!', *Business Standard* (27 May 2014), business-standard.com/article/news-ians/meet-punjab-s-ministerial-family-the-badals-114052700997_1.html.

44. Baljit Balli, 'Portfolios Allocated to New Cabinet Ministers', *Babushahi* (15 March 2012), babushahi.com/full-news.php?id=5079.

45. I.P. Singh, 'Turmoil in Badal's Punjab—From Total Control to Leadership Vacuum', *Times of India* (blog, 26 October 2015), blogs.timesofindia.indiatimes.com/punjab-point-blank/turmoil-in-badals-punjab-from-total-control-to-leadership-vacuum/.

46. Amandeep Sandhu, 'It Is Becoming Clear That The SGPC No Longer Speaks for the Sikh Community', *Caravan* (5 January 2016), caravanmagazine.in/vantage/sgpc-no-longer-speaks-for-the-sikh-community.

47. Khalsa Press, 'Sirsa Cult Leader Makes Mockery of Guru Sahib!', *Panthic.org* (16 May 2006), panthic.org/articles/3288.

48. PTI, 'Pardon to Ram Rahim: SGPC Asks Sikhs to Accept Akal Takht Decision', *Hindustan Times* (27 September 2015), hindustantimes.com/punjab/pardon-to-ram-rahim-sgpc-asks-sikhs-to-accept-akal-takht-decision/story-GjbLFJW4SJyg8JcIsht6HL.html.

49. Kirpal, 'Not on TRP Radar, Yet Govt Ad Windfall for Badal Family Channel', *Firstpost*.

50. Nicolas Martin, 'Rural Elites and the Limits of Scheduled Caste Assertiveness in Rural Malwa, Punjab', *Economic and Political Weekly* (26 December 2015), epw.in/journal/2015/52/review-rural-affairs/rural-elites-and-limits-scheduled-caste-assertiveness-rural.

51. Rajshekhar, 'How the Badals Spread Their Control over Punjab', *Scroll.in*; 'A Report on Land Grab and Farmers Displacement in District Patiala',

PUDR Bulletin (June–August 2015), pudr.org/sites/default/files/2019-03/
CDRO%20201505%20June%20July%20August%20%281%29.pdf.

52. Talmiz Ahmad, 'Indians in Iraq—A Reverie', Ministry of External Affairs, India (2 July 2014), mea.gov.in/in-focus-article.htm?23545/Indians+in+Iraq++A+Reverie.

53. Rajshekhar, 'Has Punjab's Obsession with Cancer Robbed Its Poor of Healthcare?', *Scroll.in.*

54. Rajshekhar, 'Why Is Punjab Increasingly Turning to New Gurus for Comfort?', *Scroll.in* (28 March 2016), scroll.in/article/804145/why-is-punjab-increasingly-turning-towards-new-gurus-for-comfort.

55. Mark Juergensmeyer, *Religious Rebels in the Punjab: The Ad Dharm Challenge to Caste* (India: Navayana, 2009), 273.

56. Anurag Tripathi, *Dera Sacha Sauda and Gurmeet Ram Rahim: A Decade-Long Investigation* (India: Penguin Random House, 2018), 166.

57. Amartya Sen and Jean Drèze, *An Uncertain Glory: India and Its Contradictions* (UK: Penguin, 2014).

4: THE STATE THAT EMBRACED MESSIANIC POPULISM

1. K.K. Shahina, 'Love in the Time of Caste Politics', *Open* (26 June 2013), openthemagazine.com/features/india/love-in-the-time-of-caste-politics/.

2. Soumya Sivakumar, 'Ilavarasan's Death Was Definitely "Not a Suicide", Says Doctor Who Examined Body', *Wire* (15 March 2017), thewire.in/uncategorised/ilavarasan-death-not-suicide-says-doctor-who-conducted-autopsy.

3. Kavitha Muralidharan, 'When Kausalya Met Divya: Coming Together of 2 Women Who Remind Us of the Ugliness of Caste', *News Minute* (15 April 2017), thenewsminute.com/article/when-kausalya-met-divya-coming-together-2-women-who-remind-us-ugliness-caste-60388.

4. Shahina, 'Love in the Time of Caste Politics', *Open.*

5. Sivakumar, 'Ilavarasan's Death Was Definitely "Not a Suicide", Says Doctor Who Examined Body', *Wire*; Sivakumar, 'Despite Holes in Police Story, Death of Dalit Youth Ruled a "Suicide"', *Wire* (21 February 2017), thewire.in/caste/did-ilavarasan-of-dharmapuri-commit-suicide-holes-emerge-police-version.

6. M. Rajshekhar, 'Why Tamil Nadu Is Erecting Cages around Statues (Hint: It's Linked to Caste)", *Scroll.in* (26 September 2016), scroll.in/article/815377/why-tamil-nadu-is-erecting-cages-around-statues-hint-its-linked-to-caste.

7. Rohini Mohan, 'Jeans, "Love Drama" and the Electoral Spoils of Tamil Nadu's Hidden Caste Wars', *Wire* (6 May 2016), thewire.in/politics/tamil-nadus-hidden-caste-wars.

8. Anand Teltumbde, 'Attack on Dalits of Dharmapuri: A Fact Finding Report', *Countercurrents.org* (6 December 2012), countercurrents.org/teltumbde061212.htm.

9. Sandhya Ravishankar, 'Why Caste Is As Important to Tamil Nadu Politics As Amma vs Karunanidhi', *Scroll.in* (27 March 2016), scroll.in/article/804885/why-caste-is-as-important-to-tamil-nadu-politics-as-amma-vs-karunanidhi.

10. Special Correspondent, 'Ambedkar Statue Damaged', *Hindu* (26 August 2013), thehindu.com/todays-paper/tp-national/tp-tamilnadu/ambedkar-statue-damaged/article5060143.ece.

11. V. Geetha, 'Tracing Periyar's Thinking and Struggles', *Forward Press* (24 June 2019), forwardpress.in/2019/06/tracing-periyars-thinking-and-struggles/.

12. Rajshekhar, 'A Tsunami of Debt Is Building Up in Tamil Nadu—And No One Knows Where It Is Headed', *Scroll.in* (2 August 2017), scroll.in/article/810138/a-tsunami-of-debt-is-building-up-in-tamil-nadu-and-no-one-knows-where-it-is-headed.

13. K.J.S. Satyasai, 'Farmers' Income: Trend and Strategies for Doubling', *Indian Journal of Agricultural Economics* 71, no. 3 (July–Sept 2016); Rajshekhar, 'A Tsunami of Debt Is Building Up in Tamil Nadu—And No One Knows Where It Is Headed', *Scroll.in*.

14. Rajshekhar, 'Great Rural Land Rush: 3 to 100-fold Rise in Farm Land Prices May Not Bode Well', *Economic Times* (12 November 2013), economictimes.indiatimes.com/news/economy/agriculture/great-rural-land-rush-3-to-100-fold-rise-in-farm-land-prices-may-not-bode-well/articleshow/25607513.cms.

15. Personal Communication with V. Geetha.

16. K.S. Duralarasu, 'Ramadoss's Caste Cauldron Reheats Anti-Dalit Call', *India Today* (10 December 2002), indiatoday.in/india/south/story/pmk-founder-s-ramadoss-caste-cauldron-anti-dalit-inter-caste-marriages-123868-2012-12-10.

17. B. Kolappan, 'Ramadoss Consolidates Intermediate Caste Groups against Dalits', *Hindu* (2 December 2012), thehindu.com/news/national/tamil-nadu/Ramadoss-consolidates-intermediate-caste-groups-against-Dalits/article12432099.ece.

18. K. Balagopal, *Ear to the Ground* (New Delhi: Navayana, 2011), 257.

19. Rajshekhar, 'Tamil Nadu's Healthcare Numbers Look Good—But Its People Aren't Getting Healthier', *Scroll.in* (12 December 2016), scroll.in/article/820861/part-1-tamil-nadus-healthcare-numbers-look-good-but-its-people-arent-getting-healthier.

20. Pavitra Mohan, 'In Rural India, Less to Eat Than 40 Years Ago', *IndiaSpend* (25 August 2016), archive.indiaspend.com/cover-story/in-rural-india-less-to-eat-than-40-years-ago-90780.

21. P.V. Srividya, 'With Caste on Menu, Tribal Children Go Hungry', *Hindu* (7 August 2016), thehindu.com/todays-paper/tp-national/tp-tamilnadu/With-caste-on-menu-tribal-children-go-hungry/article14556261.ece.

22. Rajshekhar, 'Think Tamil Nadu Has Good Public Healthcare? It's Hard to Find It on the Ground', *Scroll.in* (13 December 2016), scroll.in/article/822044/think-tamil-nadu-has-good-public-healthcare-its-hard-to-find-it-on-the-ground.

23. *Tamil Nadu, State Report Card, National Achievement Survey, Class X* (Education Survey Division, National Council of Education, Research and Training).

24. Rajshekhar, 'Tamil Nadu's Schools Are in Crisis (but Nobody Is Talking about It)', *Scroll.in* (24 November 2016), scroll.in/article/821820/tamil-nadus-schools-are-in-crisis-but-nobody-is-talking-about-it; Rajshekhar, 'Tamil Nadu Tried to Reform Its Schools—But Made Them Much Worse', *Scroll.in* (26 November 2016), scroll.in/article/822028/tamil-nadu-tried-to-reform-its-schools-but-made-them-much-worse.

25. Rajshekhar, 'Tamil Nadu Tried to Reform Its Schools—But Made Them Much Worse', *Scroll.in*.

26. Personal Communication with V. Chandrasekhar; Rajshekhar, 'Sand Mining in Tamil Nadu Is Incredibly Destructive—But It's Also Unstoppable', *Scroll.in* (21 September 2016), scroll.in/article/815140/why-sand-mining-in-tamil-nadu-is-unstoppable-even-though-its-destructive.

27. Rajshekhar, 'Politicians Aren't Only Messing with Tamil Nadu's Water—They're Making Rs 20,000 Crore from Sand', *Scroll.in* (19 September

2016), scroll.in/article/815138/tamil-nadus-political-parties-are-making-money-from-sand-worth-a-whopping-rs-20000-crore-a-year.

28. J. Jeyaranjan, 'Sand and the Politics of Plunder in Tamil Nadu, India', in *The Wild East: Criminal Political Economies in South Asia* (UK: University College London Press, 2019), 92–112; Rajshekhar, 'Politicians Aren't Only Messing with Tamil Nadu's Water—They're Making Rs 20,000 Crore from Sand', *Scroll.in*.

29. Rajshekhar, 'Politicians Aren't Only Messing with Tamil Nadu's Water—They're Making Rs 20,000 Crore from Sand', *Scroll.in*.

30. Rajshekhar, 'Politicians Aren't Only Messing with Tamil Nadu's Water—They're Making Rs 20,000 Crore from Sand', *Scroll.in*.

31. Jeyaranjan, 'Sand and the Politics of Plunder in Tamil Nadu, India', in *The Wild East: Criminal Political Economies in South Asia*, 92–112; Rajshekhar, 'Politicians Aren't Only Messing with Tamil Nadu's Water—They're Making Rs 20,000 Crore from Sand', *Scroll.in*.

32. Rajshekhar, 'Politicians Aren't Only Messing with Tamil Nadu's Water—They're Making Rs 20,000 Crore from Sand', *Scroll.in*.

33. Ilangovan Rajasekaran, 'The Mother of All Loot', *Frontline* (24 July 2015), frontline.thehindu.com/cover-story/the-mother-of-all-loot/article7391496.ece.

34. Jayaraj Sivan, 'Illegal Sand Mining in Tamil Nadu Worth Rs 15,000 Crore?', *Times of India* (21 August 2013), timesofindia.indiatimes.com/india/Illegal-sand-mining-in-Tamil-Nadu-worth-Rs-15000-crore/articleshow/21948643.cms.

35. [Staff report], 'Stockyard Owners Hoarding Sand', *The New Indian Express* (13 July 2012), newindianexpress.com/cities/chennai/2011/jul/13/stockyard-owners-hoarding-sand-271009.html.

36. Rajshekhar, 'Politicians Aren't Only Messing with Tamil Nadu's Water—They're Making Rs 20,000 Crore from Sand', *Scroll.in*.

37. Personal Communication with S. Neelakantan, former director of the Madras Institute of Development Studies.

38. Rohini Mohan, 'As Tamil Nadu Votes, Cash Seizures are a Reminder of Where Real Power Lies', *Wire* (16 May 2016), thewire.in/36358/as-tamil-nadu-votes-cash-seizures-are-a-reminder-of-where-real-power-lies; HT Correspondent, 'Polling in Tamil Nadu's Aravakurichi Postponed over Bribery Concerns', *Hindustan Times* (15 May 2016), hindustantimes.com/assembly-elections/polling-in-tamil-nadu-s-aravakurichi-

postponed-over-bribery-concerns/story-Mz138uuFcIn9v5ZLnORcmI. html.

39. A.S. Nazir Ahamed, 'Cash-for-Vote: Genesis of the "Thirumangalam Formula"', *Hindu* (14 May 2016), thehindu.com/elections/tamilnadu 2016/cashforvote-genesis-of-the-thirumangalam-formula/article 8601057.ece.

40. Barbara Harriss-White and J. Jeyaranjan, 'Building on Sand? Criminal Markets and Politics in Tamil Nadu', in *Rethinking Markets in Modern India: Embedded Exchange and Contested Jurisdiction*, ed. Ajay Gandhi, Barbara Harriss-White, Douglas E. Haynes and Sebastian Schwecke (UK: Cambridge University Press, 2020), 358.

41. Harriss-White and Jeyaranjan, 'Building on Sand? Criminal Markets and Politics in Tamil Nadu', in *Rethinking Markets in Modern India*, 358.

42. *Annual Audit Report (2013–2014)*, All India Anna Dravida Munnetra Kazhagam, eci.gov.in/files/file/5136-all-india-anna-dravida-munnetra-kazhagam%09-annual-audit-report-2013-14/.

43. Rajshekhar, 'Think Sand Mining Damages the Ecology? It Ruins Politics As Well', *Scroll.in* (20 September 2016), scroll.in/article/815139/think-sand-mining-damages-the-ecology-it-ruins-politics-as-well.

44. S. Narayan, *The Dravidian Years* (India: Oxford University Press, 2018), 219.

45. Rajshekhar, 'Sand Mining in Tamil Nadu Is Incredibly Destructive—But It's Also Unstoppable', *Scroll.in*.

46. Sibi Arasu, 'Holding His Ground against the Sand Raiders of Tamil Nadu', *Wire* (26 June 2016), thewire.in/46026/holding-ground-against-sand-raiders-in-tamil-nadu/.

47. K.V. Lakshmana, 'Determined Women Take Lead in Battle Against Sand Mafia in Tamil Nadu', *Hindustan Times* (25 April 2015), hindustantimes. com/india/determined-women-take-lead-in-battle-against-sand-mafia-in-tamil-nadu/story-eal7eQajL01nA6P9f3SWgO.html.

48. Dhanya Rajendran, '"Touch Me Not": Tamil Nadu Government Has Filed Over 70 Defamation Cases on Media', *News Minute* (17 January 2015), thenewsminute.com/politics/286.

49. TNM Staff, 'SRM Group Chairman TR Pachamuthu Arrested by Chennai Police', *News Minute* (26 August 2016), thenewsminute.com/ article/srm-university-chancellor-tr-pachamuthu-arrested-chennai-police-48879.

50. Personal Communication with S. Neelakantan.

51. T. Ramakrishnan, 'Adieu to Tamil Nadu Groundwater Law', *Hindu* (20 September 2013), thehindu.com/news/national/tamil-nadu/adieu-to-tamil-nadu-groundwater-law/article5147072.ece.

52. Rajshekhar, 'How a River in Tamil Nadu Turned into a Sewage Canal', *Scroll.in* (29 August 2016), scroll.in/article/812450/how-a-river-in-tamil-nadu-turned-into-a-sewage-canal.

53. Rajshekhar, 'How a River in Tamil Nadu Turned into a Sewage Canal', *Scroll.in*.

54. Sunetra Chowdhury, 'Respond to "VIP Complaint", Smriti Irani's Ministry Told Hyderabad University', NDTV (19 January 2016), ndtv.com/india-news/respond-to-vip-complaint-smriti-iranis-ministry-told-hyderabad-university-1267496.

55. Express News Service, 'Sedition Case against JNUSU President: Lawyers, BJP MLA Take Law in Their Fists', *Indian Express* (16 February 2016), indianexpress.com/article/india/india-news-india/jnu-kanhaiya-kumar-patiala-house-court-lawyers-media-attacked/.

56. TNN, 'Lawyers Attack Arrested JNUSU President Kanhaiya Kumar in Patiala House Court Complex', *Times of India* (17 February 2016), timesofindia.indiatimes.com/india/Lawyers-attack-arrested-JNUSU-president-Kanhaiya-Kumar-in-Patiala-House-court-complex/articleshow/51024005.cms.

57. 'Chhattisgarh Police Intimidates Jagdalpur Legal Aid Group and Journalist Malini Subramaniam', *Caravan* (18 February 2016), caravanmagazine.in/vantage/chhattisgarh-police-intimidate-jagdalpur-legal-aid-group-malini-subramaniam.

58. Staff Report, 'India Tribal Activist Soni Sori Attacked with Chemicals', BBC (21 February 2016), bbc.com/news/world-asia-india-35624548.

59. Madhu Ramnath, *Woodsmoke and Leafcups: Autobiographical Footnotes to the Anthropology of the Durwa People* (India: HarperCollins Litmus, 2015), 16.

60. Rajshekhar, 'How Do So Many Industrialists Get into the Rajya Sabha?', *Scroll.in* (21 March 2016), scroll.in/article/805332/how-do-so-many-industrialists-get-into-the-rajya-sabha.

61. Prem Shankar Jha, 'Where Indian Democracy Went Wrong', unpublished essay accessed digitally with author's permission.

62. K.C. Suri, 'Parties under Pressure: Political Parties in India Since Independence', paper prepared for the Project on State of Democracy in South Asia (Delhi: CSDS).

63. Bhanu Dhamija, 'In Democratic India, Why Do We Still Have Autocratic Parties?', *Quint* (25 April 2017), thequint.com/voices/blogs/no-inner-party-democracy-internal-elections-in-india.

64. Nilanjan Mukhopadhyay, 'Narendra Modi Is Right about Lack of Intra-party Democracy. But Is BJP an Exception?', *Economic Times* (1 November 2017), economictimes.indiatimes.com/news/politics-and-nation/narendra-modi-is-right-about-lack-of-intra-party-democracy-but-is-bjp-an-exception/articleshow/61426433.cms.

65. Ward Berenschot, *Riot Politics: Hindu-Muslim Violence and the Indian State* (India: Rupa Publications, 2013).

66. Francis Fukuyama, *Political Order and Political Decay: From the Industrial Revolution to the Globalisation of Democracy* (UK: Profile Books, 2014), 29.

67. Fukuyama, *Political Order and Political Decay*, 161–164.

68. Oliver Heath and Louise Tillin, 'How to Get Rid of Clientelism in Politics', *Hindu* (15 August 2017), thehindubusinessline.com/opinion/columns/how-to-get-rid-of-clientelism-in-politics/article9818611.ece.

69. Berenschot, *Riot Politics*, 146.

70. Biswajit Mohanty, *Chasing His Father's Dreams: Inside Story of Odisha's Longest Serving Chief Minister* (New Delhi: AuthorsUpFront, 2017), ebook.

71. V. Prem Shanker, 'Jaya's Three Commanders: Jayalalithaa's Trusted Aides on Whom She Banks for Her Decisions', *Economic Times* (1 August 2014), economictimes.indiatimes.com/news/politics-and-nation/jayas-three-commanders-jayalalithaas-trusted-aides-on-whom-she-banks-for-her-decisions/articleshow/39384756.cms.

72. Personal Communication with Abhijit Sen.

73. Tzvetan Todorov, *The Inner Enemies of Democracy* (UK: Polity Books, 2014), 9.

5: THE ABSENT STATE

1. M. Rajshekhar, 'Fear and Loathing in Chhapra: How a Peaceful Bihar Town Became a Communal Tinderbox', *Scroll.in* (3 July 2017), scroll.

in/article/838619/fear-and-loathing-in-chhapra-how-a-peaceful-bihar-town-became-a-communal-tinderbox.

2. Ashish Jain, 'Bajrang Dal Chapra Relly', YouTube video (4 October 2014), youtu.be/DkJVaGch_XM.

3. Mohammad Sajjad, 'The Scary Messages from the Saran Riots', *Rediff.com* (17 August 2016), rediff.com/news/column/the-scary-messages-from-the-saran-riots/20160817.htm.

4. Personal Communication with Arshad Ajmal

5. Warisha Farasat and Prita Jha, *Splintered Justice: Living the Horror of Mass Communal Violence in Bhagalpur and Gujarat* (India: Three Essays Collective, 2016), 30.

6. Tarique Anwar, 'Indicted for His Role in Bhagalpur Riots, KS Dwivedi Takes Over as New Bihar DGP', *Sabrang* (1 March 2018), sabrangindia.in/article/indicted-his-role-bhagalpur-riots-ks-dwivedi-takes-over-new-bihar-dgp.

7. Tarique Anwar, 'Indicted for His Role in Bhagalpur Riots, KS Dwivedi Takes Over as New Bihar DGP', *Sabrang*.

8. Farasat and Jha, *Splintered Justice*, 58.

9. George J. Kunnath, *Rebels from the Mud Houses: Dalits and the Making of the Maoist Revolution in Bihar* (London and New York: Routledge, 2018).

10. Rajshekhar, 'Caste Calculus: How the BJP Is Expanding Its Footprint in Bihar', *Scroll.in* (4 July 2017), scroll.in/article/839171/caste-calculus-how-the-bjp-is-expanding-its-footprint-in-bihar.

11. Rajshekhar, 'Fear and Loathing in Chhapra: How a Peaceful Bihar Town Became a Communal Tinderbox', *Scroll.in*.

12. Rajshekhar, 'Caste Calculus: How the BJP Is Expanding Its Footprint in Bihar', *Scroll.in*.

13. Jairus Banaji, 'The Political Culture of Fascism', South Asia Citizens Webs (September 2002), sacw.net/2002/BanajiSept02.html.

14. Rajeev Ranjan Chaturvedy and Atul K. Thakur, 'The Rise and Fall of Nitish Kumar', *Hindu* (28 June 2014), thehindu.com/opinion/op-ed/the-rise-and-fall-of-nitish-kumar/article6155878.ece.

15. Anand Yang, *Bazaar India: Markets, Society, and the Colonial State in Bihar* (Berkeley: University of California Press, 1998), 27, sourced from: publishing.cdlib.org/ucpressebooks/view?docId=ft4779n9tq&chunk.id=d0e5191&toc.depth=1&toc.id=&brand=ucpress.

16. Yang, *Bazaar India*, 76.

17. Yang, *Bazaar India*, 69.

18. Athakattu Santhosh Mathew, 'State Incapacity by Design', Dphil thesis submitted to the University of Sussex (December 2011), sro.sussex. ac.uk/id/eprint/7599/1/%282012.12.07%29_Mathew%2C_Athakattu_ Santhosh.pdf.

19. Jeffrey Witsoe, *Democracy against Development: Lower Caste Politics and Political Modernity in Postcolonial India* (USA: University of Chicago Press, 2013), ebook.

20. *Economic Survey 2006–2007* (Department of Finance, Government of Bihar), 177, finance.bih.nic.in/Reports/ESR-2006-07-EN.pdf.

21. *Bihar Budget Analysis 2016–2017* (PRS Legislative Research), prsindia. org/sites/default/files/budget_files/Bihar%20Budget%20Analysis%20 2016-17.pdf.

22. Rajshekhar, 'Cancer Has Exploded in Bihar as Lakhs of People Drink Water Poisoned with Arsenic', *Scroll.in* (24 April 2017), scroll.in/ pulse/835431/ignored-arsenic-contamination-in-bihars-water-has-led-to-an-explosion-of-cancer.

23. Personal Communication with Ashok Ghosh.

24. Rajshekhar, 'Cancer Has Exploded in Bihar as Lakhs of People Drink Water Poisoned with Arsenic', *Scroll.in*.

25. Matthijs Brouns, Merijn Janssen and Andrew Wong, 'Dealing with Arsenic in Rural Bihar, India' (Delft University of Technology, February 2013), indiawaterportal.org/sites/indiawaterportal.org/files/dealing_ with_arsenic_in_bihar_india_-_third_version_merged.pdf.

26. Rajshekhar, 'Lessons from Bihar's 2016 Dengue Outbreak: Migration, Poverty, Garbage Are Spreading New Diseases', *Scroll.in* (10 May 2017), scroll.in/pulse/837083/lessons-from-bihars-2016-dengue-outbreak-migration-poverty-garbage-are-spreading-new-diseases.

27. Rajshekhar, 'Lessons from Bihar's 2016 Dengue Outbreak: Migration, Poverty, Garbage Are Spreading New Diseases', *Scroll.in*.

28. Rajshekhar, 'Bihar Can't Even Count How Many Dengue Cases It Has Had, Let Alone Fight the Disease', *Scroll.in* (11 May 2017), scroll.in/ pulse/837091/bihar-cant-even-count-how-many-dengue-cases-it-has-had-let-alone-fight-the-disease.

29. Rajshekhar, 'Bihar Is Struggling to Improve the Lives of the Poor Even after 27 Years of Backward Caste Rule', *Scroll.in* (14 June 2017), scroll.in/ article/839031/bihar-is-struggling-to-improve-the-lives-of-the-poor-even-after-27-years-of-backward-caste-rule.

30. Deepu Sebastian Edmond, 'What the Photo Didn't Show: 1700 Students, 5 Rooms, 2 Math Teachers', *Indian Express* (27 March 2015), indianexpress.com/article/india/india-others/what-the-photo-didnt-show-1700-students-5-rooms-2-math-teachers/.

31. Raksha Kumar, 'In Bihar, a Land Programme for Dalits Improved Many Lives—Until Nitish Kumar Allied with the BJP', *Scroll.in* (22 February 2018), scroll.in/article/868266/in-bihar-a-land-programme-for-dalits-improved-many-lives-until-nitish-kumar-allied-with-the-bjp.

32. Rajshekhar, 'As MNREGA Work Dries Up, Even the Elderly in Bihar Are Migrating to Brick-Kilns', *Scroll.in* (28 October 2016), scroll.in/roving/820042/as-mnrega-work-dries-up-even-the-elderly-in-bihar-are-migrating-to-brick-kilns.

33. Rajshekhar, 'Bihar's Nitish Kumar Has Been in Power for 12 Years. Why Has He Failed to Change Its Fortunes?', *Scroll.in* (15 June 2017), scroll.in/article/839032/bihars-nitish-kumar-has-been-in-power-for-12-years-why-has-he-failed-to-change-its-fortunes.

34. Alok Gupta, 'Millionaire Mukhiyas', *Down to Earth* (11 June 2015), downtoearth.org.in/coverage/millionaire-mukhiyas-42170.

35. Rajshekhar, 'Bihar Is Struggling to Improve the Lives of the Poor Even after 27 Years of Backward Caste Rule', *Scroll.in*.

36. Milan Vaishnav, *When Crime Pays: Money and Muscle in Indian Politics* (India: HarperCollins Publishers, 2017), 171–174.

37. Rajshekhar, 'What's Common between Coaching Classes in Bihar and Its Bahubali Leaders?', *Scroll.in* (16 June 2017), scroll.in/article/839033/whats-common-between-coaching-classes-in-bihar-and-bahubalis.

38. Jeffrey Witsoe, *Democracy against Development*, ebook.

39. Rajshekhar, 'Off Beat: What the Popularity of South Indian Films in Bihar Says about How the State Is Changing', *Scroll.in* (6 June 2017), scroll.in/magazine/838382/off-beat-what-the-popularity-of-south-india-films-in-bihar-says-about-how-the-state-is-changing.

40. Sudhish Kamath, 'Cinema of Cruelty', *Hindu* (20 December 2013), thehindu.com/features/cinema/Cinema-of-Cruelty/article11634657.ece.

41. Rajshekhar, 'Work in Progress: What Bihar's Changing Village Bazaars Say about the State', *Scroll.in* (21 May 2017), scroll.in/article/837603/work-in-progress-what-the-changing-landscape-of-its-village-markets-says-about-bihar.

42. Rajshekhar, 'Demonetisation Has Left India's Food Markets Frozen—And the Future Looks Tense', *Scroll.in* (18 November 2016), scroll.in/article/821834/demonetisation-has-left-indias-food-markets-frozen-and-the-future-looks-tense.

43. Rajshekhar, 'Ground Report: In Bihar, Murmurs of Protest Break the Sullen Silence against Demonetisation', *Scroll.in* (16 December 2016), scroll.in/article/824203/ground-report-in-bihar-murmurs-of-protest-break-the-sullen-silence-against-demonetisation.

44. Eugene Lyons, *Assignment in Utopia* (USA: Transaction Publishers, 1991), 283.

45. PTI, 'CBI Arrests Sekar Reddy in Rs 170 Cr Cash Seizure Case', *Hindu Businessline* (11 January 2018), thehindubusinessline.com/news/cbi-arrests-sekar-reddy-in-rs-170-cr-cash-seizure-case/article9438488.ece.

46. DHNS, 'I-T Dept Raids on TN Chief Secy's Office, Home Net 30L, 5 Kg Gold', *Deccan Herald* (22 December 2016), deccanherald.com/content/587757/i-t8200dept-raids-tn-chief.html.

47. Laura Bear, *Navigating Austerity: Currents of Debt along a South Asian River* (USA: Stanford University Press, 2015), 7.

48. Zygmunt Bauman, *Liquid Modernity* (UK: Polity Books, 2000).

49. Zygmunt Bauman and Leonidas Donskis, *Moral Blindness: The Loss of Sensitivity in Liquid Modernity* (UK: Polity Books, 2013), 65.

50. Bauman and Donskis, *Moral Blindness*, 107.

51. Scroll Staff, 'Over 50% Indians believe That Autocracy or Military Rule Would Be Good for the Country, Finds Survey', *Scroll.in* (17 October 2017), scroll.in/latest/854370/over-50-indians-believe-that-autocracy-or-military-rule-would-be-good-for-the-country-finds-survey.

52. Rajshekhar, 'Guess Who Calls Lodi Gardens a Forest?', *Economic Times* (5 April 2012), economictimes.indiatimes.com/news/news-by-industry/et-cetera/Indias-forests-are-in-serious-decline-both-in-numbers-and-health/articleshow/12540825.cms.

53. Staff, 'The Elephant in the Stats', *Economist* (9 April 2016), economist.com/finance-and-economics/2016/04/09/the-elephant-in-the-stats.

54. Chaitanya Mallapur, 'Narendra Modi's "7 Million Jobs" Speech: Relying on EPF Data Alone Paints Incorrect Picture of Employment in India', *Firstpost* (30 January 2018), firstpost.com/india/narendra-modis-7-million-jobs-speech-relying-on-epf-data-alone-paints-incorrect-picture-of-employment-in-india-4326779.html.

55. Rajshekhar, 'Can the Courts Save India's Rivers from Pollution? Tirupur Shows the Answer Is No', *Scroll.in* (30 August 2016), scroll.in/article/812470/can-the-courts-save-indias-rivers-from-pollution-tirupur-shows-the-answer-is-no.

56. Bauman and Donskis, *Moral Blindness*, 107.

57. Vasily Grossman, *Life and Fate* (UK: Vintage Books, 2006), 197.

58. Robert Sapolsky, *Behave: The Biology of Humans at Our Best and Worst* (UK: Penguin Random House, 2017), 487.

59. Robert Sapolsky, *Behave*, 561.

60. Robert Sapolsky, *Behave*, 570.

61. Bauman, *Liquid Modernity*, 109.

62. M.S.S. Pandian, *The Image Trap: M.G. Ramachandran in Film and Politics* (India: Sage Publications, 1992, 2015)

63. Jacob S. Hacker and Paul Pierson, *Winner-Take-All Politics: How Washington Made the Rich Richer—And Turned Its Back on the Middle Class* (NY: Simon and Schuster, 2010), 105–106.

64. Staff, 'Congress Alleges Deliberate Manipulation in Telangana Voters List', *Outlook* (16 September 2018), outlookindia.com/newsscroll/congress-alleges-deliberate-manipulation-in-telangana-voters-list/1384150.

65. Hacker and Pierson, *Winner-Take-All Politics*, 105–106.

66. Anurag Tripathi, *Dera Sacha Sauda and Gurmeet Ram Rahim: A Decade-Long Investigation* (India: Penguin Random House, 2018), 176–177.

67. Personal Communication with Tridip Suhrud.

68. H.L. Seneviratne, *The Work of Kings: The New Buddhism in Sri Lanka* (USA: University of Chicago Press, 1999).

69. Soli J. Sorabjee, 'Babasaheb's Warning: In Politics, Hero-worship Is a Path to Degradation and Eventual Dictatorship', *Indian Express* (15 October 2019), indianexpress.com/article/opinion/columns/constitution-babasaheb-ambedkar-warning-hero-worship-6069022/.

70. Ushinor Majumdar, *God of Sin: The Cult, Clout and Downfall of Asaram Bapu* (Penguin, 2018), 212; Tripathi, *Dera Sacha Sauda and Gurmeet Ram Rahim*, 165.

6: THE STATE THAT CHOSE MAJORITARIANISM

1. J.D. Taylor, *Island Story: Journeys through Unfamiliar Britain* (UK: Repeater, 2016), 87.

2. Amita Shah and Itishree Patnaik, 'High Growth Agriculture in Gujarat', in *Growth or Development: Which Way Is Gujarat Going?*, ed. Indira Hirway, Amita Shah and Ghanshyam Shah (India: Oxford University Press, 2014), 225–269.

3. M. Rajshekhar, 'In Surat's Textile Hub, Small Businesses Are Afraid of GST—But Big Companies Are Not', *Scroll.in* (28 June 2017), scroll.in/article/841882/in-surats-textile-hub-small-businesses-are-afraid-of-gst-but-big-companies-are-not.

4. Rajshekhar, 'Beyond Surat's GST Strike: New Technologies, Chinese Imports Are Causing a Churn in Textile Sector', *Scroll.in* (29 June 2017), scroll.in/article/842004/beyond-surats-gst-strike-new-technologies-chinese-imports-are-causing-a-churn-in-textile-sector.

5. Paranjoy Guha Thakurta, 'Polyester Prince Revisited', *Economic and Political Weekly* (13 September 2014), epw.in/journal/2014/37/insight/polyester-prince-revisited.html.

6. Rajshekhar, 'Why Small Businessmen in Gujarat Are Quitting Industry and Turning to Financial Speculation', *Scroll.in* (26 September 2016), scroll.in/article/851343/why-small-businessmen-in-gujarat-are-leaving-industry-for-financial-speculation.

7. Hirway, Shah and Shah, *Growth or Development*, 153.

8. Achyut Yagnik and Suchitra Sheth, *The Shaping of Modern Gujarat: Plurality, Hindutva and Beyond* (India: Penguin Books, 2005), 228.

9. Rajshekhar, 'Why Small Businessmen in Gujarat Are Quitting Industry and Turning to Financial Speculation', *Scroll.in*.

10. Rajshekhar, 'How Palm Oil from Malaysia Fired the Patel Agitation in Gujarat', *Scroll.in* (4 October 2017), scroll.in/article/852012/how-palm-oil-from-malaysia-fired-the-patel-agitation-in-gujarat.

11. M.V. Kamath, *Milkman from Anand: The Story of Verghese Kurien* (Delhi: Konark Publishers, 1996).

12. *Report of the Committee on Rationalisation of Customs and Excise Duties on Edible Oils and Oilseeds* (13 January 2006), 7, dea.gov.in/sites/default/files/ReportRationalEC.pdf.

13. Rajshekhar, 'How Palm Oil from Malaysia Fired the Patel Agitation in Gujarat', *Scroll.in*.

14. Rajendra Jadhav and Emily Chow, 'India's Refined Palm Oil Imports to Fall as Duty Change Makes Crude Palm Cheaper', *Reuters* (18 August 2017), in.reuters.com/article/india-palmoil-imports/indias-refined-

palm-oil-imports-to-fall-as-duty-change-makes-crude-palm-cheaper-idINKCN1AY0LA.

15. Rajshekhar, 'How Palm Oil from Malaysia Fired the Patel Agitation in Gujarat', *Scroll.in*.

16. Rajshekhar, 'The Amul Story: How Politics Is Hurting the Economics of Gujarat's Milk Cooperatives', *Scroll.in* (30 November 2017), scroll.in/article/858576/the-amul-story-how-politics-is-hurting-the-economics-of-gujarats-milk-cooperatives.

17. Rajshekhar, 'The Amul Story: How Politics Is Hurting the Economics of Gujarat's Milk Cooperatives', *Scroll.in*.

18. Arvind M. Patel, 'A Performance Appraisal of Dairy Industry in Gujarat, 2005', thesis submitted to Saurashtra University, Gujarat (December 2005), shodhganga.inflibnet.ac.in/bitstream/10603/291203/5/certificate.pdf.

19. Rajshekhar, 'The Amul Story: How Politics Is Hurting the Economics of Gujarat's Milk Cooperatives', *Scroll.in*.

20. Prashant Rupera, 'Manpower Milking Baroda Dairy Dry', *Times of India* (23 September 2007), timesofindia.indiatimes.com/city/ahmedabad/Manpower-milking-Baroda-Dairy-dry/articleshow/2394081.cms.

21. Rajshekhar, '"Amul Is Now a Congress-mukt Federation": How BJP Took Control of India's Largest Milk Cooperative', *Scroll.in* (1 December 2017), scroll.in/article/858585/amul-is-now-a-congress-mukt-federation-how-bjp-took-control-of-indias-largest-milk-cooperative.

22. Rajshekhar, '"Amul Is Now a Congress-mukt Federation": How BJP Took Control of India's Largest Milk Cooperative', *Scroll.in*.

23. Uday Mahurkar, 'Verghese Kurien Quits Gujarat Co-operative, Dairy Body Faces Politicking Risk', *India Today* (17 April 2006), indiatoday.in/magazine/economy/story/20060417-verghese-kurien-quits-gujarat-co-operative-diary-body-faces-politicking-risk-783289-2006-04-17.

24. Staff, 'BJP Leader Jethabhai Patel Surrenders in Post-Godhra Riot Case', *Outlook* (18 October 2004), outlookindia.com/newswire/story/bjp-leader-jethabhai-patel-surrenders-in-post-godhra-riot-case/256430.

25. Staff, 'Summarily Dismissed', *Hindu* (22 August 2004), thehindu.com/todays-paper/tp-national/tp-tamilnadu/summarily-dismissed/article27657423.ece.

26. *Analysis of Criminal, Financial and Other Details of MLAs of the Gujarat Assembly Elections 2012* (Association of Democratic Reforms, 24 December 2012); 'Election Affidavit of Jethabhai G. Bharwad

(Jetha Bharwad), Gujarat 2012', National Election Watch, myneta.info/gujarat2012/candidate.php?candidate_id=1612.

27. Yagnik and Sheth, *The Shaping of Modern Gujarat*, 261.

28. Rajshekhar, 'Few People Seem Happy with BJP's Rule in Gujarat, Yet the Party Still Controls the State. Why?', *Scroll.in* (9 December 2017), scroll.in/article/860639/few-people-seem-happy-with-bjps-rule-in-gujarat-yet-the-party-still-controls-the-state-why.

29. PTI, 'PM Modi Attends Meeting of Somnath Trust', *Times of India* (23 August 2018), timesofindia.indiatimes.com/india/pm-modi-attends-meeting-of-somnath-trust/articleshow/65521515.cms.

30. Revati Laul, 'In Gujarat, BJP Has Consistently Delivered on One Front—Instilling Fear among Its People', *Wire* (20 December 2017), thewire.in/politics/gujarat-election-results-2017-bjp.

31. Poorna Swami, 'A Template for Violence', *Caravan* (18 September 2019), caravanmagazine.in/history/the-riots-that-changed-the-course-of-gujarats-political-history.

32. Laul, 'In Gujarat, BJP Has Consistently Delivered on One Front—Instilling Fear among Its People', *Wire*.

33. Vinod Jose, 'Narendra Modi's Shadow Lies All Over the Haren Pandya Case', *Caravan* (6 July 2019), caravanmagazine.in/politics/haren-pandya-narendra-modi-murder-case-supreme-court.

34. Personal Communication with Girish Patel.

35. Indira Hirway, 'The Truth Behind the Gujarat Growth Model', *Wire* (8 December 2017), thewire.in/economy/the-truth-behind-the-gujarat-growth-model.

36. Rajshekhar, 'Gautam Adani: Meet the Man Who Built Rs 47,000 Crore Infrastructure Empire', *Economic Times* (5 September 2013), economictimes.indiatimes.com/industry/indl-goods/svs/construction/gautam-adani-meet-the-man-who-built-rs-47000-crore-infrastructure-empire/articleshow/22304960.cms.

37. Rajshekhar, 'Adani Power Project Was on the Brink of Bankruptcy—But the BJP Government in Gujarat Saved It', *Scroll.in* (6 March 2019), scroll.in/article/915109/adani-power-project-was-on-the-brink-of-bankruptcy-but-the-bjp-government-in-gujarat-saved-it.

38. Vinod Jose, 'The Emperor Uncrowned', *Caravan* (1 March 2012), caravanmagazine.in/reportage/emperor-uncrowned-narendra-modi-profile.

39. Charlotte Thomas, 'What Juhapura Tells Us About Being Muslim in Modi's India', *Wire* (28 May 2015), thewire.in/culture/what-juhapura-tells-us-about-muslims-in-modis-india.

40. Rajshekhar, 'Few People Seem Happy with BJP's Rule in Gujarat, Yet the Party Still Controls the State. Why?', *Scroll.in*.

41. Manisha Sethi, *Kafkaland: Prejudice, Law and Counter-Terrorism in India* (India: Three Essays Collective, 2014); Warisha Farasat and Prita Jha, *Splintered Justice: Living the Horror of Mass Communal Violence in Bhagalpur and Gujarat* (India, Three Essays Collective, 2016).

42. Rajshekhar, 'Few People Seem Happy with BJP's Rule in Gujarat, Yet the Party Still Controls the State. Why?', *Scroll.in*.

43. Mohit M. Rao, 'Why Continuous Rain Failed to Raise Groundwater Level in Bengaluru', *Hindu* (9 November 2017), thehindu.com/news/national/karnataka/why-continuous-rain-failed-to-raise-groundwater-level-in-bengaluru/article20006721.ece.

44. *Ahmedabad Heat Action Plan 2017: Guide to Extreme Heat Planning in Ahmedabad, India* (Amdavad Municipal Corporation), nrdc.org/sites/default/files/ahmedabad-heat-action-plan-2017.pdf.

45. Julien Bouissou, 'Indian City of Surat Anticipates Worst Effects of Climate Change', *Guardian* (15 September 2014), theguardian.com/cities/2014/sep/15/indian-cities-climate-change-surat.

46. Skymet Weather Team, 'Rajkot Receives 95 Mm of Heavy Rains, Flood Threat Continues', Skymet Weather (16 July 2017), skymetweather.com/content/weather-news-and-analysis/with-348-mm-rains-rajkot-breaks-a-decade-old-record-flooding-likely/.

47. Rajshekhar, 'Gujarat Is Battered by Heat Waves, Floods, Drought. How Are Its Cities Coping?', *Scroll.in* (4 December 2017), scroll.in/article/859203/gujarat-is-battered-by-heat-waves-floods-drought-how-are-its-cities-coping.

48. DNA Web Team, 'Killer Heat Wave: Hottest Day in Ahmedabad in 6 Years; Mercury Soars to 50 Degree Celsius', *DNA* (18 May 2016), dnaindia.com/india/report-killer-heat-wave-hottest-day-in-ahmedabad-in-6-years-mercury-soars-to-50-degree-celsius-2213768.

49. PTI, 'Heat Breaks 100-year Record for Ahmedabad, Touches 48 Degrees Celsius', *Deccan Chronicle* (19 May 2016), deccanchronicle.com/nation/current-affairs/190516/heat-breaks-100-year-record-for-ahmedabad-touches-48-degrees-celsius.html.

50   *Draft Comprehensive Development Plan 2031 (Second Revised)* (Rajkot Urban Development Authority), rajkotuda.com/pdf/RUDA-Report-PART-1-13-07-2015-2031.pdf.

51. Rajshekhar, 'Urban Planning: Why Gujarat's Cities Are Losing Their Fight against a Changing Climate', *Scroll.in* (5 December 2017), scroll.in/article/859205/urban-planning-why-gujarats-cities-are-losing-their-fight-against-a-changing-climate.

52. Deepa Padmanabhan, 'How Indian Cities Are Being Shorn of Trees', *IndiaSpend* (29 March 2016), indiaspend.com/cover-story/how-indian-cities-are-being-shorn-of-trees-67909.

53. Rajshekhar, 'The Majoritarian Project in Gujarat Only Serves the Rich, Says Political Scientist Ghanshyam Shah', *Scroll.in* (16 November 2017), scroll.in/article/857070/the-majoritarian-project-in-gujarat-only-serves-the-rich-says-political-scientist-ghanshyam-shah.

54. B.R. Ambedkar, *Riddles in Hinduism: The Annotated Critical Edition* (India: Navayana, 2016), 168–172.

55. K. Balagopal, *Ear to the Ground* (New Delhi: Navayana, 2011), 51.

56. Paul Oliver, *Blues Fell This Morning: Meaning in the Blues* (UK: Cambridge University Press, 1990), 272.

57. Oliver, *Blues Fell This Morning*, 275.

CONCLUSION

1.   David Runciman, *How Democracy Ends* (UK: Profile Books, 2018), 3–4.

2.   Masha Gessen, *The Future Is History: How Totalitarianism Reclaimed Russia* (UK: Granta Books, 2017), 386.

3.   Sebastian Strangio, *Hun Sen's Cambodia* (USA: Yale University Press, 2014).

4.   Runciman, *How Democracy Ends*, 44.

5.   Runciman, *How Democracy Ends*, 45.

6.   Eugene Lyons, *Assignment in Utopia* (USA, Transaction Publishers, 1991), 647.

7.   Tarunabh Khaitan, 'Killing a Constitution with a Thousand Cuts: Executive Aggrandizement and Party-State Fusion in India', *Law and Ethics of Human Rights* 14, no. 1 (January 2007), doi.org/10.1515/lehr-2020-2009.

8. Nitin Sethi, 'Electoral Bonds: Seeking Secretive Funds, Modi Govt Overruled RBI', *Huffington Post* (18 November 2019), huffingtonpost. in/entry/rbi-warned-electoral-bonds-arun-jaitley-black-money-modi-government_in_5dcbde68e4b0d43931ccd200.

9. Sanya Dhingra, 'Election Commissioner Ashok Lavasa Resigns, Set to Join ADB', *Print* (18 August 2020), theprint.in/india/governance/election-commissioner-ashok-lavasa-resigns-set-to-join-adb/484219/.

10. Prabhash K. Dutta, 'Narendra Modi Government Will Not Have Leader of Opposition in Lok Sabha Again', *India Today* (24 May 2019), indiatoday.in/elections/lok-sabha-2019/story/17th-lok-sabha-leader-of-opposition-bjp-congress-1533766-2019-05-24.

11. Alok Prasanna Kumar, 'By Passing Aadhaar Act as Money Bill, Has the SC Saved or Sacrificed the Rajya Sabha?' *Wire* (27 September 2018), thewire.in/law/aadhaar-verdict-money-bill-rajya-sabha.

12. Jagdeep S. Chhokar, 'Justice P Sathasivam as Kerala governor: Why It's a Bad Sign for Indian Judiciary', *Firstpost* (7 September 2014), firstpost. com/india/justice-p-sathasivam-kerala-governor-bad-sign-indian-judiciary-1700995.html.

13. V. Venkatesan, 'CJI Ranjan Gogoi's Nomination to the Rajya Sabha: More than a Sinecure', *Frontline* (24 April 2020), frontline.thehindu.com/the-nation/article31248619.ece.

14. Rohan Venkataramakrishnan, 'From CBI to RBI, an Incomplete List of Institutions That Narendra Modi Has Undermined or Threatened', *Scroll.in* (31 October 2018), scroll.in/article/900097/from-cbi-to-rbi-an-incomplete-list-of-institutions-that-narendra-modi-has-undermined-or-threatened.

15. Prasanna Mohanty, 'RTI Bill 2019: Undermining Autonomy of Information Commissions and Transparency in Governance', *India Today* (19 July 2019), indiatoday.in/india/story/rti-bill-2019-undermining-autonomy-of-information-commissions-and-transparency-in-governance-1571439-2019-07-19.

16. Rajshekhar, 'Opinion: New RBI Chief Shaktikanta Das's Actions after Note Ban Show Why He Is a Poor Choice', *Scroll.in* (12 December 2018), scroll.in/article/905356/opinion-shaktikanta-dass-actions-after-note-ban-suggest-that-he-is-a-poor-choice-to-be-rbi-chief.

17. Aruna Chandrasekhar, 'Scorched Earth', *Caravan* (1 August 2019), caravanmagazine.in/law/suffocation-national-green-tribunal.

18. Gessen, *The Future Is History*, 59.

19. Vidya Krishnan, 'India Did Not Stockpile COVID Protective Equipment for Health Workers Despite Clear WHO Guidelines', *Caravan* (22 March 2020), caravanmagazine.in/health/india-did-not-stockpile-covid-protective-equipment-health-workers-despite-clear-who-guidelines.

20. Rema Nagarajan and Shobita Dhar, 'How Covid War Is Hurting Non-Covid Patients', *Times of India* (3 April 2020), timesofindia.indiatimes.com/india/how-covid-war-is-hurting-indias-non-covid-patients/articleshow/74949121.cms.

21. S. Rukmini, 'COVID-19 Disrupted India's Routine Health Services', (27 August 2020), indiaspend.com/covid-19-disrupted-indias-routine-health-services/.

22. Banjot Kaur, 'COVID-19: We Will Write to States to Resume Immunisation, Says Centre', *Down to Earth* (31 March 2020), downtoearth.org.in/news/health/covid-19-we-will-write-to-states-to-resume-immunisation-says-centre-70139.

23. Jean Drèze, 'India Is in Denial about the COVID-19 Crisis', *Scientific American* (25 August 2020), scientificamerican.com/article/india-is-in-denial-about-the-covid-19-crisis/.

24. Richard Horton, *The COVID-19 Catastrophe: What's Gone Wrong and How to Stop It Happening Again* (UK: Polity Books, 2020), ebook.

25. Prabhash K. Datta, 'PM Cares vs PMNRF: What Is the Fuss about?', *India Today* (18 August 2020), indiatoday.in/news-analysis/story/pm-cares-vs-pmnrf-what-is-the-fuss-about-1712468-2020-08-18.

26. Rohini Singh, 'Behind Ahmedabad's Ventilator Controversy, a Backstory of Connections to Top BJP Leaders', *Wire* (21 May 2020), thewire.in/political-economy/modis-monogrammed-suit-rajkot-ventilator-vijay-rupani.

27. Vidya Krishnan and Aathira Konikkara, 'Members of PM's COVID-19 Task Force Say Lockdown Failed Due to Unscientific Implementation', *Caravan* (19 May 2020), caravanmagazine.in/health/members-pm-covid-19-task-force-say-lockdown-failed-due-to-unscientific-implementation.

28. Jean Drèze, 'India Is in Denial about the COVID-19 Crisis', *Scientific American*.

29. The Wire Staff, 'COVID-19 Blow: India's GDP Shrinks a Record 23.9% in First Quarter of FY '21', *Wire* (31 August 2020), thewire.in/economy/india-gdp-record-shrinks-fy21-q1-covid-19-lockdown.

30. Isabelle Guerin et al, 'Surviving Debt, Survival Debt in Times of Lockdown', working paper (2020), ideas.repec.org/p/sol/wpaper/2013-309493.html.
31. Gayathri Vaidyanathan, 'India Will Supply Coronavirus Vaccines to the World—Will Its People Benefit?' *Nature* (3 September 2020), nature. com/articles/d41586-020-02507-x.
32. Rajshekhar, 'Capital Bows before the State', *Seminar* (October 2020), india-seminar.com/2020/734/734_m_rajshekhar.htm.
33. Rajshekhar, 'Crony Capitalism on Modi's Watch Means Invisible Hands Ensure You Never Go Bankrupt', *Wire* (29 July 2020), thewire.in/ political-economy/crony-capitalism-on-modis-watch-means-invisible-hands-ensure-you-never-go-bankrupt.
34. Stephen Kotkin, *Uncivil Society: 1989 and the Implosion of the Communist Establishment* (USA: Modern Library, 2010).
35. Kotkin, *Uncivil Society*, 69–93.
36. Prabhjit Singh and Arshu John, 'Crime and Prejudice', *Caravan* (1 September 2020), caravanmagazine.in/politics/the-bjp-and-delhi-police-hand-in-the-delhi-violence.
37. Singh and John, 'Crime and Prejudice', *Caravan*.
38. Samanway Rautray, 'Justice Muralidhar's Transfer Timing Raises Eyebrows', *Economic Times* (28 February 2020), economictimes.india times.com/news/politics-and-nation/justice-muralidhars-transfer-timing-raises-eyebrows/articleshow/74367002.cms.
39. Karen Dawisha, *Putin's Kleptocracy: Who Owns Russia?* (USA: Simon and Schuster, 2014).
40. Timothy Snyder, 'Hitler's World May Not Be So Far Away', *Guardian* (16 September 2015), theguardian.com/world/2015/sep/16/hitlers-world-may-not-be-so-far-away.
41. PTI, 'Wealth of India's Richest 1% More than 4 Times of Total for 70% Poorest: Oxfam', *Economic Times* (20 January, 2020), economictimes. indiatimes.com/news/economy/indicators/wealth-of-indias-richest-1-more-than-4-times-of-total-for-70-poorest-oxfam/articleshow/73416122.cms.
42. Walter Schneidel, *The Great Leveller: Violence and the History of Inequality from the Stone Age to the Twenty-first Century* (USA: Princeton University Press, 2018).
43. Lewis H. Lapham, *Age of Folly: America Abandons Its Democracy* (New York: Verso, 2016), 306.

44. Lapham, *Age of Folly*, 16–17.
45. Zygmunt Bauman, *Liquid Modernity* (UK: Polity Books, 2000), 19.
46. Robert Conquest, *Reflections on a Ravaged Century* (USA: WW Norton and Company, 2000), xii.
47. Angela Davis, *Freedom Is a Constant Struggle: Ferguson, Palestine and the Foundations of a Movement* (USA: Haymarket Books, 2016).
48. Rajshekhar, 'Chhattisgarh: How Workers Improved Healthcare for 18 Million People', economictimes.indiatimes.com/industry/healthcare/biotech/healthcare/chhattisgarh-how-workers-improved-healthcare-for-18-million-people/articleshow/5997036.cms.
49. Zygmunt Bauman and Leonidas Donskis, *Moral Blindness: The Loss of Sensitivity in Liquid Modernity* (UK: Polity Books, 2013), 40.
50. Robert Sapolsky, *Behave: The Biology of Humans at Our Best and Worst* (UK: Penguin Random House, 2017).
51. Jan Vansina, *Paths in the Rainforests: Towards a History of Political Tradition in Equatorial Africa* (USA: University of Wisconsin Press, 1990), 247–248.

ANNEXURE

1. E.N. Rammohan, 'Manipur: Blue Print for Counterinsurgency', South Asia Terrorism Portal, satp.org/satporgtp/publication/faultlines/volume12/Article1.htm.
2. Rammohan, 'Manipur: Blue Print for Counterinsurgency', South Asia Terrorism Portal.
3. Krishnadas Rajagopal, 'Manorama "Mercilessly Tortured"', *Hindu* (14 November 2014), thehindu.com/news/national/manorama-death-brutal-torture-probe-panel/article6596278.ece.
4. 'CorCom (Coordination Committee)', Terrorism Research and Analysis Consortium, trackingterrorism.org/group/corcom-coordination-committee.
5. R.N. Ravi, 'AFSPA: The Biggest Impediment to Peace', *Kangla Online* (15 July 2012), kanglaonline.com/2012/07/afspa-the-biggest-impediment-to-peace/.
6. Staff, '#NoVIP: Manipur Speaker Allegedly Watched His Team Attack Man for Not Giving Way', NDTV (13 May 2015), ndtv.com/india-news/

novip-manipur-speaker-allegedly-watched-his-team-attack-man-for-not-giving-way-762727.

7. Rajshekhar, 'Why Children in Manipur Are Writing Postcards to Prime Minister Narendra Modi', *Scroll.in* (7 June 2015), scroll.in/article/732113/why-children-in-manipur-are-writing-postcards-to-prime-minister-narendra-modi.

8. R.N. Ravi, 'AFSPA: The Biggest Impediment to Peace', *Kangla Online*.

9. *Manipur: A Memorandum on Extrajudicial, Summary or Arbitrary Executions*, report by Civil Society Coalition on Human Rights in Manipur and the UN to Christof Heyns, special rapporteur on extrajudicial, summary or arbitrary executions (March 2012), e-paolive.net/download/education/2012/03/CSCHR_Memorandum_20120328.pdf.

10. Rajshekhar, 'In Violence-Scarred Manipur, Ancient Scrolls Show Why AFSPA Will Not Work', *Scroll.in* (17 June 2015), scroll.in/article/733295/in-violence-scarred-manipur-ancient-scrolls-show-why-afspa-will-not-work.

AFTERWORD

1. Ranjana Padhi and Nigamananda Sadangi, *Resisting Dispossession: The Odisha Story* (Aakar Books, 2020).

2. Jonathan Parry and T.G. Ajay, *Classes of Labour: Work and Life in a Central Indian Steel Town* (Social Science Press, 2020).

3. Nirvikar Singh and T.N. Srinivasan, 'Federalism and Economic Development in India: An Assessment', working paper 299 (Stanford Centre for International Development, 2006).

4. David Washbrook, *The Emergence of Provincial Politics: The Madras Presidency 1970–1920* (Cambridge University Press, 1976).

5. S. Narayan, *The Dravidian Years: Politics and Welfare in Tamil Nadu* (Oxford University Press, 2018).

6. K. Balagopal, *Ear to the Ground* (Navayana, 2012).

7. See: Mythily Sivaraman, *Haunted by Fire: Essays on Caste, Class, Exploitation and Emancipation* (Leftword Books, 2012), for a nuanced contemporary account of the DMK's early years in power.

8. See: V. Geetha, 'Unhappy Anniversary: Taking Stock after Half a Century of Dravidian Rule in Tamil Nadu', *Caravan* (April 2017), for more on this argument.

Acknowledgements

In these thirty-three months of travel, I received more grace and generosity than I deserved. I had the questions of a neophyte. And yet, everyone I met was generous with their time and knowledge, helping me understand their state and the realities of their lives. Without them, this book wouldn't exist. And so, these are the debts I acknowledge first.

Within that larger set are the people who became my sounding boards as I tried to make sense of what I was seeing. In Mizoram, that list included Piju Sharma, Adam Halliday, Pu Vanlalruata, T.R. Shankar Raman, Priya Singh, David Thangluaia, Pi Lalremruati, Pu Vanneitluanga, William Singh and a clutch of state government officials and one Intelligence Bureau officer who spoke to me off the record.

In Manipur, Pradip Phanjoubam, Amitabh Arambam, Mary Beth, Babloo Loitongbam and many others. From Nagaland, Aheli Moitra.

In Odisha, Debjeet Sarangi, Sudhir Patnaik, Satish Pradhan, Kedar Mishra, Priyaranjan Sahu, Biswajit Mohanty, Uday Patel, Mahammad Ashlam, and the many bureaucrats and whistle-blowers who spoke off the record. I also need to thank Barikbhai and Patnaik Saheb at Rashmi Annexe.

In Punjab, I benefitted immensely from an early chat with Sumail Singh Sidhu. His questions about how societies can course-correct stay with me till today. Apart from him, I am grateful to Desraj Kali, Ronki Ram, Devinder Pal Singh, K.R. Lakhanpal, Sucha Singh Gill, Kanwar Sandhu, Surinder Sen, Jagjit Cheema, R.S. Bains, Jagroop Singh Sekhon, Daljit Ami, Surendar Paul, Jaspal Singh Manjhpur, Ruchika

Khanna, Lali Majithia, and the cable operators, stone crushers, liquor businesspeople, cabinet ministers and bureaucrats who spoke to me. I also need to thank the Sainis at Ranjit Avenue, Amritsar.

In Tamil Nadu, Nethi Mani, V. Chandrasekhar, Aruna Rathnam, Senthil Babu, V. Geetha, V. Suresh, P.V. Srividya, Vijay Baskar, Father Jeyapathy, J. Jeyaranjan, Venkat Subramaniam, Vincent Raj of Evidence, Sadanand Menon, Nityanand Jayaraman, Rakhal Gaitonde, Aadhavan Deetchanya, Nagasaila, Perumal Murugan, Srinivasan Seetharaman, Josephstalin of Denkanikottai, Sidhu at Springhaven and his staff, Thangam Thennarasu, Justice Chandru, M.G. Devasahayam, A.R. Venkatachalapathy and the bureaucrats who spoke to me on the condition of anonymity.

In Bihar, Shashi Bhushan, Sridhar Srikantiah, Arshad Ajmal, D.N. Gautam, Shakeel Ur Rahman, Ratnakar Tripathy, Manas Bihari Verma, Deepak Raj, Sanjay Paswan, D.M. Diwakar, Ashok Ghosh, Nupur Bose, Shaibal Gupta, Shrikantji, Vyasji, Deepak Anand, M.N. Karn, Shyam Jaipuriyar, Mohammad Sajjad and the state bureaucrats who spoke on the condition of anonymity.

In Gujarat, Tridip Suhrud, Anand Yagnik, Achyut Yagnik, Kaushikbhai, Sanjay Saraogi, Nirjhari Sinha, Pratik Sinha, Hassan Jowher, Martin Macwan, Lancy Lobo, Saswat Bandopadhyay, G.K. Bhat, M. Rajsekar and a clutch of officials who preferred to stay anonymous.

If my reporting methodology was one constant across states, former Planning Commission member Abhijit Sen was another. As each state stint ended, I met him to discuss what I had found. For his insights, generosity of time and amused interest, I am deeply grateful.

At *Scroll.in*, not only did Supriya Sharma, Naresh Fernandes and Samir Patil buy into the itinerant idea of *Ear to the Ground* but also stayed patient and supportive even as the series billowed from fifteen months to thirty-three months. Few newsrooms would have been as accommodating.

Barbara Harriss-White, Judith Heyer, M.S. Sriram and Bhanupriya Rao read everything I wrote and kept me on my toes. Mridula Chari, Malika Rodrigues, Abheek Barman (who I so miss) and others put up with my incredulous calls as I discovered 'cow cess', 'borrowed documentation' and other surrealities of emergent India.

The first draft of *Despite the State* was written during a family health crisis. Dr S. Manohar, Dr Kishore G.S.B., Dr Vineet Gupta and the day care team at Bengaluru's Sakra World Hospital—Kavi, Seena, Jisha, Aleena and others—shepherded us through. I am very grateful to them.

V.K. Karthika and Venkatesh Karthik of Westland Publications spotted a book inside that clunky first draft. Praveen Donthi, Prem Panicker, Rahul Bhatia and Avinash Singh helped me rework it into something approaching readability. Manas Chakravarti, Aniruddha Ghosal, T.R. Shankar Raman, M.S. Sriram, Usha Ramanathan, Hema Ramanathan, V. Geetha and P.V. Srividya helped me improve those interim drafts further. And then, my editor, Janani Ganesan, took that manuscript and stripped it of illogic, cumbersome phrasing, flab and puns.

My debts run deeper yet. Much of the theoretical scaffolding of this book rests on the work of Zygmunt Bauman and Tzvetan Todorov, two thinkers who helped me understand our times. I also need to thank all the authors cited in this book (and Polity Books), who so generously allowed me to cite from their work.

Usha Ramanathan, Barbara Harriss-White, Tridip Suhrud, M.S. Sriram, Madhu Ramnath, Abhijit Sen and T.K. Arun read the final manuscript. Vikas Khot captured the central themes of this book—State failure and how people respond to it, often at heavy costs to their lives—in his image featured on the cover, which I am thrilled to have for this book. V. Geetha wrote the afterword and came up with the title. And then, Saurabh Garge, Jojy Philip, John Varghese, Gavin Morris and Sanghamitra Biswas pulled all these elements together to produce the book you hold.

I am grateful to all of them.

Finally, some older founts of support need to be acknowledged.

Aradhana Takhtani and Bharadwaj Wuppalapati, who suggested that I try journalism. Aresh Shirali, who gave me my first job in the trade. Indrajit Gupta, who taught me my journalism. Rohan D'Souza and Neelima Mahajan, who pushed me towards higher studies. The University of Sussex, which selected me for an MA. S. Sivakumar, who gave me a window to rural India. Rahul Joshi, who gave me my first job as a reporter on rural India and environment. And M. Anand, my boss at the *Economic Times*.

And then, there is the kinship structure I fall back on. Rafat Ali, Indrajit Gupta, Dinesh Narayanan, Archana Chaudhary, Dinesh Krishnan, Vidya Athreya, Jaideep Hardikar, Usha Ramanathan, Murali, Maya Ratnam, T. Sundararaman, Ramana Athreya, K.V.C. Rao, T.R. Shankar Raman, M.S. Sriram, Barbara Harriss-White, Judith Heyer, Ben Rogaly, Madhusree Mukerjee, Neelabh Dubey, Chulani Kodikara, Maya Indira Ganesh, Ifeanyi Okekearu, Maria Gruending, Avinash Singh, Avinash Celestine, Praveen Thampi, Subodh Varma, Devangshu Datta, Shankar Raghuraman, Nilanjana Roy, John Samuel Raja, Ravi Chellam, Faiza Ahmed Khan, Latha Jishnu, V. Geetha, Tridip Suhrud, Anand Yagnik, Usha Thorat, Senthil Babu, Bhaskar Goswami, P.S.V.N. Sharma, Divakar Dhaveji, T.K. Arun, Rahul Bhatia, Dr Mani and Latha, Bhatia uncle and aunty and many others.

A big thanks, also, to my mother, M. Lalitha; my sister, M. Madhu; and my partner, P.V. Srividya. I wish too that my father, M. Ramam and my dear friends, Shashi Rajagopalan, Samir Acharya, Pallavi Narain, Seshadri Ratnam and Abheek Barman were around to see this book.